About the Author

Arthur MacEwan is Professor of Economics at the University of Massachusetts Boston. Educated at Chicago and Harvard, his work *Development Alternatives in Pakistan: A Multisectoral and Regional Analysis of Planning Problems* (Harvard University Press, 1971) was awarded the Harvard University Department of Economics Wells Prize. From 1968 to 1975, he taught at Harvard before moving to the University of Massachusetts Boston. His editorial positions have included *Dollars & Sense* (1974–90), *Review of Radical Political Economy* (1980–82) and the *Quarterly Journal of Economics* (1972–75).

His books include:

Edited jointly with Hollis B. Chenery and others, *Studies in Development Planning* (Harvard University Press, Cambridge, MA, 1971)

Edited jointly with Thomas E. Weisskopf, *Perspectives on the Economic Problem: A Book of Readings in Political Economy* (Prentice-Hall, Englewood Cliffs, NJ, 2nd edn, 1973)

Revolution and Economic Development Planning in Cuba (Macmillan Press, London and St. Martin's Press, New York, 1981)

Edited jointly with William K. Tabb, *Instability and Change in the World Economy* (Monthly Review Press, New York, 1989)

Debt and Disorder: International Economic Instability and US Imperial Decline (Monthly Review Press, New York, 1990)

Neo-liberalism or Democracy? Economic Strategy, Markets, and Alternatives for the 21st Century

Arthur MacEwan

Pluto Press
AUSTRALIA

Fernwood Publishing
HALIFAX, NOVA SCOTIA

Oxford University Press
KARACHI · LAHORE · ISLAMABAD

Hong Kong University Press
HONG KONG

IPSR Books
CAPE TOWN

University Press Ltd
DHAKA

White Lotus
BANGKOK

Zed Books
LONDON · NEW YORK

Neo-liberalism or Democracy? Economic Strategy, Markets, and Alternatives for the 21st Century was first published by Zed Books Ltd, 7 Cynthia Street, London N1 9JF, UK and Room 400, 175 Fifth Avenue, New York, NY 10010, USA in 1999.

Published in Hong Kong by Hong Kong University Press, 14/F Hing Wai Centre, 7 Tin Wan Praya Road, Aberdeen, Hong Kong
ISBN 962 209 506 2

Published in South Africa by IPSR Books, Community House, 41 Salt River Road, Salt River 7925, Cape Town, South Africa
ISBN 0 9584267 1 6

Published in Bangladesh by The University Press Ltd, Red Crescent Building, 114 Motijheel C/A, PO Box 2611, Dkaha 1000
ISBN 984 05 1504 7

Published in Burma, Cambodia, Laos, Thailand and Vietnam by White Lotus Company Ltd, GPO Box 1141, Bangkok, 100501, Thailand
ISBN 974 7534 16 9

Published in Canada by Fernwood Publishing Ltd, P.O. Box 9409, Station A, Halifax, Nova Scotia, Canada B3K 5S3.
ISBN 1 55266 019 2

Published in Australia and New Zealand by Pluto Press, 6a Nelson Street, Annandale, NSW 2038, Sydney, Australia
ISBN 1 86403 108 5

Published in Pakistan by Oxford University Press, 5-Bangalore Town, Sharae Faisal, PO Box 13033, Karachi-75350
ISBN 0 19 579 372 2

Distributed exclusively in the USA by Palgrave, a division of St Martin's Press, LLC, 175 Fifth Avenue, New York, NY 10010, USA.

Copyright © Arthur MacEwan, 1999

Second impression, 2001

Cover designed by Andrew Corbett
Set in Monotype Ehrhardt and Franklin Gothic by Ewan Smith
Printed and bound in the United Kingdom by Biddles Ltd,
www.biddles.co.uk

The right of Arthur MacEwan to be identified as the author of this work has been asserted by him in accordance with the Copyright, Designs and Patents Act, 1988.

A catalogue record for this book is available from the British Library.

US CIP data is available from the Library of Congress

ISBN 1 85649 724 0 cased
ISBN 1 85649 725 9 limp

Contents

Tables and Figures

Tables

Figuro

Acknowledgements

In writing this book I have accumulated many debts, and I would like to note my appreciation to several people. To begin with, I have received a great deal of useful reaction from students in my classes, colleagues at the University of Massachusetts Boston, participants in seminars and lectures at the University of Massachusetts Amherst and the Universidad Nacional Autonoma de Mexico, and members of the Boston area Communities of Resistance Seminar Group.

In addition, the following people helped me with their comments on particular parts of the manuscript, by important suggestions, or in some other useful manner: Randy Albelda, Rashid Amjad, David Barkin, Jean-Pierre Berlan, Jim Campen, Susan Druding, Alexander Fraser, Nance Goldstein, Arthur Goldsmith, Allen Hunter, Jacques-Antoine Jean, Richard Lewontin, Susan Lowes, Mary MacEwan, John Miller, Laura Renshaw, Carlos Salas, Jake Sterling and David Terkla.

Partial support for the preparation of Part II was provided by the McCormack Institute of Public Affairs at the University of Massachusetts Boston to which I am accordingly grateful.

I am especially thankful to Bob Sutcliffe, who read virtually the entire manuscript and provided me with detailed criticisms; in addition, our conversations on these matters over the years have been invaluable to me. Margery Davies read and commented on the whole thing, forcing me to make my arguments clear and my grammar correct. Also, in so many other ways, her support has been essential to this project – as well as to about everything else I do!

None of the above, however, is responsible for any errors or poor arguments that remain.

This book is dedicated to
Karla, Anna, Peter and Julia
and to
Andy

There are Alternatives

It is remarkable how much our economic lives changed during the twentieth century.

It is also remarkable how little our economic lives changed during the twentieth century.

Most people, confronted with these two statements, will have no trouble accepting the first but are likely to baulk at the second. After all, the century saw a huge expansion of material production, technological changes that were almost unthinkable at the end of the nineteenth century, and an increase of average life expectancy – perhaps the best single measure of material well-being – far, far greater than that of any other era. Not only are things very different, but, in material terms at least, it appears that they are very much better. The change is certainly remarkable.

Yet in spite of the huge material progress that virtually defined the twentieth century, we continue to live in a world of dramatic inequalities. If we define material well-being in relative terms, which corresponds to the way people generally appraise their economic situations, things have not changed very much in the last 100 years. Income and wealth are, as they were at the end of the nineteenth century, highly concentrated in a few countries and in small, elite groups in most other countries. What's more, with a few notable exceptions, the list of rich countries at the end of the century was pretty much the same as at the beginning of the century. (Of course, in the rich countries inequality is also substantial and, in some notable cases, on the increase.) In spite of the tremendous rise in production, rapid technological change, and great increase of life expectancy, the 'development gap' appears as large as it was 100 years ago. The lack of change is certainly remarkable.

The persistence of the 'development gap' continually confronts us with the question: How can people in poor countries most effectively organize their economic lives and improve their material conditions? This broad question immediately spawns a long series of related questions about how economic development should be pursued. For example, what does an analysis of the historical record tell us about the respective roles of markets and states in advancing economic development? Does the remarkable experience of economic expansion suggest that development comes when the state directs and regulates markets? Or does it suggest that we should 'leave things to the market'? What would it mean to 'leave things to the market'? And are state and market the only options? What are the roles of democracy and equality in economic development? Are these goals for the future or instruments of change? And what is it that we want when we speak of 'economic development'? Is it simply more material goods? Or is our concept of progress and change defined by a broader set of goals?

This book is motivated by these sorts of questions. Like many other people, I look at the remarkable change of the twentieth century and am stunned by the remarkable lack of change. So in the chapters that follow, I will say what I can that might make some contribution to overcoming the lack of change that has left so many of the world's people in material poverty and degradation.

Primarily, what I have to say is an argument for organizing our economic lives democratically. One basis for this argument is that democracy is a good thing in itself. In addition, if people organize their economic lives democratically, then they will be likely to achieve economic development. Democracy is an effective means by which to obtain material well-being for society. Organize economic affairs democratically, and you get two 'good things': democracy and development.

When I advocate 'democracy' as the basis for an economic development strategy, I mean political democracy as it is usually understood: elections, civil liberties and the right to organize. But beyond these essential forms of democracy, I mean something more substantive. A democratic economic development strategy is one that puts people in a position to participate in decisions about and effectively exercise political power over their economic lives. It puts people in a position where their lives are not dominated by either the market or the state. A democratic strategy also delivers the benefits of development to the population generally (what else could be the result of people having effective power?) and thereby enhances their power.

The economic development that lies at the base of my argument is also broadly conceived. It involves economic growth, the increase in the amount of goods and services available to a people. But it also involves something more: an improvement in the basic standard of living of the great majority of the people, something that can be accomplished only with a relatively equal distribution of income; the preservation, and repair, of the physical environment; the maintenance and strengthening of social community; and broad participation in decision-making about political, social and economic affairs.

The argument that I will develop in this book is very much at odds with the orthodox view that has dominated the discussion of economic development in recent decades. Much of what I have to say can, in fact, be summed up in the simple proposition that *there are alternatives* to the current orthodoxy.

Events that emerged around the globe in the late 1990s have made the search for alternatives all the more urgent and have forced a widening of the discussion of development issues. In 1997, at a time when it seemed that there were virtually no effective challenges to the economic liberalism that was often called the 'Washington Consensus', financial disruption spread through East Asia. Financial disorder very quickly turned into widespread economic crisis, sending South Korea, Indonesia, Malaysia and Thailand into sharp depressions, affecting virtually all countries of the region, and threatening the economies of countries around the globe. Both the crisis itself and the rapidity with which it spread were generally viewed as a result of the way many countries had developed unregulated connections to international financial markets. These financial policies were a hallmark of the liberal orthodoxy that had been pushed by the International Monetary Fund (IMF), the World Bank and the US government in the preceding years. Then, as efforts by the IMF to manage the Asian crisis only made it worse, the entire orthodoxy came up for criticism and reassessment. By late 1998, even the World Bank was joining the attack against the IMF; though the Bank's attack was confined to tactical issues, it abetted the more general questioning of what had been widely accepted economic policies.

The economic difficulties that began to undermine the credibility of the Washington Consensus in the late 1990s were by no means confined to East Asia. Continuing economic instability in Latin America, the widespread development failures in Africa, the débâcle in Russia, and the weakness of the South Asian economies have all played roles in creating the opportunity for a new discussion of economic development policy, a new search for alternatives.

While the problems of orthodox economic liberalism have become increasingly apparent, it is also evident that older orthodoxies that placed the state in a dominating economic role are not viable. The various sorts of state-guided development that were pursued in many low-income countries up until the 1980s had, at best, an erratic economic record; and often where they achieved well-recognized economic growth successes, as in South Korea, Brazil or Indonesia, those successes came along with authoritarian, repressive, military dictatorships. Also, in East Asia, where state-led development had its most enduring economic growth accomplishments, the crisis that appeared in the late 1990s undermined confidence in that approach to economic policy. As to the communist version of statist economic policy, the demise of the Soviet Union provided a final death blow.

Thus, as the twenty-first century opens, it is both possible and necessary to consider alternative economic development strategies. I will devote much of this book to the question of alternatives, by both providing a conceptual foundation on which to build alternative policies and setting out in concrete details many elements of a democratic economic development strategy. In spite of the events I have noted in the previous paragraphs, however, the liberal orthodoxy that has defined the direction of economic development policy in recent years is not dead. The early part of this book will accordingly provide a critique of that orthodoxy, a critique that will establish a foundation for the examination of alternatives. To begin to get at the issues of the book and introduce the outline of what is to follow, let me say a bit about the orthodox policy and positions that have increasingly come to dominate discussion of economic development in recent years.

Neo-liberalism and Alternatives

The economic policy that became dominant in most of the world during the final decades of the twentieth century has given greater and greater rein to unregulated, private decision-making. The policy calls for reducing the economic roles of government in providing social welfare, in managing economic activity at the aggregate and sectoral levels, and in regulating international commerce. The ideas at the foundation of this policy are not new. They come directly from the classical economic liberalism that emerged in the nineteenth century and that proclaimed 'the market' as the proper guiding instrument by which people should organize their economic lives. As a new incarnation of these old ideas, this ascendant economic policy is generally called 'neo-liberalism'.

While the basic tenets of neo-liberalism operate in the rich countries, the policy plays its most powerful role in many of the low-income countries of Latin America, Africa, Asia and Central and Eastern Europe. Within these countries, influential groups see their fortunes tied to neo-liberalism, but the conflict over economic policy is seldom confined within a nation's borders. Officials from the international lending agencies, particularly the IMF and the World Bank, from the governments of the economically advanced countries, particularly the United States, and from private internationally operating firms use their economic and political power to foist 'market-oriented' policy on the peoples of the low-income countries. (The use of the term 'Washington Consensus' to sum up the neo-liberal prescription underscores the role of the US government, the IMF and the

World Bank in its promulgation, as well as the complementary role of various US research and policy institutes in providing intellectual support; see Williamson 1990.)

This rise of market-oriented policy is a major obstacle to democratic economic development. By reducing explicit social regulation of private economic activity and 'leaving things to the market', neo-liberalism prevents the implementation of programmes that would allow people to exercise political control over their economic affairs, involve people in solving their own economic problems, and serve the material needs of the great majority. A long list of development initiatives that could be democratic in this sense – of the people, by the people and for the people – are proscribed or severely limited by neo-liberalism. For example:

- A programme to protect the viability of small-scale producers of basic foodstuffs would not be developed because its implementation would require restrictions on imports or subsidies to the small-scale producers, and thus the programme would directly interference with markets.
- Efforts to extend the rights of wage workers, secure their union power and protect their health and safety would be very limited because such efforts would restrict the operation of markets.
- Programmes to preserve the stability of local communities, in both rural and urban settings, would be greatly hampered because the market has no way of valuing the social bonds of community life, and thus they have no role in a neo-liberal programme.
- Direct efforts by the government to provide employment through, for example, public works programmes or public enterprises are not implemented because in the neo-liberal scheme of things production activity must be left in the private sector.
- Reconstruction and protection of the natural environment would be severely constrained because environmental issues are not readily valued in private market operations and, what's more, require extensive government involvement in the economy.
- The rapid expansion of literacy programmes and other educational efforts would be hampered because they would require a major role for the public sector.
- Likewise, heavy investment in health-care programmes runs contrary to neo-liberalism's prescription of a minimal role for government in economic affairs.
- Programmes directed at improving the distribution of income would be greatly limited, if not ruled out all together, because they could not be accomplished without extensive government intervention in the economy.

In spite of the fact that it would prevent the adoption of these sorts of democratic development programmes, programmes that would meet the basic material needs of the majority, neo-liberalism continues to define the policy agenda in many countries. It is easy to conclude that the governments of these countries have little interest in promoting either democracy or the material needs of the majority, and there is no doubt that neo-liberalism is often used as an ideological cover for powerful, elite groups to pursue their own, narrow interests. However, the issue cannot be dispensed with quite so simply because the advocates of neo-liberalism argue that, in fact, their policies will serve democratic goals. They claim that their policies, however much dislocation and pain they may cause in the short run, will lead to a higher standard of living in the long run. This higher standard of living, they then maintain, is the key to democracy. Neo-liberals also argue that the sorts of programmes listed above – programmes that would serve the immediate economic and social needs of the majority – and a broader democratic system of economic development are not viable. The neo-liberals maintain not simply that their favoured development policies are best. *They claim that there is no alternative.*

In large part, this claim that there is no alternative is based on the argument that the 'globalization' of economic affairs forces virtually all countries of the world to embrace the world market if they wish to achieve economic development. Globalization in the current era has involved, first of all, a progressive deregulation of the international movement of goods and capital. Also, globalization today is taking place in a world which is more and more uniformly capitalist. In this homogenized world economy, businesses can do the same things in the same ways at a great variety of locations, and, with the declining regulation of international commerce, they will accordingly continually relocate to the lowest cost production sites. Thus, the neo-liberals contend, if the government of a particular country attempts to regulate private activity in order to achieve some desired social goal – greater income equality or environmental preservation, for example – businesses will simply leave the country for higher profits elsewhere in the world. On the other hand, the argument continues, if a country eliminates both external and internal barriers to commerce, globalization will allow it to reap the benefits: low-cost goods from abroad, access to foreign markets for its own exports, and higher levels of investment by both foreign and domestic businesses.

This argument, the 'logic' of globalization, has been applied over and over again. In post-apartheid South Africa, for example, when popular movements have demanded social policies that would directly improve the material conditions of the majority, they have been told that they must wait. Direct improvements would require programmes to redistribute income – heavily progressive taxes, minimum wages, and land reform, for example. Also, programmes designed to meet the immediate needs of the majority would involve the government, either directly or through heavy regulation, in production – for example, in building housing. All of this would be anathema to private investors; South Africans with capital would take it out of the country, and foreigners would not invest in South Africa. So, argue the neo-liberals, efforts directly to improve material conditions of the majority would be thwarted by the 'logic' of the global system.

Similar arguments were applied in Mexico during the debate over the North American Free Trade Agreement (NAFTA) in the early 1990s. Advocates of the agreement maintained not only that this opening of international trade was the best policy, but that it was the only policy that could bring economic development to the country. If Mexico did not accept NAFTA, its proponents claimed, the country would be frozen out of the globalized economy. It would not have access to international capital markets; its exports would be seriously restricted; and imports would be costly. Efforts to restrict foreign investment and trade had to be ruled out because they would alienate both foreign and domestic investors.

The situation in the former Soviet Union and Eastern and Central European countries after the demise of the communist regimes affords another example. At the beginning of the 1990s, a large segment of the population favoured political democracy and a maintenance of the social welfare programmes that had been established during the communist era. Many people looked to Scandinavia as providing a 'third way', an alternative to both the oppressive statist systems that had been thrown off and the inequality and instability of a market system. Yet political leaders in these countries, their advisers from the IMF, the representatives from international business and officials from the wealthy nations all proclaimed that an unregulated market economy was the only option available. The freedom of the market was essential, they claimed, in order to overcome the inefficiencies and distortions of the old regime.

Still another example is provided by the Haitian experience in the mid-1990s. When, after decades of dictatorship, Jean Bertrand Aristide ran for President of Haiti, he campaigned against neo-liberalism generally and the programmes of the IMF in particular. Aristide was elected in 1991 with two-thirds of the vote, was ousted a few months later by a military coup, and then was returned to power by the US military in 1994. Back in the presidential palace, Aristide began to accept the neo-liberal platform. The IMF, World Bank and the US government asserted that no other course of action was possible – and if their analytic arguments were not sufficient, the leverage of financial assistance and military support carried the day. There was no alternative.

In all of these cases the rhetoric of neo-liberalism has been considerably stronger than the reality, and many countries have moved slowly if at all towards the neo-liberal policy regime. Behind the rhetoric of neo-liberalism, large firms and wealthy individuals have often enriched themselves through favours from the government. What's more, although neo-liberalism touts a minimal role for government in economic affairs, it generally depends upon a very strong, repressive government. Because it would deny gains to the majority in the name of longer-run economic growth, implementation of neo-liberal policy generally suffers strong popular opposition that can only be contained with military or police action. Chile, which is sometimes presented as a success story for market-oriented policies, provides a prime example. While the success of that policy is open to question, there is no dispute over the fact that its implementation took place under a harsh military dictatorship. Likewise in Mexico, the implementation of neo-liberalism – for which few people were making great claims of success after the financial collapse at the end of 1994 – depended on the power of an authoritarian state. (Mexico also provides perhaps the best example of the way well-connected individuals were showered with government favours that turned several into billionaires while their benefactors in government preached the gospel of neo-liberalism.) Nevertheless, although the implementation of the neo-liberal programme may be uneven and the claim of minimal government is belied by the repression that implementation requires, the move towards a reduction of traditional economic roles for the state and a deregulation of market activity has become a powerful, global phenomenon.

This book argues against this powerful global phenomenon of neo-liberalism. To achieve my primary purpose of establishing the validity and desirability of organizing our economic lives democratically, I am going to have to refute central aspects of neo-liberalism along the way. *Contrary to the claims of its proponents, there are alternatives to the neo-liberal course, and these alternatives are far preferable both in terms of immediate and long-term consequences.*

As powerful as neo-liberalism is, however, it is not a monolithic ideology. The advocacy of 'market-friendly' policies comes in various forms, and even within those institutions that are most active in pressing neo-liberal policies around the world – the IMF and the World Bank – caveats, qualifications and modifications of neo-liberal doctrine have emerged. Especially in the wake of the East Asian crisis in the late 1990s, with the World Bank and the IMF publicly at odds over the proper tactics to pursue, divisions have appeared in the ranks of neo-liberalism.

During the 1980s, Ronald Reagan and Margaret Thatcher established an international political climate that allowed the spread of neo-liberalism in an extreme form. The demise of the Soviet Union gave further impetus to extreme arguments about the limits of state action in economic affairs and the miracles that could be performed by markets. Yet even ideologues are forced, eventually, to take some account of reality. One especially important aspect of reality was the great economic success of several countries in East Asia that could not be explained by the extreme neo-liberal position because in that success the states of the region played such important, directing roles in promoting economic growth. In its 1993 report, *The East Asian Miracle*, the World Bank attempted to reconcile its neo-liberalism with the reality of experience in the region. The report attempted to limit the damage by arguing that the East Asian experience was not readily generalizable and, in any case, the role of the governments was, according to the Bank, properly characterized as 'market-friendly'. The Bank was nonetheless forced to acknowledge the positive role that an active state could play in economic development.

The neo-liberal revisionism in the 1990s has been further developed in the Bank's annual *World Development Report* and in various articles and speeches by World Bank and IMF economists. In its *World Development Report 1997*, for example, the Bank acknowledges the essential role of the state in promoting and providing the framework for economic development. Furthermore, in 1998 the Bank's chief economist claimed that 'we have broadened the objectives of development to include [in addition to economic growth] other goals like sustainable development, egalitarian development, and democratic development' (Stiglitz 1998a). Both World Bank and IMF top-level economists have recognized that a relatively equal distribution of income can be a foundation for successful economic growth (Stiglitz 1998a, 1998b; and Fischer 1995).

This revisionism in the Bank and the IMF is certainly positive, partly simply because it brings official doctrine more into line with reality but also because it contributes to the legitimacy of egalitarian, democratic and environmentally sound economic programmes. Moreover, in part this revisionism has been a response to pressures from international democratic movements. For example, in recent years the World Bank has given in-creasing attention to gender issues in economic development, and the Bank has in some cases attenuated its long-established practice of backing huge water control projects.

Nevertheless, this revision of ideology has not dramatically altered the approach of these institutions to economic policy. As the predominant international lending agencies, the Bank and the IMF have great influence over polices in many nations, and they consistently use this influence to push policies guided by central propositions of neo-liberalism, policies that lower governments' spending and open nations' economies to international trade and investment. The former tends to reduce social programmes that would be the foundation for egalitarian and democratic development. The latter undermines the possibilities for the social control of economic activity, a control that is necessary to promote both positive social policies and effective technological change. Furthermore, the ideological revisionism in the Bank and IMF is usually accompanied by reaffirmation of central propositions of neo-liberalism (Stiglitz 1998a, 1998b; and World Bank 1997).

Although the revision of neo-liberalism has not altered either the basic policies of the IMF and World Bank or the basic arguments of the ideology itself, it does complicate the chore of developing a critique of neo-liberalism. The caveats, modifications and qualifications can obscure the core of the ideology. Similarly, a critique of neo-liberalism is complicated by various developments in mainstream economics. Major propositions of neo-liberalism that I will deal with in the following chapters are today the conventional wisdom of economics as it is presented in most English-language textbooks. (English-language economics textbooks are important because of the dominant, perhaps domineering, role of Anglo-American economics.) Yet at the same time, much of this conventional wisdom is in direct conflict with positions that have been well established in the foremost, mainstream English-language professional journals (Gordon 1994). For example, while economics textbooks argue the case for free trade, it is now generally recognized, as I will discuss in Chapter 2, that one cannot defend free trade as an optimal policy simply on economic grounds. Similarly, while textbooks often argue the case that economic growth is dependent on policies that increase income inequality, articles in the professional journals have established rather clearly that empirically there is no positive relation between inequality and growth and perhaps the opposite is true – a matter I will address in Chapter 3. On the one hand, the journal studies are useful in aiding a refutation of the conventional wisdom. On the other hand, the studies reported in the journals can be used to deflect the refutation with the claim that they have sufficiently qualified the conventional wisdom. Yet the conventional wisdom of mainstream economics expressed in texts, like the practices of the World Bank and IMF, remains largely unaffected by qualifications and revisionism.

Thus it is both legitimate and important to develop a full-fledged critique of neo-liberalism. In its basic propositions it is an ideology that is still clearly alive and, in spite of its retreat and modifications in recent years, is playing a central role in shaping and rationalizing policies that are pursued in many countries. It is largely incorrect or misleading, or both, in the view of the world that it promulgates. As a result it shapes a view of economic affairs that is highly detrimental to the creation of an egalitarian development programme. Neo-liberalism, in its extreme or revised form, presents us with a view of the world in which there are only two choices, an economy organized by markets or an economy organized by a dictatorial – or at best inept and inefficient – statist bureaucracy. When the choices are framed in this way, many people will accept the conclusion that there really is no alternative to submitting to the world of markets. In the remainder of this book, however, I will argue that there is another way to understand the situation, a way in which the world of markets does not offer a meaningful or positive option and in which there is the option of a democratic economic development strategy.

Plan of this Book

In Part I, I will focus first on neo-liberalism, particularly on some of the central myths that are the foundation of the neo-liberal argument. Although neo-liberal policy holds sway because it serves the interests of powerful groups, its effective operation depends upon its widespread ideological acceptance. Like other ideologies, neo-liberalism relies on a set of myths about history and about the way the economic world works. My purpose in chapters 2 and 3 will be to examine some of the central myths about the market and show how and why they are false. In Chapter 2, I will discuss the 'free trade' myth, the claim that international commerce without government regulation holds the key to successful economic expansion. In discussing international commerce, I will also examine the role of globalization and the extent to which this phenomenon really does eliminate alternatives to neo-liberalism. In Chapter 3, I will deal with the relationship between income distribution and economic growth and attack the seemingly paradoxical neo-liberal myth that substantial inequality is necessary for economic growth and economic growth brings about greater equality. These sets of myths about international trade and income distribution, while not the entire foundation of neo-liberalism, are central pillars on which the ideology is erected. Without them, the whole neo-liberal edifice cannot stand.

The neo-liberal ideology is also held together by a belief in the legitimacy of markets. To establish this legitimacy, neo-liberals treat markets, usually without explicit acknowledgement, as existing outside society and outside history. 'The Market' is simply there, to be called upon as the arbitrator of human affairs. We are told to 'leave things to the market', as though in doing so we will necessarily achieve a socially desirable solution. In Chapter 4, I will argue that *the market is a historically contingent phenomenon*. At any given time, market relations involve a set of arrangements – property rights, physical and social infrastructure, a distribution of income and wealth, and a set of rules and regulations – that reflect history as it has come to us, as it has been created by ourselves and those who have come before us. Like history, the market is not a fixed institution, but is continually evolving. Also like history, it has no particular legitimacy. The invocation that we 'leave things to the market' is no more reasonable than the demand that we accept history as it has come to us. In order to establish these points, I will devote considerable attention in Chapter 4 to explaining basic aspects of what markets are, how they operate and their connections to social relations more generally.

Chapter 4 thus provides some conceptual cohesion for the arguments of preceding chapters, and it also establishes a foundation on which to develop alternatives to market-based policies. Once I have explained this historical construction of the market, I will have set the stage for talking about conscious intervention in history. Arguing in Chapter 4 that markets are socially constructed, I intend to lay a basis for the discussion in Part II about the different ways they can be constructed (which includes how they can be limited and constrained).

In Part II, I will present a strategy for democratic economic development, explaining in some detail how it could be organized. Chapter 5 provides a framework for examining alternatives, first, through an examination of how democratic economic development is most usefully defined. Here is where I elaborate on the definition of development referred to above, and also where I say something about the meaning of democracy in the development context. Beyond clarifying the meaning of these important concepts, I want to establish the point that, while economic growth is a necessary part of development, any programme that would meet the material needs of the majority of the people must include a multi-dimensional set of goals. This set of goals includes: economic and social equality, environmental restoration and preservation, the security and social cohesion of communities, and popular participation in social, economic and political affairs. Even if economic growth is accomplished, this does not assure that other, equally essential goals will be attained. Also, if isolated from a broader set of social goals, economic growth itself is likely to become a chimera.

In Chapter 5, I will also explain the context in which I will present a democratic strategy. I am concerned with economic policy that is realistic. As compared to the way 'policy' and 'realistic' are usually interpreted, however, I will define 'policy' more broadly and 'realistic' rather differently. With regard to policy, I am not simply concerned with what governments should do (policy in the usual sense), but also with the economic changes that could be pursued by popular social movements. As to my criteria for a realistic strategy, I will argue that it must be realistic in the sense that its promise of social change is real, that it can gain popular support and that it is economically (or technically) feasible without a prior change of the economic system. This matter of 'policy that is realistic' lies at the heart of my argument, and I will discuss it further here in Chapter 1 as well as in Chapter 5.

Chapter 6 takes up macroeconomic policy in the usual sense, dealing first with the question of where the money would come from to pay for the social programmes that would lie at the heart of a democratic development alternative. The claim that 'there is no alternative' to neo-liberalism rests in large part on the contention that efforts to push economic life in a more egalitarian direction would lead to macroeconomic instability, disrupting economic growth, and thoroughly undermining the egalitarian efforts. In Chapter 6, I refute this claim.

It is then possible in Chapter 7 to turn to the central aspects of a democratic alternative, social programmes that would both serve people's direct needs and provide a foundation for long-term economic well-being. While I will discuss the general role of social programmes and will also comment on a variety of particular types of programmes, I will give major attention to education. Education or, more precisely, schooling is widely recognized to play a very important role in economic development, but the focus of the discussion about education and development is usually narrowly quantitative. I will argue that in shaping a democratic economic development strategy the qualitative aspects of education are also of great importance. The same is true, I will suggest, of other social programmes as well.

In Chapter 8, I will give attention to policies that would shape the private sector in a democratic strategy. This alternative that I am discussing is one in which markets still exist and in which the private sector continues to play a large role. Society, operating partly through the state and partly through the organizations of civil society, would none the less take an active role in giving direction to the private sector. After setting out some principles that would guide the way in which policies towards the private sector could be structured, I will examine some particular investment incentive programmes and then turn attention to programmes that would encourage local production – that is, programmes that would regulate international commerce. A unifying idea of Chapter 8 concerns technology, and I will argue that a democratic strategy is one that would push the private sector along a 'high road' of technological progress. Also, I will argue that an important factor guiding regulation of the private sector is a recognition of the value of local production.

In concluding the book, in Chapter 9, I will offer some comments on the political problems associated with an effort to establish a democratic economic development strategy. I will not pretend to offer a prescription for political strategy, but will only suggest some of the basis for the political work that could lead towards democratic development. At the centre of my argument is the proposition that people can take advantage of the democratic openings in society to build popular organizations; these organizations can increasingly involve people in having a say in the economic and social programmes that affect their lives; and thus the organizations and the people in them can become the agents of change. Also, however, the problem of democratic development is an international problem, and imperialism, in many forms, limits change. Thus, to bring progress, forces pursuing democratic development must work towards a globalization of their politics.

The Political Context of Economic Alternatives

In proposing 'economic alternatives', my goal is to conceive of alternatives that are practical in the sense that they could actually be implemented within the existing socio-economic framework and that are significant in the sense that they would bring about, or at least have the potential to bring about, substantial changes in the social organization and power. This is not an easily attainable goal.

On the one hand, arguments about economic development are usually confined to a relatively narrow set of alternatives. The choice among the different options is little more than a technical exercise because they do not involve significant differences in social structure or in the relative power and well-being of different groups. The entire discussion is based on the assumption that basic structures of social organization and economic power cannot be changed. For example, rural development programmes in low-income countries often focus on alternative technologies, methods of agricultural extension work and the ways in which infrastructure can be improved; they accept as given the existing land tenure arrangements. Another example is the debate in the 1980s over how low-income countries should meet their foreign debt obligations; the debate was based on the premise that the debt would in fact be repaid, and it then focused on such issues as methods of debt rescheduling, terms of new loans and the degree of support from the international lending agencies. These sorts of disputes involve disagreements over how a social economic system should be managed. They are not disputes over the nature of the system.

On the other hand, when discussions of alternatives do question the nature of the social system, they often become thoroughly impractical. Impractical ideas have their uses, and there are very good reasons to question the basic structures of society in the low-income countries of the world (to say nothing of the basic structures in the wealthy countries). But in order to bring about change it is not sufficient to state what should be done. We need to begin with the question: What should be done? But it is also necessary to figure out what *can* be done. However desirable sweeping change may be, it is not enough to advocate revolution or particular programmes that have no chance of implementation without revolution. If the goal is to alter the nature of the system and make a real difference in people's lives, then we need to formulate and implement practical programmes that both improve economic conditions and challenge the structure of social–political power.

Programmes of this type are similar to what André Gorz (1964) dubs 'non-reformist reforms' or 'revolutionary reforms'. These are 'reforms which advance toward a radical transformation of society' and can be contrasted with 'reformist reforms'. In Gorz's terms:

> A reformist reform is one which subordinates its objective to the criteria of rationality and practicability of a given system and policy. Reformism rejects those objectives and demands – however deep the need for them – which are incompatible with the preservation of the system.

> On the other hand, a not necessarily reformist reform is one which is conceived not in terms of what is possible within the framework of a given system and administration, but in view of what should be made possible in terms of human needs and demands.

> … a struggle for non-reformist reforms – for anti-capitalist reforms … bases the possibility of attaining its objective on the implementation of fundamental political and economic changes. These changes can be sudden, just as they can be gradual. But in any case they assume a modification of the relations of power; they assume that the workers will take over powers or assert a force (that is to say, a non-institutionalized force) strong enough to establish, maintain, and expand those tendencies within the system which serve to weaken capitalism and to shake its joints. They assume structural reforms. (Gorz, 1964: 6–8)

Gorz was writing about the situation in the advanced capitalist countries – France of the 1960s, in particular – where political democracy prevailed and revolutionary change, in the sense of a violent insurrection, was clearly not on the historical agenda. The basic idea, however, is generally applicable in many of today's low-income countries where a substantial degree of political democracy exists and where there is no immediate likelihood of revolutionary upheaval. Gorz's formulation is helpful in establishing a set of criteria for democratic initiatives that would neither accept the system as it is and focus on management nor define change in terms of impractical goals:

- Democratic initiatives – or 'reforms' or 'programmes' – must make a positive difference in people's lives. They should not demand that a sacrifice be made in the name of some greater good; they must bring something good in themselves. Their goals are defined by what should be.

- Democratic initiatives must challenge the existing relations of power and authority and in some way move society towards a more democratic structure. They need not overturn or destroy the existing social structures. Yet in some manner they must pose a threat to the existing social and economic structures. The essence of this threat is that these initiatives expand the realm of democracy and enhance democratic authority.

- Democratic initiatives must be possible in the sense that their implementation does not require a prior revolutionary, structural reorganization of society. They may set in motion a process of change that pushes society in the direction of dramatic structural reorganization – that is precisely their point. Yet, because they are particular and partial and therefore are not themselves dependent on that reorganization, they are possible.

Gorz's non-reformist reforms or democratic initiatives are not in conflict with revolutionary upheaval (and Gorz himself certainly did not see such a conflict), but they are not themselves the programme of a revolutionary upheaval. The politics of the relationship between a revolutionary struggle and a struggle for non-reformist reforms would be complex. It is not an issue I will deal with in this book. Suffice to say that in most of the world's low-income countries, where some political democracy exists, revolutionary upheaval is not an immediate issue as the twenty-first century opens.

Although in Part II of this book I will examine democratic initiatives within the context of a discussion of an overall democratic economic development strategy, in order to introduce the issues here it will be useful to say just a bit about one such initiative that I will deal with towards the end of Part II. Consider a programme to protect the viability of small-scale producers who have traditionally played a major role as food suppliers. In many parts of the world, a large percentage of the population lives in rural areas and is immediately involved in agriculture; also, poverty, including low levels of food consumption, is concentrated in the rural population. So a policy that promoted the viability of small-scale producers could directly raise the incomes of the rural poor, supporting them as producers and as consumers. The policy could provide some stability for the large rural population and could strengthen rural communities. Stronger rural communities with a growing stake in agriculture could be a foundation for improving environmental conditions. By creating a better situation in the countryside, a programme of this sort could slow rural-to-urban migration and be a first important step in dealing with the country's urban problems as well. Also, for a food programme to work, it would require extensive organization of the rural population, providing, for example, an impetus to the emergence of cooperatives. For all of these reasons, a programme protecting the viability of small-scale producers would be defined in terms of social needs.

At the same time, protecting the viability of small-scale producers would conflict with and challenge the principle of minimal regulation of markets. For in order for the programme to be effective, it would be necessary to protect local food production from competition with imports or provide direct subsidies to local agriculture or both. Market advocates would argue that unregulated markets would provide the population, including the poor, with the lowest cost foods, and therefore be preferable to a policy involving regulation. Yet this sort of argument ignores the non-market gains, such as stabilization of rural communities and the emergence of rural co-operatives, that could come with a food support programme. Also, a market food policy would mean that the food supplied would be disproportionately the food demanded by the wealthy, and that would entail a pattern of production and foreign trade in conflict with social goals. Finally, reliance on market policy would not take sufficient account of the changes in the organization of rural production (the changes in technology) that could take place over time as a result of the structural changes involved in a programme that would protect the viability of small-scale producers of foodstuffs.

So an initiative to support the viability of small-scale food producers would be a 'non-reformist reform' in Gorz's sense. It would serve social needs, which is why it is worth pursuing, and it would challenge the existing economic structures. It could be a good thing in the short run, and it could generate positive social change and economic expansion in the longer run. Also, such an initiative would be possible in the sense that it could be implemented in many places without prior revolutionary or major structural socio-economic change.

The challenge that a programme to support small-scale farmers, or any other democratic initiative, presents to 'the logic of capital' does not depend only on the content of the reform. In addition, the means by which a particular reform is developed and implemented is an important basis for challenging the status quo. It makes a great deal of difference, for example, whether the peasants of a country are presented by government authorities with a programme to support their viability or are themselves engaged *from the start* in the formulation of that programme, whether the programme emerges through the formal organs of political authority or arises as a consequence of popular struggle, whether the programme relies primarily on support and direction from above or leads peasants to build primarily on their own resources. Even where significant political democracy exists, and certainly where it does not, maintenance of the status quo depends upon people being excluded from involvement in the economic decisions that affect their lives and in the formulation and implementation of economic policy. Regardless of the content of reforms, if the method of reform does not challenge the alienation of most people from control over their economic lives, its positive, democratic implications will be limited. Democratic initiatives, non-reformist reforms, cannot simply be for the people; they need to be of the people and by the people as well.

Yet how is it possible to implement economic programmes, such as a support programme for small-scale farmers, that challenge the structure of social–political power? Won't such programmes be squelched by the people who actually hold power and do not want to see change? Isn't that what it means to 'hold power'? Well, no, it turns out that power is seldom if ever so clear and absolute. For example, even during the era of apartheid in South Africa, there were niches of opposition activity in the trade unions and elsewhere. In Brazil, during the military dictatorship that lasted from the early 1960s to the early 1980s, reform struggles that challenged the structure of power began to emerge during the 1970s in unions and in the Catholic Church. In many other dictatorial situations, examples exist where opposition groups could throw up challenges, however limited, to the existing authorities. Yet in the circumstances of dictatorship, where not even a façade of democracy exists, policy can be contested only within a very narrow realm, and doing so always carries a high degree of risk. These dictatorial situations are not, then, what I am dealing with in this book.

In many countries of today's world, however, political democracy, sometimes only a façade and sometimes much more than a façade, does allow substantial space for the articulation and even implementation of alternative economic initiatives. In much of Latin America today – in Brazil, Chile, Mexico, Haiti and Nicaragua, for example – it is possible to push initiatives that would both amount to practical reforms and challenge existing authority. Post-apartheid South Africa is another example, a particularly important one because of the political attention that the country has received over the years. India, as the experience in the state of Kerala amply illustrates, is another case where it is possible to implement reforms that both improve people's lives and challenge the existing structure of power. In addition, in several countries, regardless of a lack of effective democratic political forms, power is in flux. Different groups are vying for control over the political apparatus, and, while political democracy is very limited, the unstable political situation opens up possibilities for mounting democratic initiatives. Many of the former communist countries fall into this category.

These sorts of situations, where some degree of political democracy or a certain amount of flux or both allow the political space of opposition activity, are the political context I am dealing with in this book. They are situations where it is meaningful to talk about structural reforms and to take practical steps towards democratic initiatives. (Proposing structural reforms or democratic initiatives in a context where they are not practical – in a dictatorial political environment, for example – is not necessarily useless. It is often useful to articulate politically impractical proposals; they can expose the regime and inspire opposition. Also, in a revolutionary context, concrete proposals can be useful in establishing a programme that could help gain support for the revolution and serve as a guide after the change of political power. But proposals in these sorts of dictatorial or revolutionary situations are not the same as putting forth practical programmes, which is my concern here.)

The Limits of State Action

An attack of the sort I am mounting in this book on neo-liberalism and on market-based economic policies might be interpreted as an argument for a powerful state. Advocates of market policies present their position as an alternative to reliance on the state, and many opponents of market policies have offered state planning as their alternative to the market. Yet it is highly misleading to present the state–market relation as a simple dichotomy and to ignore mechanisms of economic organization that are neither market institutions nor fully state institutions.

Market-based economic policies, as I have pointed out above, generally rely upon strong states. As I will argue extensively in Chapter 4, in market societies the state plays a central role in constructing and organizing markets. Even when the state does not intervene directly in markets, its indirect interventions are essential and permeate economic affairs. Markets are always infused with state actions, and the neo-liberal position is not in reality an advocacy of a weak state; it is an advocacy of a particular kind of strong state.

Strong states, whether under a neo-liberal or explicitly statist rubric, present problems for any advocate of democracy. In a great variety of settings, powerful states have maintained themselves through political repression, have established bureaucracies that usurp popular authority and have diverted resources from socially useful functions. Sometimes they operate as the representatives of a dominant class or coalition of elites, and other times they are relatively autonomous. In the communist countries and in many low-income countries during recent decades, the state has been openly hostile to political democracy. In the advanced capitalist countries, the state has generally embraced formal political democracy, but has relied on bureaucratic control and the thoroughly undemocratic structure of economic life to limit the diffusion of power (and also on numerous occasions has not shied away from repression). Any glance at history – even leaving aside such horrors as the Nazi genocide, the ravages of Stalinism, the slaughters of indigenous peoples and the sponsorship of slavery by several states – can uncover a long list of state atrocities. There is good reason why the neo-liberal attack on the state finds popular resonance. Even when we recognize the importance of strong state action to limit or eliminate the social devastation and inept operations of markets, limits on state power should still be an important concern.

The specific initiatives that I will present later in this book often depend on state intervention in the economy. The state, whatever other roles it may play, is a central mechanism that society has for collective action. Also, only a powerful state would be able to control powerful private actors, and only a strong state would be able to raise sufficient funds (taxes) for the social programmes that are essential to democratic economic reforms. So, as much as our experience with state power raises problems, the importance of the state is a reality that cannot be wished away or ignored. What might be possible, however, is to formulate democratic initiatives that are alternatives to the market strategies and also build popular autonomy and people's independence from the state.

In all societies there are alternatives to markets that do not rely principally on the state. Even in the most advanced capitalist societies, as I point out in Chapter 4, a considerable amount of economic activity takes place outside the market: in families, in volunteer associations, among friends, between the citizens and the government, within firms and within governments. A great deal of this activity does not involve the state, and often where the activity formally falls within the state domain institutions operate with considerable autonomy. These activities which fall outside the market and outside the direct authority of the state remind us that such activity is possible.

One place where we might look for a useful illustration of such activities is in primary, elementary and, perhaps, secondary public schools, not as they generally exist but as they sometimes exist and as many people would like them to exist. (I am using the term 'public schools' in the US sense of the term; the British equivalent would be 'state schools'.) Public schools are formally a part of the state. Yet it is widely recognized that effective public schools are embedded in the communities where they exist, involving considerable parent participation. Effective schools, while an arm of the state, are also an arm of local communities. They are effective in part because students feel the schools are their own. The community influences the organization of the schools and affects issues of resource allocation within the schools through a variety of mechanisms, ranging from the election of school boards ('governing bodies' in Britain) to direct parent involvement. The state, both through its local and centralized structures, also affects the operation of schools and usually has ultimate authority over them. Yet when they are embedded in the community, they are not simply state institutions. Similarly, in a market society, the market has a great deal of influence over what goes on in the public schools, but they are certainly not market institutions. They are a relatively autonomous social 'space' in which economic decisions are made outside the normal channels of state and market, though fully independent of neither. (The emphasis I place on education in Chapter 7 is partly motivated by this view of schools as a potentially autonomous 'space,' and thus as basis for popular participation in development policy.)

Various cooperative enterprises – peasant production cooperatives, for example – provide another illustration of such relatively autonomous space. Cooperatives in market societies are connected to and formally part of the market (analogous to the relation of community-based schools to the state), and they are in part subject to the 'discipline of the market'. Yet their internal organization, their decisions about resource allocation, and their distribution of payments are not necessarily controlled by the same market 'logic' as an individually owned or corporate firm. Members of a peasant cooperative need not be simply profit maximizers, and their activities can be directed by a broader set of goals including, for example, the stability of their communities. Cooperatives also function within a framework established by the state and cannot ignore its regulations and demands, but they are certainly not state institutions. They offer the possibility of relatively independent 'space'.

Any effort to create a more democratic society is presented with the conundrum of how to influence and use the power of the state in this effort while at the same time limiting the power of the state. The examples I have just described, of schools and cooperatives closely connected to communities, give some suggestion of the solution to this problem, or at least of the direction in which a solution may lie. When the institutions of civil society are strong, popular authority is likely to be more effective in both constraining the state and providing alternatives to market-based policies. Certainly one of the goals of any democratic initiatives should be to strengthen the institutions of civil society, both because the resulting popular participation is a good thing in itself and because it is an important insurance of wider democracy.

Part I

Neo-liberal Myths and the Meaning of Markets

2

International Commerce and Economic Development

In 1993, scientists at the University of Vienna announced that through microscopic, infra-red and chemical analyses they had determined that strands of cloth found in the hair of an Egyptian mummy were clearly silk and almost certainly from China. The mummy had been interred around 1000 BC. Prior to this discovery, it had been generally believed that trade between China and the Mediterranean had not developed until several centuries later (Wilford 1993).

While we are fond of thinking that 'globalization' is some new phenomenon, the story of the Egyptian mummy illustrates that commerce over great distances and across local political boundaries is an ancient practice. We know relatively little about long-distance trade around the year 1000 BC, and perhaps the silk in the hair of the mummy represents a marginal aspect of commercial affairs, a small trade in luxury items. Yet we do know that at least for the last 2,5000 years long-distance economic relations have played important roles in economic changes at many times. Globalization, in the sense of a major surge of commerce across political boundaries that brings about new patterns of economic organization and generates far-reaching social, political and cultural change, is not new.

Long-distance commerce, whether in ancient times or today, is distinctive because it crosses political boundaries. When the geographic realm of commerce is different from the geographic realm of politics, it takes on a separate dynamic and poses distinctive problems of regulation, as compared to commerce within political boundaries. International commerce poses some special threats to local commerce, and it offers the possibilities of special gains. Also, it can threaten the strength and authority of local government, and it can provide local government with an exceptional source of revenue and power. For better or for worse – or perhaps for better *and* for worse – long-distance trade has been a powerful engine of disruption and change. For these reasons, globalization takes on an important role in economic development.

Each of history's great empires marks a wave of globalization, a move towards a larger and larger sphere of economic interaction. The consolidation of Han hegemony in what is now China, the various phases in the development of Mogul power through Asia, the emergence of the Roman Empire around the Mediterranean, the expansion of the Ottoman Empire in the Middle East, the growth of the Incan Empire in the Andes – all are examples of early globalizations; all involved the establishment of commercial relations over a spreading geographic realm. When we turn to more recent centuries, it is possible to identify three great waves of globalization that are distinguished because they have been cumulative, each phase clearly building on the preceding one: a first that began at the end of the fifteenth century with the extension of European control over the western hemisphere and the opening of truly global sea routes; a second in the nineteenth century, with the great surge of trade and international investment associated with the industrial revolution; and the third in which we are now engulfed. Each of these steps in globalization has involved great extensions of trade, investment and migration, as well as profound political, social and cultural changes.

The Context: Current Globalization

Recognizing that globalization is an age-old process and that the current phase of globalization is the most recent stage of a continuous and connected phenomenon that dates back some 500 years, we are less likely to overstate the 'unique' character of current events. It also helps place current world affairs in perspective to note that although various major quantitative changes in the world economy are often cited to illustrate the importance of the current globalization, these changes are not quite so impressive on more careful inspection. For example:

- Throughout the post-Second World War period, international trade has grown substantially faster than national commerce. Between 1960 and 1988, for example, world exports more than quadrupled while world output did not quite triple (Dicken 1992: 16). Yet, this rapid growth of trade has generally brought the world back to where it was at the beginning of the century, before two wars and the depression of the 1930s wreaked havoc on international commerce. Data for a set of advanced capitalist countries illustrate the general phenomenon: for six countries (France, Germany, Japan, the Netherlands, UK and the USA), between 1950 and 1987 the ratio of commodity exports and imports to gross domestic product (GDP) grew from 28.8 per cent to 40.2 per cent; yet in 1913, the ratio was 42.6 per cent (Maddison 1989: 149).[1]
- Foreign direct investment (FDI), the activity of multinational firms,

has become a hallmark of the current globalization. Between 1973 and 1991, the world stock of FDI grew (in current dollars) from $211.1 billion to $1,836.5 billion, a growth rate of roughly 13 per cent per year. From the perspective of the advanced capitalist countries, the origins of the vast majority of FDI, this stock grew substantially faster than GDP, amounting to about 6.7 per cent of GDP in the early 1970s and rising to nearly 9 per cent at the beginning of the 1990s.' Yet, again, in aggregate quantitative terms it is not clear that these changes did more than return things to early twentieth-century levels. Estimates place the world stock of FDI in 1913 at 9 per cent of world output; in 1960 the figure was 4.4 per cent; in 1991, it stood at 8.5 per cent (UNCTAD 1994: 130). For the United States alone, by far the largest home base of FDI, the pattern is the same: on the eve of the First World War, the ratio of the value of US FDI to US GDP was slightly greater than it was at the end of the 1980s, about 7 per cent at both times (MacEwan 1991: note 3).

- Perhaps the most impressive figures on the current globalization are those for international financial activity. Between the mid-1960s and the mid-1980s, the volume of international banking grew from about 1 per cent of the GDP of the world's market economies to 20 per cent. Whereas in the mid-1960s cross-border banking activity was about 10 per cent of the volume of world trade, by the mid-1980s the volume of cross-border lending exceeded the volume of international trade of the market economies.[3] These are imposing and important figures. Yet, if we measure the degree of international financial integration by the correspondence in the variation of the prices of financial assets in different markets (New York, London, Frankfurt, Tokyo), then the integration of the current era appears to be no more, and perhaps less, than that of the later part of the nineteenth century (Zevin 1992).

Nevertheless, the current globalization does have distinctive characteristics. More important than any aggregate quantitative changes, the principal distinctive features of the current globalization are qualitative:

- The global economic integration taking place at the end of the twentieth century is occurring in a world that is almost entirely capitalist. Virtually everywhere, production is increasingly organized for profit and increasingly based on wage labour. The growing economic ties are therefore ties that bind one socio-economic system together, not ties between different systems (as was often the case in earlier eras of globalization). In this sense, the current globalization is the first that is truly global; there is no longer any substantial part of the world that is generally outside the one international economic system.

- National and regional differences have continued to exist in many aspects of economic life, as well as in social and cultural spheres, and income gaps between different parts of the world are huge and growing. Nevertheless, in terms of the organization of production and finance, we are moving towards a thoroughly homogenized world economy. In many parts of the world, the same commodities are produced in the same ways for the same markets, frequently in enterprises owned by the same companies. In earlier eras of globalization, when production was linked across international boundaries, it was often linked in a complementary manner, with workers in different regions engaged in different segments of production. For example, in the classic North–South relationship, workers in the low-income countries, often working under non-capitalist conditions, produced raw materials that were then processed by workers in the advanced countries. Such links continue to exist and in some cases have been extended, as, for example, when the labour-intensive part of a manufacturing process is carried out in one country and the skill-intensive part in another. Yet an increasing amount of the same work can be and is carried out in the same way in a variety of low- and high-income locations. (The capacity of firms to switch the location of production is a reflection of their longer-term success at deskilling many aspects of work; see Braverman 1974. With knowledge of the production process in the hands of managers and with the nature of technology often embodied in the equipment rather than in the workers themselves, it is relatively easy to relocate production to an area with a relatively unskilled workforce. While many activities are not so readily deskilled, considerable manufacturing work and an increasing amount of service activity – data entry and aspects of computer programming, for example – do fit the description.)
- Because of the domination of the world economy by capitalism and because of the economic homogenization that goes with that domination, the degree of competition is particularly intense. National boundaries provide only limited protection for national firms, and in several industries a few large internationally operating firms, which continue to compete with one another, have eliminated their smaller competitors. As many firms operate internationally and almost all firms have ready access to international sources of supply, workers in different countries are forced into immediate competition with one another. Homogenization of the world economy underlies this worker-versus-worker competition: workers producing the same goods in the same ways for the same markets (and sometimes in different branches of the same company) can easily replace one another.
- There is a general effort on the part of businesses and their government

supporters to deregulate international commerce. The conclusion in 1994 of the Uruguay Round of negotiations of the General Agreement on Tariffs and Trade (GATT) and the creation of the World Trade Organization (WTO), mark the considerable success of these efforts. In the advanced capitalist countries, larger firms have become more and more international in their operations and depend for their continued expansion on a deregulated international environment. In the low-income countries, businesses have increasingly rejected the national option, tying their fortunes to international operations as *de facto* (and sometimes *de jure*) junior partners of firms from the advanced countries.

The spread of capitalism, homogenization, increasing competition and deregulation are certainly not new phenomena. Yet, while these forces have been important tendencies in previous eras, they have moved to the fore, become dominant and serve to define the current globalization. From a political or ideological perspective, the focal point of controversy in all of this is the issue of deregulation. For the large firms that dominate world economic affairs, homogenization and the spread of capitalism create a whole new set of opportunities for gains from international expansion. Rising competition works in the same direction, forcing the firms to obtain new sources of profits through expansion. Furthermore, geographic expansion and technological change have been mutually supportive; advances in transport and especially communications have raised the returns to firms' geographic expansion while, at the same time, the emergence of opportunities for geographic expansion have raised the returns to technological innovations that facilitate the expansion.

In spite of the very real changes that have taken place in recent years, globalization is far from a completed or fully defined process. Capitalism may appear ubiquitous, but even in a thoroughly capitalist world a great deal of economic activity remains outside markets – a point I will discuss further in Chapter 4. While homogenization of economic life and growing competition are powerful tendencies, there are also social and political limits on these tendencies. National economic policies continue to exist, and they make a difference, as I will explain more fully later in this chapter. National regulation of international commerce and sometimes the regulation of international agreements loom as constraints on the expansion by large firms and provide barriers to their even greater success. In the low-income countries, the move towards neo-liberal policies has been relatively successful in recent years. Among wealthy nations, however, the 1980s saw a general increase of protectionism (with that protectionism aimed more at the products of the low-income countries than at the products traded among the high-income countries; see World Bank 1991b: 9). Also, deregulation and increases of regulation are, paradoxically, sometimes tied together, as in the formation of regional trading agreements that, while they reduce trade regulation among the countries of the region, pose the spectre of dividing the world into trading blocks; the North American Free Trade Agreement provides a case in point. So globalization is a very real and important process, but it is also an incomplete and contested process.

This incomplete and contested process of globalization is the context of the neo-liberal ideological offensive on the issue of international commerce. Arguments for 'free trade' have a long history within economics, but they have come to the fore again in recent years as the pressure for deregulation has increased. The advocacy of free trade that lies at the heart of the neo-liberal position on international commerce is by far the dominant position among economists, at least in the English-speaking world which has defined the teaching and theoretical development of economics for many decades. The basic arguments behind the position, as I describe them shortly, can be found in innumerable basic economics textbooks. While many professional economists might demur on the larger package of neo-liberal policies, there are few who do not genuflect at the altar of free trade. This is especially strange, since, as I will explain in a later section of this chapter, it is now generally recognized within the economics profession that the theoretical case for free trade is not valid.

Great gains, however, certainly can be obtained from international commerce, both material gains and socio-cultural gains. Widespread commerce allows us to obtain a larger variety of goods than otherwise, and it allows different regions to specialize and make most effective use of their resources and abilities. Also, the social and political contact that comes with commerce spreads ideas and can enrich our lives through exposure to different cultures. There is nothing automatic about these benefits from commerce, and international commerce has often been closely connected to war and devastation. Yet few people would argue that commerce in and of itself should be avoided. The issue is not *whether* we take part in world commerce, but *how* we take part. Any democratic development alternative would include international commerce. It would also, however, require that a society regulate its foreign commerce, and thus it would be in direct conflict with the neo-liberal prescription. In order to establish a critique of neo-liberalism and build a foundation for democratic alternatives, it is necessary to examine the historic arguments for free trade and their role in the neo-liberal ideology.

Neo-liberal Theory

The essence of the neo-liberal position on international commerce is the proposition that economic growth will be most rapid when the movement of goods, services and capital is unimpeded by government regulations. The proposition is applied to all nations engaged in world commerce, whether they are rich or poor, agricultural or industrial, creditors or debtors. If governments wish to pursue economic growth, then the neo-liberal argument says that they should adopt 'free trade', a practice that allows unregulated international movement of goods and services and of capital – though not necessarily of labour, a point to which I will return shortly. (The neo-liberal position also identifies economic growth as the key to the larger process of economic development, but I will leave the growth–development relationship for later chapters.)

A simple logic lies at the basis of the free-trade position. If, for whatever reasons, countries differ in their abilities to produce various goods, then they can all benefit if each specializes in the production of those items it produces most effectively (that is, at least cost). They can then trade with one another to obtain the entire range of goods they need. In this manner, each country is using its resources to do what it can do best. (In the basic argument, countries, not individual people or groups of people, are the units of analysis, and no attention is given to how the benefits from trade are distributed among people within a country.)

As an illustration of this logic, consider two countries, one with an abundance of good farmland and the other with a good supply of energy resources (hydro power, for example). It seems likely that each of these countries will gain from trade if the first specializes in the production of agricultural goods and the latter specializes in the production of manufactures. Moreover, if the governments impose no constraints on international trade, then this specialization is precisely what will occur. Without constraints on trade, people attempting to produce manufactured goods in the country with abundant good farmland will not be able to do so as cheaply as people in the country with a good supply of energy resources – and vice versa for people attempting to produce agricultural goods in the latter country. Without constraints, competition will lead to least-cost specialization. If, however, the government of the country with abundant farmland bans the import of manufactures, then the only way its people can obtain manufactures will be to remove some of their resources from agriculture and devote them to manufacturing. This means shifting their resources from an activity where they are low-cost producers to an activity where they are high-cost producers, and, relative to the situation before the ban was imposed, they will be wasting resources. People in the other country will also lose under these circumstances because, unable to obtain agricultural goods by selling their manufactures to people in the country with good farmland, they will have to produce their own agricultural goods. (The argument is easiest to understand if we think of costs in terms of units of labour time. However, the argument is not qualitatively changed if costs are viewed in a more complex manner.)

The theory appears to run into trouble if one country produces everything more efficiently than the other. Yet the trouble is only apparent, not real. Under these circumstances, all will gain if each country specializes in the production of those goods where it has a *comparative advantage*. For example, the case described in the previous paragraph can be slightly elaborated (and, as we will see, the nature of specialization is reversed). Let's assume that the country with abundant farmland produces agricultural goods at half what it costs to produce them in the other country. At the same time, this country with abundant farmland has a workforce with great capacity for industrial labour, and it therefore can produce manufactured goods at one-quarter of what it costs to produce them in the other country. Under these circumstances the country's skilled labour force gives it a greater advantage in the production of manufactures than the advantage that its abundant farmland gives it in the production of agricultural goods. Thus it has a *comparative* advantage in the production of manufactures. Similarly, the second country, even though it is less efficient in the production of both categories of goods, has a *comparative* advantage in the production of agricultural goods. To produce manufactures would cost four times as much in this country as in the other, whereas to produce agricultural goods would only cost twice as much. Consequently, both countries can gain if each specializes where it has a comparative advantage, and they then trade to obtain their full set of needs. (The theory does not resolve the question of how the overall gains are distributed between the different partners in a trading relationship. However, if free trade exists and all the participants have the option not to trade, then it seems clear that no country will lose absolutely because of engaging in trade.)

The theory of comparative advantage has played an important role in the history of economics, for it has provided an intellectual rationale for free-trade policies. An intellectual rationale has been necessary because, whatever the larger efficacy of the policy, free trade is always costly to groups that have prospered under any prior trade restrictions. The first full and clear articulation of the theory is credited to David Ricardo, an early nineteenth-century English businessman and economist.

The ideological nature of Ricardo's argument is suggested by the fact that, in developing his case for free trade and specialization, he uses as a prime example the trade between Britain and Portugal, in which British cloth was exchanged for Portuguese wines (Ricardo 1966 [1817]: ch. VII). As a matter of fact, this cloth-for-wine exchange was not the result of free trade at all, but had been established through the 1703 Methuen Treaty in which Portuguese wines had been given preference in the British market over French wines as a means by which to open the Portuguese market to British cloth. As Adam Smith had noted in *The Wealth of Nations*:

> By the famous treaty of commerce with Portugal, the [British] consumer is prevented by high duties from purchasing of a neighbouring country [France], a commodity which our climate does not produce, but is obliged to purchase it of a distant country [Portugal], though it is acknowledged, that the commodity of the distant country is of a worse quality than that of the near one. The home-consumer is obliged to submit to this inconveniency, in order that the producer [of cloth] may import into the distant country some of his productions upon more advantageous terms than he would otherwise have been allowed to do. (Smith 1937 [1776]: 625–6)

At the beginning of the nineteenth century when Ricardo developed his argument, British manufacturing and financial interests were increasingly developing their international operations. They had become sufficiently well established that they were relatively unconcerned about foreign competitors. (I will return shortly to the means by which they had become so well established.) Success in the international realm, however, required that restriction elsewhere in the world on the imports of British manufactures be eliminated and also that restrictions on imports of agricultural goods into Britain be removed (because those restrictions on imports, whether they be foodstuffs or raw materials, raised the costs of British industry). In their struggle to obtain these ends, British business interests built on their prior economic success to gain dominant power in Parliament. In 1846, the Corn Laws were repealed, eliminating protective tariffs on grains. Elsewhere in the world, either through direct colonial control, as in India, or supported by the persuasive authority of the British navy, as in much of Latin America, British business achieved considerable success in securing open access. Neither political nor military power, however, is fully effective unless it is buttressed by a well-developed ideology. In the realm of commercial policies, the theory of comparative advantage was a foundation stone of such an ideology.

The theory of comparative advantage, however, is a static theory. It deals with the situation in a single time period, explaining how the countries participating in international trade maximize their incomes in that time period through free trade. In order to make it an argument for economic growth, the static theory must be transformed into a dynamic theory, in which maximizing income in a given time period also maximizes growth over an extended period of time. The steps in this transformation are simple, deceptively simple. Economic growth, it is argued, depends primarily on the level of investment. Investment in turn depends on the level of savings, and savings tend to rise and fall with the level of income. Free trade, then, leads to a higher current level of income, which leads to a higher level of savings, which leads to a higher level of investment, which leads to a higher rate of economic growth. Proponents of the theory do not claim that in the real world these steps are automatic, but they do argue that the end result of a higher level of economic growth is more likely if the current level of income is higher (as accomplished, they claim, through free trade) than if it is lower (the apparent result of regulation).

One of the critical steps in this simplest form of the argument is that the level of investment depends on the level of savings. Within a country, however, the level of investment is not directly linked to the level of savings in so far as capital is internationally mobile. This observation – which brings out the fact that savings, and therefore investment and growth, can be augmented by an inflow of foreign capital – provides the foundation for another important part of the neo-liberal argument for unregulated international commerce: capital movements as well as the movement of goods and services should be unrestricted. The lack of restriction on capital movements is, according to this position, the best means to assure a flow of foreign capital into a country. More foreign capital will allow more investment, and more investment will yield more growth. Attempts to prohibit foreign investors from certain realms (agriculture, 'key' industries or mining, for example), requirements that foreign investors take on national partners or develop national sources of supply, restrictions on the repatriation of profits, or other such policies will reduce the amount of foreign capital that comes into a country as investors find some of the particular conditions too costly and are inhibited generally by this restrictive business environment.

The neo-liberal argument about international commerce thus becomes dynamic through a theory of economic growth in which the level of a country's capacity to invest is the critical issue. The argument sees free trade as optimal because it allegedly raises the level of income and therefore raises domestic savings. Unrestricted capital movement is optimal because it supposedly raises the availability of foreign funds.

The acceptance of an economic theory depends in part on its internal coherence, the validity of its assumptions and the logical deductions from those assumptions. Also, the acceptance of a theory depends upon the extent to which the relationships it describes and its predictions are consistent with reality. Advocates of the neo-liberal position, accordingly, base their policy prescriptions as much on certain myths about history as on the internal coherence of their theory. They argue that their theory is validated by the history of successful economic growth, both in the longer experience of the relatively advanced economies and in the recent experience of successful growth in newly industrialized countries. They cite, in particular, the history of economic development in the United Kingdom, other countries of Western Europe, and the United States, and the more recent experiences of countries in East Asia.

An examination of these experiences, however, quickly demonstrates that the neo-liberal claims are but crude myths, having only a vague connection to reality. Such an examination, a short excursion into the history of economic development, also provides a basis for understanding the internal flaws in the theory of free trade. As it turns out, there are in fact great gains to be obtained from international commerce, gains that are socially valuable as well as profitable to those who directly engage in the trade. Yet there is no reason to believe that social gains are greatest when regulation is least.

However, before turning to historical experience and then to a re-examination of the theory, it is necessary to give some attention to the significance of neo-liberals' failure to include the free movement of labour across international boundaries as part of their platform. This failure, this special exception made for labour in the free-trade doctrine, is generally not given much attention in policy debates. Yet *neo-liberals' failure to advocate unregulated movement of labour along with unregulated movement of capital and commodities is a fatal flaw in the logic of their position.* If one were to accept the neo-liberal axioms that social welfare is maximized when government regulation is minimized and, in particular, national boundaries should be fully open to commercial intercourse, then the question must immediately arise: why regulate labour markets by preventing the movement of labour across national boundaries? The only conceivable answer is that because the movement of labour necessarily involves the movement of people it is socially disruptive and politically unacceptable. Yet *once social and political considerations are allowed to override the market, the whole neo-liberal position disintegrates.* Isn't it true that if capital is allowed to move across national boundaries the result will often be socially disruptive, in both the communities from which capital departs and the communities in which it arrives? And what about jobs lost to import competition when barriers to the movement of commodities are removed? Doesn't this often create social and political turmoil? There is no logic other than that of political opportunism by which social and political considerations can be used to justify government regulations on the movement of labour but cannot be used to justify government regulations on the free movement of capital and commodities. While my discussion that follows will focus on trade and investment, the issue of international labour migration should not be forgotten.

Historical Experience: a Brief Sketch[4]

Virtually all of our experience with economic development suggests that extensive regulation of foreign commerce by a country's government has been an essential foundation for successful economic growth. In the United Kingdom, perhaps the case most frequently cited to demonstrate the success of free trade, textile producers secured protection from import competition at the end of the seventeenth century, and high tariffs served British manufacturing well through the era of the country's rise to world economic pre-eminence. At the beginning of the nineteenth century, the average tariff rate on manufactures was 50 per cent – high by almost any comparative standard (World Bank 1991a: 97; the figure is an unweighted average for 1820). Later in the century, the UK did eliminate its tariffs on manufactures, but then it had passed the early stage of development and its industry was well established. As E. J. Hobsbawm (1968: 31) notes: 'British industry could grow up, by and large, in a protected home market until strong enough to demand free entry into other people's markets, that is "Free Trade".' Moreover, state support for industry in the United Kingdom came through the creation and maintenance of empire. While the British textile industry might have prospered without the captive Indian market, the fact of the matter is that it did prosper through regulations which stifled the Indian textile industry and forced that colony to import its linens from Lancashire (R. Dutt, 1963 [1884]: ch. 14).

Tariff protection also played a large role in the emergence of US industry. The textile industry, which was especially important in the country's economic development, got its start when the hostilities leading up to and through the War of 1812 provided implicit protection by limiting international shipping. After the war, the protection became explicit as a tariff was established (Taussig 1931). According to the World Bank (1991a: 97), the average US tariff on manufactures was 40 per cent in 1820. There were other factors that encouraged expansion of the US textile industry in the early nineteenth century; the relatively high wages of US workers induced innovation, and the relatively high level of education facilitated that innovation and its effective application. Yet a rapidly growing protected market was certainly a key element in the success of US textiles.

While the average tariff for the United States varied considerably in the early part of the nineteenth century, southern planters did manage to restrict the full extension of the tariff until they lost the Civil War. Then, in the last third of the nineteenth century, with tariff protection well established at an average of around 30 per cent for most of the 1870 to 1910 period (Schiavo-Campo 1978: Table 8.1), the United States experienced a great industrial expansion. Only after the Second World War, when US industry's dominant position in the world economy was secure, did a steady and lasting reduction of tariffs take place. As with the textile industry, many factors engendered the growth of US industry in the late nineteenth and early twentieth centuries, but tariff protection was of considerable importance. (In any comparison of levels of protection over time, it is probably reasonable to assume that protection due to costs of transportation have declined substantially over the last 200 years. Thus, for example, a formal 40 per cent tariff rate in 1820 involved a substantially greater degree of protection than would a formal rate of 40 per cent today. However, I am aware of no studies that provide a systematic analysis of transportation costs as a share of production costs.)

While the early development experiences of Britain and the United States demonstrate a role for trade protection, state regulation of foreign investment does not seem to have been an issue. In the case of Britain, foreign investment was not substantial in its early development, and during the nineteenth century Britain became a major capital exporter. Foreign-source funds do appear to have played a role in Britain's early industrial expansion, but these were the spoils of empire and slavery as opposed to private investment (Williams 1966 [1944]; Solow and Engerman 1987).[5]

In the United States, foreign investment was substantial but not dominant in nineteenth-century industrial expansion (Lewis 1938). Foreign finance was important in particular industries at particular times – for example, in the early development of the railways – and foreign owners were directly involved in several industries. Yet, overall, both sources of capital and control were predominantly from the US. Just before the First World War, foreign financial investments in the USA amounted to about $6 billion, roughly 15 per cent as large as the gross national product. Foreign direct investments totalled $1.3 billion, and payments on all foreign investments in the United States amounted to less than 10 per cent of merchandise export earnings (USDC 1975). Foreign investment in the United States during the nineteenth century was not heavily regulated. In particular, foreign-owned enterprises (direct investments) generally stood 'on an equal footing before the law with those under domestic control' (Lewis 1938: 78). Yet the lack of restrictions did not bring massive foreign investment and, while a factor, foreign investment does not appear to have been of dominant importance in US economic development.

Countries that achieved their developmental advance at a later historical period were generally characterized by a significantly greater role for the state in the regulation of foreign commerce, both with regard to trade and investment (Gerschenkron 1962; and Rosovsky 1961). Japan's experience in joining the ranks of advanced capitalist countries provides the prime example. In the post-Second World War era, the Japanese government rejected free trade and extensive foreign investment, and instead promoted its national firms. In the 1950s, for example, the government protected the country's fledgeling auto firms from foreign competition. At first, quotas limited imports to $500,000 a year, and then in the 1960s quotas were replaced by prohibitively high tariffs. Furthermore, foreign investment in Japan was virtually prohibited; allowed only in so far as it contributed to the development of the domestic industry. Japanese companies were encouraged to import foreign technology, but they were required to produce 90 per cent of parts domestically within five years. Success was also obtained through protecting the Japanese computer industry. In the early 1970s, as the industry was developing, a foreign machine could be purchased only if a suitable Japanese model was not available. IBM was allowed to produce within the country, but only when it licensed basic patents to Japanese firms (and IBM computers produced in Japan were covered by the restrictions on purchases of foreign machines) (Armstrong et al. 1984).

In so far as any country has broken out of underdevelopment in more recent decades, South Korea would provide the most important case study. In broad terms, the South Korean experience is very similar to that of Japan. From the early 1960s, the South Korean state followed policies of protecting domestic markets, heavily favouring Korean-owned firms, and using state-owned industries to develop national production in certain 'strategic' sectors. In addition to all the traditional mechanisms of intervention in foreign commerce, the Korean government relied heavily on credit policies and, in important cases, price controls to guide the country's industrial development (Hart-Landsberg 1993; and Amsden 1989). South Korea, with a per capita income of $9,700 in 1995, is at least on the verge of entering into the league of the world's rich countries, the financial crisis that appeared in 1997 notwithstanding. In any case, its extremely rapid growth rate over an extended period – an average over 7 per cent per year in the growth of real per capita income between 1965 and 1995 – and its role in world markets of such goods as automobiles and electronic equipment attest to a considerable degree of economic success. A heavy state role in regulating the country's international commerce, which led to a rapid transformation of technology, appears to have been a fundamental part of this success.

One of the important aspects of the South Korean experience is that in protecting and supporting the development of national industry the government did not by any means encourage Korean firms to abjure exports and follow an 'inward-looking' policy. On the contrary, the government used a firm's ability to compete in export markets as a measure of whether or not it was succeeding in becoming more efficient (Amsden 1989). The South Korean experience shows how economic policy can both regulate foreign commerce but at the same time make sure that national firms reap the many advantages associated with international commerce – including, especially, the transfer of knowledge and technology that come with foreign exposure. (Some authors – Rudiger Dornbush [1992], for example – attempt to build a case for free trade by pointing out these advantages of foreign commerce and act as though the only policy options are free trade or autarky. Their arguments are thoroughly refuted by South Korean and other East Asian experiences.)

South Korea and also Taiwan provide useful perspectives on the role of foreign capital in development. Both countries attained relatively rapid economic growth in recent decades without relatively large amounts of foreign direct investment (FDI). Table 2.1 and Table 2.2 present data on FDI which indicate that the high rates of growth in South Korea and Taiwan compared to countries in Latin America cannot be explained by a high rate of foreign participation in the economies of the East Asian high performers.

TABLE 2.1 Share of foreign firms in industrial production, selected countries (%)

South Korea (1978)	19
Taiwan (1976)	16*
Argentina (1972)	31
Brazil (1977)	44
Chile (1979)	28
Colombia (1974)	43
Mexico (1970)	35
Uruguay (1978)	12

* Share of employment.
Source: R. Jenkins (1991).

Table 2.1 shows that, in the 1970s, the level of participation by foreign firms in industrial production was substantially lower in South Korea and Taiwan than in several Latin American nations (though Uruguay provides an exception). Table 2.2 shows that, in the late 1970s and early 1980s, the inflows of FDI (and the outflows of earnings on FDI) were very much larger in relation to GDP in Brazil and Mexico than in South Korea and Taiwan. (Comparisons of GDP with stocks of FDI are available only for Brazil and South Korea, and fit the same pattern.) Thus, in so far as they

TABLE 2.2 The extent of foreign direct investment (FDI) in Mexico, Brazil, South Korea and Taiwan, various measures (millions of dollars)

	Inflows of FDI		Outflows of FDI profits		Stock of FDI	GDP
	Annual averages 1975–80	1981–85	Annual averages 1975–80	1981–85	1985	1985
Mexico	1,023.5	1,106.7	819.5	1,224.3	–	177,360
Brazil	1,835.8	1,992.8	1,102.7	1,825.7	22,967.9[1]	188,250
South Korea	60.7	116.3	47.9	102.2	1,679.5[2]	86,180
Taiwan	91.3	189.0	93.2	207.4	–	62,062

Notes: 1. Stock of FDI in Brazil was 35 per cent US and 10 per cent Japanese.
2. Stock of FDI in South Korea was 35 per cent US and 52 per cent Japanese.

NB: These data indicate that, whatever the net impact of FDI on a country's surplus, the costs of accepting that foreign investment are high. For example, in Mexico between 1981 and 1985, the outflows of profits on FDI substantially exceeded the inflow of FDI, either in that or the previous five-year period. The fact that outflows of FDI profits exceed inflows of FDI does not necessarily mean that FDI has a net negative impact on a country's surplus. To determine the net impact, we would have to know what would have happened to the surplus in the absence of the investment. For example, if $1 of FDI increased the surplus by $2 and the resulting outflow of profits was $1.50, the net impact would be an increase of $0.50 of the surplus within the country, in spite of the fact that the outflow exceeded the inflow. Such marginal calculations, however, would not get at the central issue of the overall structural impact of foreign investment on a country's economy.

Source: FDI data from UNCTC (1988). GDP data from Republic of China (1989) for Taiwan and from the World Bank (1987) for other countries.

tell us anything about the relation between FDI and economic growth, these data suggest a negative correlation. (See Evans [1987] for a useful comparison of East Asian and Latin American experiences.)

More to the point, however, the East Asian experiences indicate that successful economic development is not associated with unrestricted access by foreign firms to a country's national economy. South Korea achieved its growth success by actively favouring its national firms in a manner similar to that employed in Japan. The country's Foreign Capital Inducement Act required that all foreign direct investment be evaluated by the government bureaucracy. In recent decades, foreign investment was allowed in 'key' sectors only when the government believed it had no alternative means to obtain technology or raw materials. When foreign investment has been allowed, it has been given very profitable incentives; but the incentives have been tied to 'very detailed agreements that specify the technology to

be transferred and/or quantity and nature of raw materials to be supplied'
(Hart-Landsberg 1993: 89).

Taiwan's practices seem to have been similar, providing highly attractive
incentives for those foreign investments that the government has seen as
useful in supporting national development but at the same time exercising
a good deal of selectivity over which foreign investments would serve the
government's ends. The selectivity increased over the 1970s, and was based
on such factors as technology transfer, opening of new markets, export
expansion and intensity of linkages, as well as on its effect upon the
country's international political relations. (Wade 1990: 150). (I should point
out that however one explains the economic growth success in South Korea
and Taiwan, to recognize that success is by no means to take the authoritarian and repressive regimes in those countries as models to be emulated.
Those experiences are important for what they show us about the connection between state regulation and successful growth, but they are also
important for what they show us about the suppression of democracy. On
this point, see Hart-Landsberg 1993; and Bello and Rosenfeld 1990.)

East Asian experiences are often contrasted with experiences in Latin
America, as I have done in Tables 2.1 and 2.2. Yet through the 1980s,
Mexico's and Brazil's foreign investment policies shared certain broad
features with those of South Korea and Taiwan. In all of these countries,
there was an effort to control and regulate foreign investment towards
national development. If anything, Mexico and Brazil obtained their relatively larger inflows of foreign investment on the basis of more restrictive
and less friendly practices than were employed in Taiwan and South Korea.
In all four countries, this broad policy worked to achieve very high rates
of economic growth. The fact that Brazil and Mexico, along with much of
the rest of Latin America, experienced debt crisis and disruption of
economic growth in the 1980s can hardly be attributed to the simple fact
that they exercised some controls over foreign investment. Perhaps they
did not manage foreign investment correctly or perhaps they allowed too
much (contributing to the outflow of funds through high rates of profit
expatriation), but the comparison with Taiwan and South Korea makes it
very clear that management per se, as opposed to allowing free access, was
not the problem.

Foreign direct investment, however, is only one category of externally
sourced funds that may affect a country's economic development. Especially
during the early phases of their rapid growth experiences, South Korea
and Taiwan received substantial amounts of foreign aid, both economic
and military, and South Korea obtained a substantial amount of foreign
financial capital during the 1970s (managing to avoid the ravages of the
debt crisis even though it was one of the world's relatively large debtor

nations at the beginning of the 1980s). In some other low-income countries, remittances by nationals living abroad have also provided significant inflows of funds. On the basis of recent experiences of successful expansion as well as from the experience of earlier developing nations, it is possible to make the case that funds from foreign sources are an important, if not necessary, foundation for placing a country on a path of economic development (Vilas 1989). Experience, however, does not support the contention that a high level of foreign direct investment is the key to economic development. Most important, there is no basis in the record to maintain that a substantial inflow of foreign funds requires minimal regulation of foreign investment.

This is not to say that regulation per se is the key to economic development. In all cases where state regulation of international commerce has been a component in the foundation of economic expansion, other policies and circumstances have also played important roles. It should be obvious, moreover, that there are wrong ways to regulate foreign commerce as well as right ways. Protectionism and the regulation of foreign capital inflows have at times contributed to economic failure instead of economic success. Yet as this brief discussion of a few notable countries' histories indicates, there is no substance to the neo-liberal claim that 'free trade' has been the foundation, historically and in the current era, of successful economic growth. (The very special case of the Hong Kong city state, in so far as it grew on the basis of free trade, may be the exception that proves the rule. It has been such an unusual sort of political and economic entity that its experience does not undermine the general conclusion of a lack of association between free trade and successful development. In recent years, Chile has been touted as a showcase for neo-liberal policies, including trade policies. Yet the Chilean success is substantially overrated and, however great the success in terms of economic growth, growth cannot be attributed simply to free trade and other neo-liberal policies; see Pieper and Taylor 1998; and Collins and Lear 1994.)

Re-examining the Theory of International Trade and Investment

So the neo-liberal theory of international commerce does not sit very well with historical experience, and this lack of congruence between theory and reality suggests that there are some problems with the theory. Indeed, there are several.

The problems in the traditional economic theory of free trade have been well known for a long time. When the theory of free trade was emerging at the end of the eighteenth and beginning of the nineteenth centuries, the critique of free trade also began to emerge. While free trade was espoused as the ideology of British business, which was the industrially most advanced and dominant power in world commerce, the opposition to free trade was articulated by individuals associated with those powers competing with and threatened by British dominance. One famous example is Alexander Hamilton's *Report on the Subject of Manufactures* (1966 [1791]). Hamilton, as the first US Treasury Secretary, was making an argument for the state's role in supporting the development of US industry. As it emerged from British colonial restraints, he argued, US economic development would be best served were US business protected by the state from the economic restraints that would result from directly facing the more advanced British industry. On the European continent, the work of the German writer Frederich List (1928 [1841]) became the most enduring early response to the British ideological offensive. List's argument, directed in large part explicitly in response to Adam Smith's rationalization of *laissez-faire*, anticipated much of the modern criticism of free trade. He maintained that certain economic activity (manufacturing) was particularly advantageous to a nation's long-run prosperity because it would stimulate the development of labour and natural resources to the general benefit of the economy. List then argued that this advantageous activity would not emerge, or not emerge as quickly, unless it were protected (by tariffs, for example) from competition with already advanced foreign industry.

The early arguments for state regulation of a country's foreign commerce have been elaborated and extended in recent decades. In spite of the fact that the doctrine of free trade remains official ideology within at least the US economics profession and is the standard fare in basic textbooks, it is now increasingly recognized by economists – though begrudgingly in most cases – that purely economic arguments are insufficient to support the free-trade position.[6] Today, then, we have a substantial list of bases on which to challenge the neo-liberal theory of international commerce.

Technology in economic growth   First on this list is that the theory of free trade is fundamentally flawed because it fails to take account of the ways in which production itself affects technological change. 'Learning-by-doing' is a particularly important form of the phenomenon. In a new activity, initial production may be very costly. Yet as time passes and experience accumulates, the people engaged in the activity learn. They change the way they do things, which is to say that they change the technology. Such an activity might never develop were it forced to compete with already established firms in other countries where the learning-by-doing had already taken place. Yet if the activity were protected from foreign competition during an initial phase in which experience could be accumulated, it could develop and become fully competitive. The same is true of situations where economies of scale are important. Without protection, the firm might never reach the size where it could produce efficiently and compete in international markets.

Yet protection involves costs. Why should society in general bear the costs of protection in order to assure the development of any particular activity? After all, any investment requires some initial period of development before profits start accruing. Why are the problems of import competition different from any other problems facing an investor? Why not let the individual investor bear the costs that are involved during the learning period or during the period where the scale of production is small?

The answer to these questions lies in the concept of *location-specific technological externalities*. Different kinds of production activities tend to bring about different kinds of changes in the overall economic environment. In the eighteenth and nineteenth centuries, for example, manufacturing tended to generate new methods of production and a development of skills that had far-reaching technological impacts. In the current era, 'high-tech' production appears to have similar far-reaching impacts. Because the gains from these sorts of changes are not confined to the industry or firm where they originate, they are not reflected in the profits of that industry or firm and will not be taken into account as a basis for investment decisions. These positive technological impacts of a particular production activity that do not affect the profits and are outside of, or external to, the purview of the people making decisions about that production, are 'technological externalities'. When positive technological externalities exist for a particular activity, then the value of that activity to society will be greater than the private value. If investment decisions take place within a free market (or if the market is not manipulated to reflect the externalities), there will be less investment in that activity than would be desirable from the perspective of society at large. Indeed, when the products of that activity can be imported from already established production facilities abroad, it is possible that no investment at all will take place in this branch of production within the country. (Externalities can be negative as well as positive. Air pollution from factory smoke stacks, for example, is a widely noted negative externality. When activities have negative externalities, unregulated market decisions will result in more of that activity taking place than is socially desirable.)

Even when the activities that generate technological externalities do not take place within a particular country, it is possible that the country may still benefit from the externalities. For example, in today's economy, where modern communications tie together economic activity in far-flung regions, technological innovations at one site may have applications and thus positive impacts globally. Nevertheless, technological externalities are often 'location-specific', having their greatest impact within relatively close geographic proximity to the site where they are originally generated; or at least having their principal impact within the same national unit, for, as I will point out in a moment, technological externalities sometimes work through the socio-political framework.

The US experience with the cotton textile industry, which I have cited above, provides a particularly good example of the generation of location-specific technological externalities. The textile industry emerged in the early decades of the nineteenth century, prospering especially in the northeastern part of the United States. Mill towns throughout southern New England became centres of growth. Not only did they create a demand for southern cotton, but they also created a demand for new machinery, maintenance of old machinery, parts, dyes, *skills*, construction materials, construction machinery, *more skills*, equipment to move the raw materials and the products, parts and maintenance for that equipment, *and still more skills*. As centres of economic activity, innovation and change, mill towns made a contribution to the economic growth of the United States that went far beyond the value of the textiles they produced.

One of the ways that the textile industry promoted change and growth was through its impact on education. Textile mills and other factories required a disciplined labour force. Early industrialists recognized that schools could provide them with the sort of people they needed to operate their factories, and they pushed for the expansion of the public educational system (Bowles and Gintis 1976: ch. 2). The educational system, in turn, was a major pillar of more general technological advance and economic growth. Thus, one form of the location-specific technological externalities of the early US factory expansion had its impact through the political and social system, to the schools, and back to myriad realms of production. It is widely recognized that schooling enhances the development of advanced industry, but it is also true that advanced industry enhances the development of the school system. In this sense, a positive circularity exists, and the state can support development by promoting industry, promoting education or promoting both. (In the United States, for reasons that need not detain us here, the public educational system has developed on the basis of state laws and local finance. Consequently, the educational impacts of early industrialization had their greatest impacts in ways that were quite 'location-specific'. Massachusetts, the site of many of the early textile mills, was particularly important as a leader in the development of public education. In countries with more centralized educational systems, parallel impacts would not be so focused, but they would take place within the country none the less.)

Any of the cases mentioned in the preceding section's brief historical discussion could provide further examples of the way certain industries have been protected by state regulation of foreign commerce and then have generated a wide range of location-specific technological externalities that have enhanced national development. Certainly the industrial revolution in Britain fits this pattern, where, under state protection and with the market and resources that came with empire, symbiosis emerged among the various branches of production. In Japan, the development of the automobile industry was nurtured by the government in such a way as to create far-flung connections among the central firms and supplying industries, generating widespread technological advances (Hill 1989). Likewise, the Japanese government protected the computer industry because of its more general impacts on economic life. South Korea and Taiwan successfully followed a similar path, using a variety of protections and state subsidies to push forward industries that would have large and general technological impacts.

The connection between protective state action and positive, general technological impacts, however, was by no means always conscious. It would be a mistake to infer cause from effect, especially among those countries that experienced early industrialization. More often than not in the history of the regulation of foreign commerce, in successful cases as in unsuccessful cases, particular tariffs (or other trade restrictions) were the result of political efforts by industrial groups seeking to enhance their own interests; broader social impacts were sometimes offered as a rationale but were seldom the actual motivating factor. In Japan and South Korea, however, as well as in some other recent East Asian success stories, the effort to generate technological change through the promotion of particular types of activity appears to have been relatively explicit and conscious.

Regardless of original causation, however, it matters which goods a society produces. For when we produce a good – cotton textiles in 1800, computers in the 1990s, or any other good – we also reproduce ourselves as a society. We create skills and opportunities, new technologies and new ideas. What we do today determines who we are and what we can do tomorrow. In so far as the gains in this production and reproduction do not accrue to private decision-makers who can appropriate a profit, there is no reason to believe that they will take place without state intervention. Indeed, for countries that are relative late-comers in the world economy, as the experience of several East Asian countries suggests, the role of the state in promoting development in the face of international competition is especially important.

These arguments can be counterposed directly with the classical theory of comparative advantage that is at the core of neo-liberal doctrines on international commerce (and, for that matter, is at the core of the official ideology of mainstream economics). The theory of comparative advantage takes no account of location-specific technological externalities. There are no economies of scale, and learning-by-doing is not a factor. In so far as technological change exists in the theory, its origin lies outside the system of production itself. The value of any particular type of production is then fully captured in the free-market prices, and thus private, profit-motivated decisions lead to socially optimal consequences. All our experience with economic growth suggests that, not only do economies of scale, learning-by-doing and location-specific technological externalities exist, but also that they are very important.

When the theory of comparative advantage is made into a dynamic theory, its focus is entirely on investment as the driving force of economic growth. No one would deny that investment is an important part of the economic growth equation, but technological change also plays a very substantial role. There is no escaping the fact that protectionism, even when it successfully enhances long-run economic growth through generating technological change, has costs. If an industry needs some form of protection from foreign competition in order to survive, this means that the goods in question could be obtained more cheaply from abroad. So protection has the immediate impact of lowering incomes, and lowering incomes will tend to mean lower levels of investment. Yet government regulation of international commerce will enhance economic growth when it leads to the development of industries that generate technological advances that outweigh the short-run income-investment losses.

It is worth underscoring the point that at the core of the argument for protection is the fact that different industries have impacts that are not captured in market prices. In the United States of the early nineteenth century, an additional $1 of manufacturing production had different impacts from an additional $1 of agricultural production. In mid-twentieth-century Japan, an additional $1 of auto production had different impacts from an additional $1 of textile production. The differences lie in the different technological externalities that are not reflected in the market prices of the goods. Yet it is also clear, as these examples suggest, that different industries play these 'key' roles in different historical periods. The cotton textiles industry was the focus of change and innovation in an earlier era, but it is unlikely to play that same role today. Manufacturing may play an especially important role in affecting technological change (Cohen and Zysman 1987), but different manufacturing sectors will play different roles at different times and even our definitions of manufacturing are amorphous and changeable. So, while recognizing the importance of promoting certain types of industries to enhance economic growth, we should be cautious in applying facile rules as to exactly which industries those are.

Furthermore, in the form of the well-developed 'infant industry' analysis, the essence of the argument presented here has been used on many occasions to justify protectionism that garners power and privilege for a small group without any resulting technological spin-offs of importance. In addition, the infant industries argument has the practical problem that, whatever the legitimacy of original protection, it is not always easy to force the 'infants' to 'grow up'. There is no automatic assurance that these protected industries will become more efficient as time passes. Moreover, those who own and work in protected industries gain income and power from that protection, and they can use that income and power to preserve the protection long after the original infant industry argument has ceased to have any relevance. These practical matters will be addressed in Chapter 8. Nevertheless, the basic premise of the argument – that in the face of competition from previously developed enterprises abroad, some form of support is necessary to assure the development of industries that have far-reaching technological externalities – is certainly sound. Also, the practice of supporting infant industries has played profound and essential roles in virtually all cases of successful economic development.

Trade and employment The theory of comparative advantage and arguments for free trade rest on the assumption that full employment exists, or at least that the level of employment is independent of the *pattern* of trade and production. In addition, the theory assumes that when patterns of trade and production change, labour will move from one activity to another instantaneously – or at least sufficiently rapidly so as to cause no great welfare loss or disruption of overall demand. In reality, most low-income countries are characterized by very high levels of unemployment and underemployment, the pattern of trade and production does affect employment levels (at least in the short run), and labour markets adjust to change relatively slowly (so that disruptions due to transitory causes can become long lasting).

An illustration of the problems is provided by experience in many low-income countries when trade restrictions on grain imports are lifted. Relative to some of the economically advanced countries (Canada, Australia, USA) and a few low-income countries (Argentina), grain production in many low-income countries is high cost. Grain is often produced on small plots of land, perhaps marginal land, by peasants who have limited access to capital and regular water supplies. In spite of the high costs, peasant grain production continues to exist because it is supported by tariffs on foreign grain (or other import restrictions), sometimes accompanied by subsidies that keep the price of basic food low for urban consumers. At the same time, where grain production is high cost, the production of agricultural export crops (fruits, vegetables, flowers) and of labour-intensive manufactures is relatively low cost. In these sorts of situations, it seems that the value of national production would be increased were labour moved out of grain production into the production of export crops or labour-intensive manufacturing. Moreover, it would seem that the elimination of the grain import barriers, a move towards free trade, would have this economically advantageous result. (The elimination of peasant grain agriculture, however advantageous in terms of national production, may have high social costs because of the role of this traditional activity in peasant culture and because of its impact on the stability of communities.)

In Mexico, where the internationalization of grain supply was proceeding apace in the 1980s, even before the establishment of NAFTA, the replacement of peasant grain production by imports has not worked out so favourably (Barkin 1990). In fact, those parts of agriculture that have expanded in recent years – meat production and vegetable exports, for example – and export manufacturing use relatively small amounts of labour. Peasants displaced by the import of inexpensive US and Canadian grain, instead of finding employment in these sectors, swell the ranks of the unemployed or underemployed, often in cities. Consequently, instead of labour resources being used more efficiently under the pressure of import competition, labour resources are wasted. Also, the strain on urban services imposes economic costs (to say nothing of social costs), either in terms of additional government spending or deteriorating services. Perhaps these 'adjustment' problems in Mexico would be less severe if labour could migrate more easily to jobs in the United States, but neither NAFTA nor the broader neo-liberal agenda allows the free international movement of workers.

Also, these sorts of difficulties in Mexico might be less severe if they were confined to a single sector, though peasant grain production in Mexico, as in many other countries, is a single sector of considerable importance. Eventually, displaced peasants might find work in the service sector or in small-scale manufacturing and construction. The early results of the implementation of NAFTA, however, suggest that such favourable results are unlikely. Large-scale retailers from the United States, for example, have been quick to take advantage of the opening of the Mexican market. The retail outlets that they have begun to establish will use far less labour than have small-scale Mexican stores, contributing further to, rather than alleviating, unemployment.

Arguments for free trade have assumed away the unemployment that comes when trade displaces domestic production partly by implicitly treating the labour force as though all workers are engaged in wage labour. In advanced capitalist countries, this may be a reasonable approximation of reality; in the rich partners of NAFTA, Canada and the United States, over 90 per cent of workers are 'wage and salary' workers. In Mexico at the beginning of the 1990s, however, only 70 per cent were 'wage and salary' workers, and some 30 per cent were 'self-employed' or 'unpaid employees' (Russell 1992). Though globalization has incorporated the bulk of the Mexican economy into a thoroughly capitalist mode of operation, a large sector of small-scale peasant producers and urban shopkeepers remains, and their occupations would be greatly reduced, if not eliminated, in a regime of free trade. The relative size of the wage-labour sector is insufficient to absorb a massive influx of labour in a relatively short time. In this regard, Mexico is typical of the situations in very many low-income countries. (James Russell [1992] points out that Puerto Rico in the 1940s and 1950s offers a historical analogy to the current Mexican situation. The integration of the Puerto Rican economy with that of the US mainland resulted in the rapid depopulation of agricultural areas. Unlike Mexicans and the citizens of other low-income countries, Puerto Ricans were able to migrate freely to the United States. 'Solving' a country's unemployment problem through massive emigration may or may not be socially desirable, but, in any case, it is not an option that is generally available.)

Even if the problems of shifting labour from one set of activities to another were only a matter of time, they would be significant. Direct suffering by the unemployed and their families would be substantial, as would the lost income that would result from these 'labour resources' sitting idle. The income losses could outweigh the gains that might be obtained from the more 'rational' allocation of resources forced upon a country by free trade. Yet there is no assurance that, after these losses, a successful adjustment would ultimately be attained. The income losses during the 'period of adjustment' would reduce aggregate demand, and the unemployment (or underemployment) would have political consequences. The result of the ensuing disruptions is not likely to be the favourable efficient organization of resources anticipated in the theory of free trade.

Free trade and large firms The neo-liberal argument for free trade is based on the assumption that if government did not intervene and regulate international commerce, then the economy would operate in a competitive manner with advantageous results. For example, competition, in particular price competition, would ensure that a country with a large, relatively low-paid labour force would specialize in the production and export of labour-intensive products; firms that obtained their goods from elsewhere would be forced out of business by competition. Likewise, price competition would assure that a country's imports would be drawn from the least-cost sources elsewhere in the world. Government restrictions on commerce would only interfere with competition and disrupt the efficient operations of markets.

International commerce, however, is often dominated by a relatively small number of very large firms that operate in a monopolistic manner. Competition among them exists, and in some cases is very intense. It is, however, monopolistic competition, not simply the price competition that is assumed in the argument for free trade. The patterns of trade and production engaged in by very large firms are determined as part of their complex global strategies – with results that do not necessarily coincide with either the price competition model of the free trade argument or the long-run development interests of a particular country.

The role of large firms in international commerce is indicated by figures on the share of international trade that is intra-firm trade, the purchase of goods and services by one branch of a firm from other branches of that same firm. In the early 1980s, more than a third of US international trade (exports and imports) and about one-quarter of Japanese trade was intra-firm trade. Although thorough data are not available for other countries, the central role of the United States and Japan in the world trading system makes these data of general significance. The share of countries' merchandise trade that is associated with multinational firms (as opposed to simply intra-firm trade) also establishes the dominating role of the large companies. For the United Kingdom, 80 per cent of export trade in the early 1980s was associated with multinational firms; for the United States in that same period, more than half of imports and some three-quarters of exports were associated with US-based multinational firms (UNCTC 1988: ch. 6).

Large firms are sensitive to price considerations, and they are often quick to relocate production to take advantage of low-cost resources. Yet resource costs, the foundation of the theory of comparative advantage, are only one element in the strategies of large, internationally integrated firms. The Japanese automobile companies, for example, established their leading role in the industry through a strategy of developing linkages to suppliers in close physical proximity to the central plant. Resource costs were secondary to the issue of strategic control, which had important impacts on technological change and the management of inventory. In the international textile industry, flexibility is a paramount concern in the strategy of large firms, and issues of market proximity and control over product supply stand alongside resource costs as factors determining the location of production. Similarly, in the semi-conductor production of the electronics industry, many firms (particularly US firms) have followed a strategy of vertical integration. When companies produce semi-conductors for use in their own final products, their location decisions tend to be dominated by concerns about control of the technology and production process; concerns about least-cost siting tend to be secondary. In all of these examples, selected from industries that are both highly international in their operations and in which very large companies play central roles, monopolistic firms employ strategies of control that enhance their own long-run profits. There is no reason to expect the outcomes to conform to those envisioned in the theoretical arguments for free trade.

Peter Dicken (1992: chs 8, 9 and 10), the source for the examples of the previous paragraph, does emphasize the fact that a great variety of strategies are employed by the multinational firms, and in some of these strategies, resource-cost considerations are important. For example, in the late 1960s and 1970s, some US auto firms, particularly Ford, pursued a 'world car' strategy that was tied to resource cost considerations. This strategy called for an integrated network of plants, each producing a particular part of a highly standardized car, which could be slightly varied for different markets, located in least-cost production sites. The 'world car' strategy, however, was based on reaping large economies of scale at each site, and thus does not conform to the world envisioned as the basis for the free-trade position. In any case, what is important is that in any industry firms follow a variety of strategies. As Dicken describes the international electronics industry:

> In such a volatile technological and competitive industry as electronics, firms inevitably employ a whole variety of strategies to ensure their survival and in pursuit of growth ... Of course, many factors influence the particular mix of strategies employed. One important variable is size of firm: large firms tend to operate in rather different ways from smaller firms. Another influence is, undoubtedly, a firm's geographic origins: the domestic context in which it has developed. There are substantial differences in behaviour between American, Japanese, and European electronics firms. (Dicken 1992: 327)

The argument of free trade theory, however, assumes that a single sort of strategy is imposed on firms by competition. The very existence of a multiplicity of strategies belies the theory.

Primary product problems When the argument for free trade was developed in the nineteenth century, it was a rationalization for the particular character of the international division of labour that emerged so clearly at that time. That division of labour placed a few countries of Europe and North America in the position of specializing in the production and export of manufactured goods, while several other countries – many of which are today's low-income countries – specialized in the production and export of primary products. Today, although the international division of labour has changed, there are still many low-income countries characterized by primary product specialization.

Primary product specialization is problematic, first of all, because the prices of primary products are highly unstable. Primary products are, by definition, the raw materials that enter at an early stage into the production of other goods. Sugar, for example, is used largely in the manufacture of a great variety of sweets, and the cost of sugar plays a small role in affecting the final price of those sweets. Copper finds its demand as an input to houses, automobiles and other machinery. Like sugar, its cost plays a small role in determining the price of the final products of which it is a part. Grains, vanilla, cocoa, cotton, coffee and several other products fit this pattern. Consequently, the demand for such a product is very insensitive to its price (that is, the demand is very price inelastic). When the supply of a primary product increases – for example, because of good weather and a resulting good crop in some region of the world – prices will decline a great deal as producers compete with one another to unload their surpluses on the very limited market. Conversely, with a small decline in the supply – resulting, perhaps, from bad weather and a resulting crop failure – producers will be able to push up the price a great deal. Even when the average price of a primary product is in some sense 'reasonable', price fluctuations create severe cyclical problems that, when the product is important, may disrupt the development of an entire national economy.

An additional problem of specialization in primary products was made famous by Raul Prebisch (1950) and Hans Singer (1950), namely that in general the average prices of primary products are not 'reasonable', in the sense that the demand for the products is subject to long-term downward pressure. Consider, for example, the case of foods – sugar, coffee, cocoa – exported from low-income countries to the advanced economies of Europe and North America. As income rises in the advanced countries, the demand for food rises less rapidly (that is, the income elasticity of demand for primary products is less than 1). Under these circumstances, in so far as countries rely on primary product exports to the advanced countries for their national income, their national income must grow more slowly than income in those advanced countries. The problem might appear in declining terms of trade (that is, a decline in the ratio of the prices of the primary product exports to the prices of manufactured imports) or it might appear simply in slower growth of production. Yet, however the problem appears, as long as a country remains dependent on a single primary product (or a narrow group of primary products), the problem will be very real.

These problems with a reliance on primary product exports have been aggravated by the development of various substitutes, the products of modern chemical and industrial innovations: corn sweeteners for sugar, synthetic fibres for cotton, artificial flavours for various natural products, and plastics for just about everything. Any lasting rise in the price of the primary products directly induces the innovations, limiting the gains that might be obtained by cartels or other price-increasing mechanisms.

There is little dispute about the existence of these problems. Free traders, however, would claim that precisely because of these problems the free market will lead countries away from specialization. Price instability, long-run downward pressure on prices and limits on price increases will all reduce the profits on primary products relative to other goods. Moreover, as these prices fall relative to goods that have been imported (the declining terms of trade), production of those other goods within the country will become more profitable. The fact that some countries have overcome primary product export dependence through diversification into non-traditional agricultural exports and manufacturing exports is then called forth as evidence that the problem is taken care of by self-correction within the context of free trade. Yet this argument ignores the fact that the context for 'self-correction' has not been free trade at all. The East Asian success stories, Brazil, Mexico, and other countries that have diversified away from primary product export reliance, have done so with active government support for the shift.

The particular flaw in free-trade theory that is relevant here is that it assumes a degree of responsiveness to relative price changes that simply does not exist, partly because it ignores the social foundations of investment and their connection to past patterns of production. In low-income countries, capital markets are poorly developed, infrastructure is weak and slow to change, and the labour force is not well prepared for new types of production. The risks of new lines of business activity are large, and investors are conservative. Under these circumstances, relative price changes do not elicit a rapid reaction. Moreover, while declining export prices raise the relative prices and profits of new sorts of production, they also weaken internal demand. So the problems are not simply overcome by waiting.

The impact of foreign direct investment The neo-liberal theory of international investment is no more consistent with historical experience and no less flawed than the traditional argument for free trade. The failure of the theory of international investment can be seen in two important issues: the way a firm's national identity affects its strategy and thereby affects its impact on a country's economic development; and the way foreign firms can pre-empt, instead of enhance, the operations of national firms in a low-income country.[7]

The neo-liberal argument for deregulation of foreign investment by low-income countries rests on the assumption that the national identity of a firm does not affect the impact of its operations on the economic development of a low-income country. Investment is the foundation of growth, the argument asserts, regardless of where it comes from. The justification for this assumption concerning the irrelevance of a firm's national identity is that, regardless of national identity, all firms are under the same pressures to maximize profits; the pressures of competition, rather than any national characteristics, will then determine their strategies. The world of the multinationals that engage in international investment, however, is a world of very large firms. For very large firms, the pressures to maximize profits are not immediate, and the firms have leeway to develop a variety of strategies (as noted just above). What's more, the historical experiences of firms have a great deal of influence on their strategies, and historical experiences vary along with national identity. This point is brought out particularly strongly by the considerable attention that has been devoted in recent decades to the difference between large Japanese and large US firms.

Aside from the issue of size, firms with different national identities operate with different sets of information and networks that constrain their operations differently and lead them to choose different strategies, even while they all follow the same goal of maximizing profits. As any elementary economics student should know, firms do not simply maximize profits; they maximize profits subject to constraints. If the constraints differ, then the strategies to maximize profits will differ. Peter Evans (1979: ch 1), in discussing the difference between Brazilian firms and foreign-based firms operating in Brazil, develops the implications of this distinction by using the concept of 'bounded rationality'. Evans argues that both Brazilian firms and foreign firms follow the same rationality, a profit-maximizing rationality, in making their decisions. Yet they do so within different boundaries (that is, within different constraints). In general, the managers of Brazilian firms have a better knowledge of and are more thoroughly connected, politically and socially, within their own nation than are their counterparts in foreign firms. The latter in general have more information and better sets of networks beyond Brazil. This difference leads the Brazilian firms to focus more on internal sources of supply (the formation of internal linkages), makes them more likely to reinvest within the country, and impels them to develop new methods of production that reflect local conditions and new products that satisfy local demand. They are also more likely than foreign firms to encourage the Brazilian state to act in ways that support national development through, for example, the expansion of social and physical infrastructure. In each of these ways, the

Brazilian firms are more likely than the foreign firms to have strategies that will positively affect economic development within Brazil. (To a large extent, the issue here is again location-specific technological externalities, including those that are generated through the political system. Import limitations that force production to take place within a country will not necessarily maximize these externalities if that production is undertaken by a foreign firm.)

Some differences between national and foreign firms are likely to mean that the foreign firms' strategies would at times be more favourable to a low-income country's economic development. The foreign firms, for example, have readier access to certain advanced techniques of production. They have experience and access to resources that place them in a better position to undertake some large, technically complex projects. Their international operations may give them better access to export markets. Also, the foreign firms generally pay higher wages and bring women into the paid labour force to a greater degree than do national firms. None of these facts, however, justifies the neo-liberal position that foreign investment has an unequivocally positive impact on a country's economic development because it raises the level of investment. On the contrary, these facts simply underscore the general observation that significant differences exist between the strategies and practices of national and foreign firms. Once it is clear that these differences exist and once it is recognized that private decisions cannot take account of the full range of social benefits and costs involved in a particular investment, there is no basis to be indifferent regarding the relative roles of foreign and national firms.

A recognition of the connections between national firms and the expansion of the national economy provided motivation for the policies of the developmental state in Brazil and also in several other countries in Latin America, East Asia and elsewhere. In Japan, South Korea and Taiwan, as I have discussed above, governments favoured national firms precisely because they would form local supply linkages, expand the technological base and reinvest within the nation. Indeed, the governments did not rely simply on the firms' 'natural' proclivities in the direction of national development, but, in addition to restricting foreign firms, pushed the national firms in this direction.

Still, even when foreign firms do not make the same degree of positive contribution to a country's development as do national firms, if they add to the total amount of investment in the country and undertake projects that would not be developed by national firms, it would seem that they would make a net positive contribution to the country's economic expansion. This 'more is better' view of foreign investment is a central aspect of the neo-liberal position. The problem is that more foreign investment in a country does not necessarily mean more total investment, especially in the long run.

Foreign investment often pre-empts investment by national firms. This pre-emption occurs most directly when foreign investors raise some of their funds within the capital market of the country where they are investing. (Ronald Muller [1979] reports that in the late 1950s and early 1960s a quarter of the funds invested in Latin America by US-based multinational firms came from sources within the 'host' countries; the figure does not include the profits that the firms obtained and reinvested in the region, which accounted for another 60 per cent of their investment funds.) A more substantial type of pre-emption occurs when foreign firms make investments that otherwise would have been made by national firms. Then the national firms, instead of simply investing in other operations, might invest less than they would have in the absence of the foreign firms, and the national savings rate declines. This could happen when high-return investment opportunities are discrete and fairly limited. The phenomenon would become especially severe if we assume, as is the case to a substantial degree (and would be even more so in a neo-liberal world without government restrictions on the international movement of funds), that savers in a low-income country could take their funds abroad to the securities markets in the advanced countries. Under these circumstances, real investment would take place in the country only in so far as the expected rate of return were higher than the expected rate of return in foreign securities markets. The amount of investment would be simply a function of available opportunities, not a function of the national savings rate. If foreign firms invested in the country, they would be replacing national investment, making no net contribution to the overall level of capital formation.

A broader, socio-political phenomenon of pre-emption is also associated with foreign investment in low-income countries. When foreign investors replace national capital to a significant degree, they pre-empt the social role of a national capitalist class. In some experiences of capitalist economic development, a capitalist class has led the process, shaping the state and obtaining its support for an economic growth agenda. In other cases, a developmental state has taken the lead, nurturing the expansion of a capitalist class along with the expansion of the economy. In general and as I have pointed out above, though reality never neatly fits broad models, the class has tended to lead in the early developing countries and the state has tended to lead in the later developing countries. Yet in all cases of successful capitalist development, a strong class has emerged alongside a strong state. This class–state alliance is essential in allowing the state effectively to provide a broad gamut of supports for economic growth, such as the formation of appropriate physical and social infrastructure, maintenance of a stable financial system, promotion of research and development, and preservation of the orderly operation of labour markets.

Yet, when foreign firms play a large role in a country, operating important industries, their presence inhibits the emergence of a strong capitalist class and undermines or perverts the essential class–state alliance (MacEwan 1990: ch. 3; and Frank 1972). Even if a dollar's worth of investment by a foreign firm were to play the same direct role as a dollar's worth of investment by a national firm, no such substitution is possible in the socio-political realm. Foreign firms cannot replace the social functions of national capital partly because they are not as effectively connected to the social and political networks of the country. Also, the interests of foreign investors are different from those of national investors. For the foreign investors, the socio-political framework in one low-income country is a small part of their larger, often global operations. For national investors, the framework in their own country is central to their operations. So when foreign investment pre-empts the role of national capital and the framework is not effectively established, investment, technological change and economic growth will all be limited.

The argument here does not imply that direct foreign investments can have no positive impact in low-income countries; sometimes they can have very positive effects, both economically and as catalysts of social change. Yet, the argument does imply quite clearly that the impact of foreign investment is much more complex than the simplistic 'more is better' nostrum of neo-liberalism. Once we have a theoretical understanding of why more is not necessarily better, it becomes possible to understand why government policies that have strictly controlled foreign investment have often led to success; it may even be possible to begin to extend those sorts of policies.[8]

International commerce, income distribution and power Much of this critique of the neo-liberal theory of international commerce has dealt with the complex and indirect way in which patterns of trade and production affect a country's development (where 'development' means economic growth). The neo-liberal theory is wrong in large part because it is simplistically narrow; it does not deal with a host of causal relationships that are central to economic development. Especially important, in a manner similar to the approach of a great deal of economic analysis, neo-liberal theory is based on the assumption that social structure is not affected by changes in international commerce. The theory is quintessentially marginal in that all changes are viewed as adjustments on the basis of a fixed set of social relationships. This approach is not only wrong; it is implicitly self-contradictory. For neo-liberal theory maintains that international commerce can be the motor force of change in economic development. Yet any process that is the motor force of change must alter social structure, and the altered social structure must perforce have its impact on both international commerce and national economic development.

In the preceding sections, I have raised this issue of the interaction between international commerce and social structure at various points – in discussing technological change, in examining the role of the state and in addressing the character of the capitalist class. The issue is pervasive, however, affecting not only the rate of economic growth but the entire, broader character of a country's economic development. Although we can talk about economic development in terms of the expansion of total output in a country or in terms of the increase in per capita income, the broader character of economic development is intertwined with social power. As I will argue later in this book, there is not one economic development, just as there is not one capitalism. The different paths of economic development involve, to a large degree, different arrangements of power and different distributions of benefits. In order to suggest some of the relevant issues of social power, let me point to the concern of the subsequent chapter, income distribution, and foreshadow part of the argument there in order to broaden the argument here.

The deregulation of international commerce that is envisioned in the neo-liberal model is largely, if not entirely, a deregulation of business. By removing constraints on the operation of business, it necessarily would give more power to the owners of capital. It would allow business to seek out profits with fewer constraints: on the location of production, on its sources of supply, on characteristics of production and so on. Power is largely a question of options, and by providing more options to the owners of capital, neo-liberal globalization would give them more power. Most clearly, within a deregulated international environment, owners of capital can resist labour's demands by exercising, or threatening to exercise, their option of shifting production to regions of the world where labour costs are lower. This is not only an option of moving from high-wage to low-wage countries, from Britain to Sri Lanka, for example. Owners of businesses in Sri Lanka may move, or threaten to move, operations to Britain if productivity is sufficiently higher in the latter country. So the power that business gains *vis-à-vis* labour by the deregulation of international commerce can be important in low-wage and high-wage countries. Perhaps if the neo-liberal model included the free movement of labour along with the free movement of commodities and capital, the power shift would not be so dramatic. Even were formal regulations on the movement of capital and labour the same, however, labour is intrinsically less mobile than capital. In any case, the neo-liberal model does not include the free international movement of labour.

Power in economic life means primarily an ability to shift more and more of the value produced by society into one's own hands. In this way, neo-liberal globalization is a *de facto* formula for shifting income to the owners of capital, that is, for increasing inequality in the distribution of income. Experience does not always reveal this shift as clearly as it might because the international economy is made up of more than two groups and there are substantial differences within the many groups; the world is not made up simply of a homogeneous group of capitalists and a homogeneous group of workers. Also, although neo-liberalism is a powerful rising ideology, the world is not yet (and never will be) organized fully according to neo-liberal precepts. Nevertheless, tendencies towards inequality, both within nations and on an international level, appear to have been substantial in recent decades. (I will review the available evidence in Chapter 3.)

So to the extent that we view equality in the distribution of income as a social goal, neo-liberal globalization would be problematic regardless of its impact on economic growth. Yet as I will argue extensively in the next chapter, there is substantial reason to believe that income inequality is bad for economic growth. The focus of that argument is not international commerce. Yet it does provide us with one more basis for seeing why deregulation of international commerce is an ineffective development policy: deregulation of international commerce shifts power to favour an increase of inequality; an increase of inequality tends to undermine economic growth (MacEwan 1995).

Globalization and Development Options

The defenders of neo-liberalism are not ignorant of the various criticisms of free trade. As I have noted above, those criticisms are as old as the arguments for free trade themselves, and in recent years they have been given mathematical formulation and entered the mainstream of economic analysis. In response, free-traders have developed defences against the criticisms, and they are worth noting.

One line of defence for the traditional theory is to accept the criticisms on a purely theoretical level but maintain that they are relatively unimportant in practice. Location-specific technological externalities, for example, can be acknowledged but then dismissed with the claim that their impact is small. Because it is difficult, if not impossible, to measure directly the quantitative importance of technological externalities, this response seems to reduce the criticism to a matter of arbitrary judgement about the size of vaguely defined variables. Likewise, defenders of neo-liberalism do not deny the existence of large firms, but they point out that the extent to which these firms deviate from the competitive outcomes cannot be readily measured and claim the criticism is therefore moot.

Yet the test of a theory is the extent to which it is consistent with and helps explain actual experience. As I have demonstrated earlier in this chapter, success in economic development, virtually wherever it has occurred, has been associated with a substantial role for government in the regulation of foreign commerce. The problem for theory is one of explaining this success, and the neo-liberal theory simply cannot do so. Experience creates a *prima facie* case that government regulation of foreign commerce provides a foundation for development. More specifically, for example, the several cases of successful economic development strongly suggest that technological externalities are large. The burden of proof falls on those who make the contrary claim.

Once it is recognized that economic arguments cannot provide sufficient support for the deregulation of international commerce, defenders of liberalism raise political arguments. Government, it is alleged, cannot pick winners. That is, if government attempts to promote economic development by picking certain industries that have high location-specific technological externalities, it will generally make the wrong selections. Supposedly the basis for this allegation is that governments by their very nature are bureaucratically inept and dominated by special interests, and they are therefore incapable of 'picking winners'. This is, on a moment's reflection, a rather silly argument. Several governments have been very successful at picking winners when they have set out to do so, as some of the East Asian stories demonstrate quite clearly. In other cases, those of the early developing countries, broad protections for industry induced development. True, there are many cases where a combination of bureaucratic ineptitude and special interests have generated waste and inefficiency, and the result has sometimes been an abysmal development record. Cases of failure, however, provide no more basis for the conclusion that government necessarily cannot pick winners than the cases of success provide for the equally silly claim that governments can always pick winners.

In any case, a government can regulate international commerce to promote development in ways that do not necessarily require the sort of fine-tuning that is implicit in the picking winners concept. Instead of picking winners, governments might establish criteria which firms would have to meet in order to merit and maintain protection. The South Korean government, for example, required firms to meet export targets in order to maintain support, thus forcing them to meet a test of international competition. Also, governments could adopt broad programmes of support, such as subsidies for research and development and for establishing domestic sources of supply. Simply in promoting a country's educational system a government would be implicitly regulating its international commerce without 'picking winners'. (These sorts of issues will come up again in chapters 7 and 8.)

There is also the allegation that regulation of foreign commerce cannot work because it will be met with retaliation that will be more costly than any gains from regulation. This claim is even less plausible than that about picking winners: the history of development could be written as a history of regulations that have had greater benefits than the costs incurred through the retaliation they generated. In many cases, however, powerful governments will use their economic strength to crush the development efforts of weaker governments when those efforts run contrary to 'openness' and 'access'. IMF conditionality, to say nothing of nastier forms of intervention, provides numerous examples. Certainly any effort to challenge neo-liberalism in low-income countries must take this threat into account. Yet, as in all bargaining situations, many factors are involved, even in the relations between relatively powerful and relatively weak states, and the outcomes are not pre-ordained.

When all other arguments in favour of free trade have failed, neo-liberal rhetoric falls back on the there-is-no-alternative defence. Ironically, and somewhat sadly, the idea that globalization simply does not allow governments to regulate their countries' foreign commerce and take control of economic development is proclaimed as gospel by many opponents of free trade, as well as by free trade's defenders. The argument is not complicated. Because the world economy has already become so integrated and homogenized, capitalist firms have myriad options as to location of production, origin of resources and the site of markets; if a government attempts to regulate the firms' behaviour, they will simply move out of the country. This logic is proudly touted by neo-liberals as an irrefutable truth. By people who recognize the damage done by free trade, both to economic growth and to broader social goals such as relative equality and the preservation of the environment, it is lamented as the unpleasant reality.

The argument does have an important, if none the less partial, element of truth. To the extent that the realm of the economy does not coincide with the realm of political authority, the power of political authority to control the economy is limited. The difficulties appear most clearly with policies directed towards the management of aggregate demand: attempts, for example, to stimulate economic expansion in a country through lower interest rates may drive capital abroad in search of higher returns; attempts to stimulate through expansion of the government deficit may raise imports, diverting some of the impact outside the country. Also, a government's capacity to tax is limited by the openness of the international economy because wealthy individuals and corporations can locate their incomes in sites where tax rates are low (an issue I will deal with more fully in Chapter 6). More broadly, any efforts to push businesses to act in ways that are not consistent with profit maximization – which, after all, is an inherent feature of any regulation – can contribute to an 'unfriendly business climate'; firms may respond by moving funds out of the country (or by declining to bring funds into the country). Under these circumstances, it could be difficult to engineer economic growth through regulation, and it may be even more difficult to attain the broader social goals of development – an improvement of basic needs and environmental preservation, for example.

Nevertheless, while the current globalization does place real constraints on government economic policy, those constraints are far from absolute. The relationship between governments and firms (or private individuals with considerable resources) is a bargaining relationship. Governments of large countries – Brazil, China, Indonesia, India, Pakistan, Mexico, South Africa and Nigeria, are obvious examples – have significant bargaining power regardless of the changes that define the current phase of globalization. These countries and many others have sizeable markets, large numbers of workers and valuable supplies of natural resources. Such factors give governments substantial leeway in placing controls on the movement of capital in and out of the country, setting tax rates at levels sufficient to finance social programmes, and implementing a wide range of development-oriented regulations. To be sure, governments in smaller countries, especially in very low-income countries, have less bargaining power. Yet for governments of countries like Haiti, Guinea, Nicaragua or Papua New Guinea, the new globalization may make their situations somewhat weaker, but it is not the origin of their bargaining difficulties in the international economy. Even for these small countries, bargaining options exist and are affected as much by political context and particular economic circumstances as by the general phenomenon of globalization.

The sorts of experiences discussed earlier in this chapter provide substantial evidence for these claims that globalization does not eliminate the abilities of governments in low-income countries to maintain considerable authority over their national economies. Both in earlier eras and recent decades, the ways in which particular countries have interacted with the world economy have been affected both by international conditions and by the particular choices of governments. It would be unreasonable to claim that the changes of recent decades that define the current globalization have not altered international conditions in ways that threaten the autonomy of some national policies. It would be equally unreasonable, however, to assert that those changes have eliminated any scope for choice by national governments.

Advocates of neo-liberalism have little basis on which to make their claim that with regard to a country's foreign commerce 'there is no alternative' to free trade. The conclusion of the argument of this chapter, to the contrary, is that free trade itself does not provide a viable development option.

Notes

1. The figure is an arithmetic average calculated at current market prices. Using data on sixteen advanced capitalist economies, Angus Maddison (1989: 326) calculates that the average ratio of merchandise exports to GDP at current market prices rose from 15.1 per cent in 1950 to 24.1 per cent in 1987. Maddison's data also show that in 1913 the average was 21.2 per cent. Bob Sutcliffe and Andrew Glyn (1999) argue, however, that Maddison's figures for the post-Second World War period exaggerate the rise of exports relative to national commerce in that period because they are in constant prices. They argue: 'It is the share of exports at current prices which most closely reflects productivity gains and thus the share of resources devoted to exporting activity. This measure shows much less dramatic change than the constant price figure.' In any case, the year 1913 marked the culmination of the previous great era of globalization, and that era too had its impressive figures on trade expansion. Between the early nineteenth century and the early twentieth century, for example, the value of Great Britain's foreign trade (imports plus exports divided by two) as a percentage of its gross domestic product more than tripled, from 8.5 per cent to 29.4 per cent (Furtado 1976: 45).

2. These statements are computed from data in UNCTC (1988: Table 1.2) and Rutter (1993: Appendix Table 1). There are numerous problems with these data, and one should take them as only very rough approximations. The data are based on book values, and the meaning of comparisons over time is complicated by issues of inflation, changing exchange ratios, and the differences between real and allowed depreciation.

3. The figures are from Harry Magdoff (1992: 56) who, in turn, cites Bryant (1987: 22). Magdoff points out: 'By the 1980s, under the impact of changing economic and political pressures, and assisted by new electronic and communications technology, a totally new stage of global finance had emerged ... A normal function of international banking is to facilitate world trade [but] ... Transcending its traditional role, global banking became the centre of a self-generating financial boom, spreading in ever-wider circles during the 1970s and 1980s.'

4. Much of this section is drawn directly from MacEwan (1995).

5. Giovanni Arrighi (1994: 159-69), however, explains London's rise as a centre of high finance in the eighteenth century in part as the result of 'a transfer of Dutch surplus capital to British enterprises'. He goes on to report that during the French wars in the late decades of the century, Britain's commanding position in European finance allowed the government to borrow heavily abroad. Britain's powerful industrial and financial positions, however, made this debt rather different in its implications from development debt.

6. During the 1980s, even while the ideology of free trade was solidifying its hegemony among economists, a major theoretical challenge appeared under the name of the 'new international economics'. Working well within the framework of mainstream, orthodox economic theory, a number of economists demonstrated that when certain crucial

and unrealistic assumptions of the traditional trade theory were altered to correspond more closely to reality, there was no theoretical foundation for the conclusion that free trade was necessarily the optimal economic policy (Helpman and Krugman 1985; Krugman 1986). Once such realities as economies of scale, technological externalities and monopolistic competition were introduced into the analysis, there was simply no foundation for the simplistic traditional claim that economic theory supported the principle that the state should not intervene in a country's foreign commerce. Yet the proponents of these new theoretical developments have declined to challenge the ideology of free trade, claiming that political reality – for example, that the state cannot pick winners or that trade restrictions will lead to detrimental retaliation – requires support for free trade (Krugman 1992). The economic arguments for free trade remain the doctrine of basic English-language textbooks.

7. In the last fifty years, as multinational firms have become a focal point in controversies in discussion of international economic relations, a substantial literature has emerged concerning the impact of foreign direct investment on economic development, and there are numerous points of contention in the debate. Dicken (1992: ch. 12) provides a useful summary. In order to refute the neo-liberal theory, however, it is not necessary to deal with the entire range of issues in this debate. The neo-liberal position is, after all, rather extreme, asserting that foreign direct investment plays an unequivocally positive role in economic development, that therefore more is always better, and that the best way to bring in more is by the absence of regulation. The position falls apart once it is established that the role of multinational firms in low-income countries is usually ambiguous and often negative.

8. In this critique of neo-liberalism, I have not tried to examine foreign financial investment (or foreign aid). With foreign financial investment, the principal controversies concern loans with which the government is in some way involved, either directly or as guarantor. Then the dispute is not one of whether or not the government should play a role, but one of what role the government should play. For example: What are the legitimate uses of foreign loans? What sort of conditions should be accepted in order to obtain foreign loans? Answers to these kinds of questions will emerge here and in later chapters, at least implicitly. Certainly there are development experiences where foreign financial capital has made an important, positive and non-disruptive contribution to a country's growth – for example, the United States in the nineteenth century and South Korea during its period of rapid expansion. Nevertheless, the experience with debt crises, in the 1980s and earlier epochs, hardly provides reason to be sanguine about the role of foreign financial capital in the economies of low-income countries (MacEwan 1990). Also, the experience of East Asia in the late 1990s led to a general recognition of the perils of unregulated capital movements (Stiglitz 1998a).

3

Economic Growth and the Distribution of Income

During the 1960s, I lived for a time in Karachi, Pakistan. Another family from the United States lived near me, with their dog, which they had brought with them to Pakistan. It was a large dog. Each day, my neighbours had their cook feed the dog a pound or more of raw hamburger, probably more meat than the cook's family – or, for that matter, most Pakistani families – ate in a month. The arrangement struck me as obscene.

It is easy to explain my reaction. I do not dislike dogs; in fact, I am rather fond of dogs. It none the less strikes me as wrong to provide so well for a pet when people all around do not have enough good food to eat. (Those were the days, I should add, when most people viewed red meat as unequivocally 'good food'.) Yet, on more thorough reflection, I was troubled by my reaction: why did it bother me so much to see my neighbours feed their dog so well in Pakistan, while I had seen many people feed their dogs equally well in the United States without having my sense of moral outrage stimulated? Leaving the dog aside, was there something wrong in my living comfortably while a million people within a five-mile radius barely survived? I suppose there was something about the cook, who himself was poor, doing the actual feeding of the dog that aroused my moral indignation. My neighbours were, in a sense, flaunting their wealth, and rubbing the cook's poverty in his face. But, thinking about the matter, I hardly would have felt better about the dog's diet had my neighbours done the feeding themselves.

I never did resolve the moral issue of the dog, the cook, my neighbours, my own position, and Pakistani poverty in general. Perhaps that helps explain why I am an economist instead of a philosopher. Thirty years later, however, I am still uncomfortable when friends, even in the very rich United States, feed their pets pounds of raw meat. (I should own up to the fact that shortly after I originally drafted the opening paragraphs of this chapter, my wife and I finally agreed to get a dog for our teenaged daughter. Throwing moral issues aside, to say nothing of our concern for all the work that is involved in caring for a puppy, we gave in to her persistent pleadings. We do not feed Ozzy, the dog, raw meat, just regular dog food – though I can hardly claim that this makes any moral difference.)

The distribution of income is often viewed as a moral issue – and well it should be. There is something deeply wrong in a society where a small group of people control the vast majority of wealth and receive incomes that allow them to live in luxury, while most of the people live in poverty. Even when relatively few people live in 'absolute poverty', most of us are troubled by the existence of great economic disparities. Those at the bottom of society's economic hierarchy may have enough to eat, roofs over their heads, and the basic amenities of modern life; yet, it seems un-reasonable and unfair when those at the top have what appears as infinitely more.[1]

Within low-income countries, the inequalities of wealth and income are particularly striking because the gap between those at the top and the bottom is so great. On the one hand, in Pakistan or India or Brazil or Peru, for example, there are people who live on a scale comparable to that of the richest people in the richest countries; the very wealthy share a common lifestyle the world around. On the other hand, in these countries there are millions of people who live in extreme material deprivation, who lack basic food and shelter. This huge gap is what struck me in Pakistan.

My Pakistan experience also underscored the international dimension of income inequality. The confrontation of extreme wealth and poverty is more evident, perhaps, when it is in one locale and when the rich and the poor are part of the same national society. Yet even in the 1960s my neighbours' and my own presence in Pakistan presented us with the stark realities of international inequality. Increasingly in today's world, where advances in communications and transportation technology have created a 'global village', we confront the realities of the income inequalities that exist across political boundaries.

Beyond the fact that these arrangements of inequality strike me, and many other people, as obscene in and of themselves, there are some more complex issues that demand attention. We sense moral outrage with our guts, but it can help if we complicate it and examine it with our minds. For example, it bothers me when I see one group of people that is very rich alongside another group that is very poor, but it bothers me even more if I believe the former group is rich *because* the latter group is poor and the latter is poor *because* the former is rich. That is clear enough. But suppose I believe something very different. Suppose I believe that the poor would be even poorer if the rich were not so rich. Suppose that in order to improve the position of the poor, it is necessary first to improve the position of the rich. What if, for example, my neighbours in Pakistan told me that if they did not have the cook feed their dog, then the cook would have no job – to say nothing of the butcher who prepared the meat and the herder who raised the steer. The morality of an act, it turns out, cannot be easily separated from its causes and consequences. I could justify my moral outrage over the dog and the hamburger only with an analysis of the economics of inequality.

What's been Happening to Income Distribution?

To begin with, in so far as we judge the world by what has been happening to income distribution, the course of events in the twentieth century does not provide much basis for a positive appraisal. The record, however, does display many ambiguities.

On the grandest level, the worldwide distribution of income appears to have been becoming more and more unequal through most of the twentieth century. (I say 'appears' because data of this sort certainly should be viewed with caution.) According to the *Human Development Report 1992*:

> Between 1960 and 1989, the countries with the richest 20% of world popu-
> lation increased their share of global GNP from 70.2% to 82.7%. The
> countries with the poorest 20% of world population saw their share fall
> from 2.3% to 1.4%. The consequences for income distribution have been
> dramatic. In 1960, the top 20% received 30 times more than the bottom
> 20%, but by 1989 they were receiving 60 times more ... Even these figures
> conceal the true scale of injustice since they are based on comparisons of
> average per capita incomes of rich and poor *countries*. In reality, of course,
> there are wide disparities within each country between rich and poor *people*.
> (UNDP 1992: 34)

The authors of the *Human Development Report* point out that when intra-country income inequality is taken into account and when estimates are made for countries for which insufficient data exist, the ratio between the income of the top 20 per cent and bottom 20 per cent of world population may more than double, rising as high as 150. On the other hand, if the estimates are recalculated using real purchasing power data rather than nominal GNP data adjusted at existing exchange rates, the ratio might be cut back in half. In any case, there is no indication that such adjustments would alter the change towards greater inequality that has taken place in recent decades.

Growing global income inequality reflects the fact that, in spite of a few important 'success stories', income has been growing more rapidly in rich countries than in poor ones. For the fifty-year period from 1938 to 1988, Giovanni Arrighi (1991) illustrates this phenomenon by comparing GNP per capita in particular countries and regions with GNP per capita in what

TABLE 3.1 Per capita income in various parts of the world as a percentage of per capita income in the 'organic core', 1938–88*

	1938	1948	1960	1970	1980	1988
Latin America	19.5	14.4	16.7	15.5	19.8	10.6
(Brazil)	12.0	11.3	12.1	12.7	17.5	12.1
Middle East and North Africa	n.a.	n.a.	11.5	8.1	11.1	7.1
(Turkey and Egypt)	14.9	13.0	12.8	7.7	8.1	5.6
Subsaharan Africa						
Western and Eastern	n.a.	n.a.	3.6	3.4	4.7	1.6
Southern and Central	25.2	18.3	10.5	11.3	n.a.	6.1
South Asia	8.2	7.5	3.6	2.8	2.0	1.8
South East Asia	n.a.	n.a.	6.6	3.8	5.7	3.7
(Indonesia and	6.0	n.a.	6.4	2.8	4.6	2.3
Philippines)						
Japan	20.7	14.5	23.2	52.1	76.3	117.9
South Korea	n.a.	n.a.	7.7	7.2	12.7	20.2
China	4.1	n.a.	n.a.	n.a.	2.5	1.8

* The aggregates are made up as follows: the 'organic core' – United States, Canada, Australia, New Zealand, the Benelux and Scandinavian countries, West Germany, Austria, Switzerland, France and the United Kingdom; Latin America – Argentina, Bolivia, Brazil, Chile, Colombia, Dominican Republic, Ecuador, El Salvador, Jamaica, Mexico, Paraguay, Peru and Venezuela; Middle East and North Africa – Algeria, Egypt, Libya, Sudan, Syria and Turkey; Western and Eastern Subsaharan Africa – Benin, Burundi, Cameroon, Chad, Ethiopia, Ivory Coast, Kenya, Madagascar, Malawi, Mali, Mauritania, Mozambique, Niger, Nigeria, Rwanda, Senegal, Somalia, Tanzania and Upper Volta; Southern and Central Subsaharan Africa – South Africa, Zaire, Zambia and Zimbabwe; South Asia – Bangladesh, India, Pakistan and Sri Lanka; Southeast Asia – Indonesia, Malaysia, Philippines, Thailand, and Singapore.

Note: The figures are aggregated and compared using existing exchange rates.

Source: Arrighi (1991: Tables II, III and IV).

he calls the 'organic core' of the world economy: Western Europe, the United States and Canada, and Australia and New Zealand. Some of Arrighi's data are presented in Table 3.1. Whether one's base of comparison is pre-war (1938), post-war (1948), or somewhat later (1960), the same general conclusion of relative deterioration across regions of the 'South' is evident. The 1970s do provide an exception to the overall trend, as the countries of the 'North' entered a period of relative stagnation while several countries of the 'South' maintained growth through debt accumulation. By the late 1980s, however, the devastation wrought by the debt crisis and the 'structural adjustment programmes' it engendered was dramatic.

Over the period examined by Arrighi, the most spectacular success story is that of Japan. Even with the death and destruction the country experienced during the Second World War, Japan grew from its position of relative poverty – a per capita income 21 per cent of that in the 'organic core' in 1938 – to a position among the wealthiest countries of the world by the end of the 1980s. South Korea, Taiwan and a few other countries have also attained quite high rates of economic growth over several decades, though they may not yet be counted as members of the exclusive club of rich countries. As important as these success stories are, however, they do not alter the overall picture. During this half century the trend was towards greater income inequality among countries. (At the same time, on some important measures of social well-being, the gap between the 'North' and the 'South' has narrowed in recent years. During the 1960 to 1990 period, North–South disparities declined in, for example, life expectancy, literacy rates, infant mortality and average caloric supply. In the same period, however, disparities rose on important indicators of economic capacity for further progress: mean years of schooling, tertiary education enrolment rates, and scientists and technicians per capita, for example (UNDP 1992: 37). When we have a full accounting of the impact of the crisis that emerged in East Asia in 1997, the overall picture is likely to get worse as some of the high performers among the low-income countries have been among the most seriously affected.)

Looking at individual countries, it is difficult to make generalizations about what has been happening to the distribution of income over time. The problem is in part that good data exist over an extended period for only a very few countries. In addition, in so far as we do have reliable data, they provide a somewhat mixed picture. For the advanced countries, it is generally (but not universally; see Kolko 1962) agreed that over the first several decades of the twentieth century within most high-income countries the distribution of income became more equal. Data presented by Simon Kuznets (1966: 208–11) show, for example, that in the United States, the ratio of the income attained by the top 20 per cent to that obtained by the bottom 60 per cent declined from about 2 at the time of the First World War to about 1.4 at the end of the 1950s; in West Germany, the decline was from 1.6 to 1.3. In the UK, the share of total income going to the top 20 per cent fell from 59 per cent in 1913 to 42 per cent in 1957.

Yet, since about 1970 in some advanced countries the trend has been towards an increase of income inequality. The United States is probably the most noted case. Between 1950 and 1970, the ratio of income going to the top 20 per cent of families to that of the bottom 20 per cent fell from 9.5 to 7.6. After 1970, this ratio rose to 9.6 in 1990 and to 11.1 in 1996 (USBC 1998). The United States, however, cannot be taken as typical. In

Western Europe, although the UK has moved in a direction similar to that of the United States, several countries have not experienced a significant rise of income inequality in recent decades. Likewise, in Japan, there is no evidence of any substantial increase of inequality.

For the low-income countries there are not sufficient data to allow any generalizations about how income distribution has been changing over time. The information that does exist reveals a very mixed set of experiences. R. M. Sundrum (1990: 117–21), for example, has brought together data for sixteen countries showing changes in the distribution of income for various time spans in the 1953 to 1985 period. Inequality rose in seven of these countries, fell in four, and the trend was mixed in the remainder. In several cases, however, the time spans are quite short, and, as Sundrum notes, the data are often not comparable, even for one country at two different times.[2]

During the early 1980s, with slow growth and high unemployment in several low-income countries, it is likely that the distribution of income worsened in many places. Data on Latin American countries, in particular, suggest a perverse pattern of change during the 1980s. A World Bank study (Psacharopoulos et al. 1993) concludes that overall poverty increased and income distribution worsened in the region during the decade. While some countries showed improvements, the distribution of income became more unequal in nine of the thirteen countries for which the study provides data. Latin American countries have relatively unequal distributions of income and are highly urbanized. Under these circumstances, it is likely that the lowest income groups have been unable to protect themselves during the hard times of recent years. Certainly in terms of absolute poverty, there is every reason to believe that the poor in Africa have suffered severely since the 1980s, but it is not clear what has happened to the distribution of income in African countries in this period. In some East Asian countries – South Korea, Taiwan and perhaps elsewhere – it is likely that growing demand for labour and the high rate of educational attainment have meant that income distribution did not worsen significantly in recent years, at least up until the crisis of the late 1990s. (Data in Sundrum [1990: 119] show a very substantial reduction of inequality for Taiwan from 1953 through the early 1960s and then a continuing decline until 1980. At that point Taiwan had a relatively low degree of inequality. Data from the World Bank [1995; 1982] indicate that in South Korea the ratio of the income received by the top 20 per cent to that received by the bottom 20 per cent fell from 7.95 in 1976 to 5.70 in 1988, but it is not clear that the data for the two years are fully comparable.)

In spite of mixed or ambiguous evidence on changes in the distribution of income, it is possible to draw some useful conclusions from this brief survey. The data do make it clear that on a global level the distribution of income is getting worse. Rising global inequality in an era of increasing international interdependence is especially disconcerting, suggesting that globalization is generating forces that lead to the concentration instead of the dispersion of wealth. The global income distribution facts are certainly consistent with the argument that 'globalization' is simply a new term for imperialism, allowing those in the advanced countries more effective access to, control over and benefit from the world's human and natural resources (Arrighi,1991; Magdoff 1992). Moreover, in so far as globalization involves a broad social and cultural, as well as economic, integration of the world (that is, the creation of the 'global village'), the political implications of the global distribution of income may be growing at the same time as it is becoming more unequal. If people increasingly use the global economy as their frame of reference for evaluating and explaining their own well-being, rising global inequality will have a larger and larger impact on their consciousness. Also, the rising inequality suggests that, for those of us who judge and analyse on this basis, there is something deeply wrong in the world economy.

The variation of intra-country experience with changes in the distribution of income allows two additional useful observations. First, it tends to belie claims that a general improvement of within-country income distribution is a 'natural' concomitant of economic growth. In recent decades economic growth in itself has simply not produced a discernible trend towards greater equality. (This is true whether we look at the individual countries or the world as a whole.) Second, the variety of national experiences suggest that alternatives are possible, that there is no 'natural' order by which the distribution of income is determined. Differences among countries with regard to the distribution of income may be determined by long-run historical factors rather than by short-run policy decisions, but in no case is it possible to claim that they must be as they are. Each of these observations, it turns out, has some direct relevance for an appraisal of the neo-liberal arguments regarding inequality.

The Neo-liberal Justification of Inequality

As with the neo-liberal argument on international commerce, the neo-liberal position on income distribution is one that both has wide acceptance among economists and has been thoroughly undermined by economic research. Also, like the position on international commerce, it has long historical roots among the classical economists.

In his *History of Economic Analysis*, Joseph Schumpeter (1954: 572) sums up a central argument of classical economists with the simple statement: 'Savings ... was the powerful lever of economic development.' The expansion of output depends, in this analysis, on an expansion of the stock of capital, that is, on investment. Investment, however, is limited by the amount of savings. A higher rate of savings allows a higher rate of investment; a higher rate of investment allows a higher level of productive capital; a higher level of productive capital allows more output; and so a higher rate of savings allows a higher rate of economic growth. Furthermore, in the classical analysis, it is the rich – capitalists and perhaps landowners – who save. Labourers, the poor, spend their income; they consume. It follows that more income in the hands of the poor means more consumption and less savings, whereas more income in the hands of the rich means more savings. A more unequal distribution of income, then, leads to a higher rate of economic growth because, by raising the share of income going to the wealthy, the inequality raises the savings rate.

The neo-liberal position on the distribution of income follows directly from this classical analysis. Understandably, however, the neo-liberal position avoids the obvious *reductio ad absurdum* of the classical argument, and does not advocate a maximization of inequality (which would, I suppose, mean placing all income in the hands of one person). Instead, *the neo-liberal position is that maximum economic growth will be obtained by allowing the distribution of income to be determined by the market; governments should not adopt policies that would redistribute income away from the rich and towards the poor.* The position rules out, for example, progressive taxes, food subsidies, minimum wage policies, protection for union rights, and government employment creation programmes. It also severely limits public social welfare programmes such as public education and public health care. (Neo-liberals generally recognize that some social welfare programmes, most notably education, contribute to economic growth and therefore might not proscribe them even though they might have income equalizing implications.)

The neo-liberal position on the distribution of income, however, does not rest solely on the origins and role of savings as set out in the classical analysis. It is also based on the argument that an unequal distribution of income serves an incentive function. Any action that would reduce the returns to investment – by high taxes on investment income, for example – would reduce the incentives for investors, reduce investment and reduce growth. The argument applies to labour income as well, asserting that a redistributive tax system would reduce the incentive to work, especially among highly paid managers and professionals, who, if one accepts the general logic of market determination of wages, are supposedly making the largest contribution to production. Moreover, the incentive impact of inequality is also supposed to work throughout the income scale via a demonstration effect: people work hard, invest their money, gain skills and, in general, give their greatest productive effort in order to raise their relative position in society; or, which leads to the same results, to avoid moving downwards. The power of this demonstration effect depends on a substantial degree of inequality.

Neo-liberals seldom proclaim the desirability of inequality per se. In part the argument depends on a belief in the ethical legitimacy of market-determined outcomes (an issue I will take up in Chapter 4). More frequently, the argument is the functional one that acceptance of inequality yields growth. With growth, even those people who are at the bottom of the income hierarchy will supposedly benefit. Indeed, a common element in the neo-liberal rhetoric is that efforts to help the poor through redistributive policies wind up hurting the poor because of their growth-reducing impacts.

Nevertheless, the neo-liberal position does not impose on society a permanent state of high inequality. Here the 'Kuznets Curve' plays a crucial role in the argument. On the basis of minimal information about historical experience in a few developed countries, Simon Kuznets (1955) hypothesized that there is a certain pattern of change that takes place in a country's distribution of income as it experiences income growth and moves from a low to a high level of development. Kuznets suggested that during the early phase of growth, 'when the transition from the pre-industrial to the industrial civilization [is] most rapid' (1955: 18), there is an increase in the extent of inequality; then, in the later phases of development, the distribution of income becomes more equal. The 'Curve', then, shows the degree of inequality plotted on the vertical axis of a graph against the level of development as measured by per capita income on the horizontal axis; as development proceeds and income rises, the curve rises (rising inequality) and then as income rises further the curve descends (declining inequality). The curve thus has the shape of an inverted U.

Kuznets offered a number of possible explanations for the inverted U-shape of this curve showing the relation between income inequality and economic growth. The explanation that fits most easily within the neo-liberal framework emphasizes the shifting supply and demand for labour. (Later in this chapter, I will look at some of the other possible explanations suggested in Kuznets's original article.) First, regarding the early phases of development, Kuznets poses for himself the question of whether or not the pattern that he discerns in the historical experience of the advanced countries is 'likely to be repeated in the sense that in the early phases of industrialization in the underdeveloped countries income inequalities will tend to widen before the levelling forces become strong enough first to stabilize and then to reduce income inequalities'. He answers:

While the future cannot be an exact repetition of the past, there are already certain elements in the present condition of the underdeveloped countries, e.g., 'swarming' of populations due to sharp cuts in death rates unaccompanied by declines in birth rates – that threaten to widen inequality by depressing the relative position of the lower income groups even further. Furthermore, if and when industrialization begins, the dislocating effects on these societies ... are likely to be quite sharp – so sharp as to destroy the positions of some of the lower groups more rapidly than opportunities elsewhere in the economy may be created for them. (Kuznets 1955: 24–5)

In speculating about historical experience in the advanced countries, Kuznets offers the following to explain the movement toward greater equality at a later stage of development:

Much is to be said for the notion that once the early turbulent phases of industrialization and urbanization had passed, a variety of forces converged to bolster the economic position of the lower-income groups within the urban population. The very fact that after a while, an increasing proportion of the urban population was 'native,' i.e., born in cities rather than in the rural areas, and hence more able to take advantage of the possibilities of city life in preparation for the economic struggle, meant a better chance for organization and adaptation, a better basis for securing greater income shares than was possible for the newly 'immigrant' population coming from the countryside or abroad. (Kuznets 1955: 17)

The argument is based on a differential rate of change in the countryside and in the urban-industrial sectors. In the early stages of development displacement from rural, agricultural activities is rapid, swelling the supply of urban labour beyond the capacity of the very small industrial sector to absorb the available workforce. This excess supply of labour is augmented, at least in the modern era, by rapid increases in the rate of population growth. Then, at a later stage, when the rural–urban shift has stabilized or at least slowed, the demand from the expansion of the now large industrial sector catches up and perhaps surpasses the expansion of the labour force. These shifts would tend to produce the inverted U.

Combined with the arguments about savings and incentives, the Kuznets Curve – sometimes enshrined as Kuznets's Law – rounds out the neo-liberal position nicely. On the one hand, the position asserts that *nothing can be done* directly about inequality and the plight of the poor in low-income countries. Direct efforts to reduce inequality will simply make the condition of the poor worse by harming economic growth. On the other hand, *nothing needs to be done*, because in the long run the conditions of inequality themselves will contribute to growth, and growth will both improve the absolute condition of the poor and reduce inequality. *The main implication* of this analysis of inequality and growth, as with other elements of the neo-liberal position, *is that government should minimize its role in the economy*.

As with the neo-liberal theory of international commerce, these contentions about growth and equality are open to challenge in terms of both the accuracy with which they describe actual experience and the coherence of the arguments themselves. Here too the neo-liberal position turns out to be essentially a myth.

Income Inequality and Economic Growth: the Record

Data on the experience of low-income countries in recent decades give no support to the argument that an unequal distribution of income enhances economic growth. There is, in particular, no pattern of association between countries with relatively unequal income distributions and countries with relatively high rates of growth of national income. A rough picture is shown by the data in Table 3.2. World Bank data allow the classification of thirty-eight 'low-income' and 'middle-income' countries on the basis of both their degree of income inequality and their rates of growth of per capita income in the 1960 to 1993 period. In Table 3.2 these thirty-eight countries are categorized by high, medium and low inequality and by high, medium and low rates of growth. (The dividing lines between the groups are arbitrary, but changing them in any reasonable manner would not affect the overall qualitative implications of the data.)

Among these 38 countries, there are those that have experienced rapid growth with inequality; Brazil stands out as an example. Yet there are several countries that have grown rapidly with equality, of which South Korea stands out as a particularly important example. Likewise, while some countries – Nepal and Ghana, for example – have stagnated with equality, others have stagnated with inequality – Honduras and Senegal, for example. Overall, the data in Table 3.2 simply do not provide any basis for a claim that greater income inequality is associated with higher rates of economic growth. (See, however, the qualification in the note to the table. Sundrum [1990: 85–8], using a somewhat different set of data in a similar set of exercises, also finds no association between the two variables.)

Data summarizing recent experience in high-income countries suggest similar results. In so far as a relationship between income distribution and economic expansion can be discerned, it appears that countries with more equal income distributions have grown more rapidly. The United States and Australia, for example, have shown both relatively great inequality and relatively slow growth. Japan and Belgium, on the other hand, have grown

TABLE 3.2 'Low income' and 'middle income' countries categorized by degree of income inequality and rate of growth 1960–93

Inequality	Rate of Growth		
	High	Medium	Low
High	Lesotho (20.7; 3.4) Brazil (32.1; 3.2)	Colombia (15.5; 2.4) Chile (18.3; 2.3) Kenya (18.2; 1.7) Panama (29.9; 1.7) South Africa (19.2; 1.3) Guatemala (30.0; 1.2) Tanzania (26.1; 1.2)	Honduras (23.5; 0.5) Zimbabwe (15.6; 0.3) Senegal (16.7; -0.1)
Medium	Thailand (8.3; 5.4) Malaysia (11.7; 4.0)	Nigeria (9.6; 2.4) Costa Rica (12.7; 2.4) Dom. Rep. (13.2; 1.4) Mexico (13.6; 1.4) Venezuela (10.3; 1.3) Bolivia (8.6; 1.0)	Mauritania (13.2; 0.6) Jamaica (8.1; 0.2) Peru (10.5; -0.4) Zambia (8.9; -1.1) Nicaragua (13.2; -1.8)
Low	S. Korea (5.9; 7.5) Indonesia (4.9; 4.1) Tunisia (7.8; 3.4) Pakistan (4.7; 2.9) Sri Lanka (4.4; 2.5)	India (4.7; 2.0) Morocco (7.0; 2.0) Algeria (6.7; 1.6) Philippines (7.4; 1.4)	Nepal (4.3; 0.9) Rwanda (4.0; 0.4) Cote d'Ivoire (6.5; -0.4) Ghana (6.3; -0.6)

Note: The figures in parentheses for each country are, first, the measure of inequality and, second, the annual average rate of growth of per capita gross national product. The measure of inequality is the ratio of the share of total income obtained by the highest income 20 per cent of the population to the share of income obtained by the lowest income 20 per cent of the population. The dividing lines for the rate of growth categories are as follows: high rate of growth – greater than or equal to 2.5 per cent per year; medium rate of growth – greater than or equal to 1 per cent per year and less than 2.5 per cent per year; low rate of growth – less than 1 per cent per year. The dividing lines for inequality are as follows: high inequality – ratio above 15; medium inequality – ratio from 8 to 15; low inequality – ratio below 8.

NB: The income distribution data used here are from various years, often late in the 1960–93 period. If we are to measure the extent to which income distribution has an impact on the rate of growth, then we should use income distribution data from the beginning of the period for which growth is measured. I have used a conceptually improper procedure here in order to include more countries, and I would seek some justification in the fact that in most countries the distribution of income changes slowly. The deficiency in the methodology behind this table should none the less be noted.

Source: Computed from data in World Bank (1995; 1982).

relatively rapidly with relative equality. Figure 3.1 shows the inverse relation between inequality and growth of labour productivity during the 1980s and early 1990s for eleven high-income countries, all of which have populations greater than 10 million. (It is possible that more recent years, with relatively slower growth in Japan and relatively more rapid growth in the United States, would alter the picture somewhat. More recent data, however, would not reverse the picture, as would be necessary to establish support for the neo-liberal claims.)

Using statistical techniques that go well beyond the sorts of illustrative or suggestive relationships of Table 3.2 and Figure 3.1, other studies have found no empirical basis for the neo-liberal claim that greater income inequality enhances economic growth (Ahluwalia 1976; Sundrum 1990: ch. 4). In fact, studies published in the mid-1990s come to exactly the opposite conclusion, namely that equality tends to support more rapid expansion. Alberto Alesina and Dani Rodrik (1994), for example, use a sample of forty-six countries, including OECD countries and poorer countries for which they were able to obtain 'high quality' data, to test the hypothesis that the growth of national income in a particular time period is more rapid when the distribution of income at the beginning of that time period is more equal. (They also test the hypothesis using a larger sample of countries, including many for which the data are less reliable.) Their results lead to a clear and statistically significant conclusion: income inequality is negatively correlated with subsequent growth. Torsten Persson and Guido Tabellini (1994) examine the same equality–growth relationship, using both historical data stretching back over 150 years for nine developed economies and post-Second World War data (different from Alesina and Rodrik's) for a sample of fifty-six countries. They also obtain statistically significant results showing that 'income equality at the start of a period has a positive effect on subsequent growth'.

These recent studies, when added to an accumulation of earlier evidence, put to rest the neo-liberal claim that, in general, inequality enhances income growth. Attention now focuses on the question of *why* equality enhances growth. I will turn to this matter shortly. First, however, it will be useful to examine the second neo-liberal claim in this realm, namely that nothing needs to be done about inequality if growth policies are adopted because, as is shown by Kuznets's inverted U, economic growth brings about a more equal distribution of income.

Kuznets's original speculation about the impact of economic growth on income distribution was a statement about what happened within particular economies – those of the advanced capitalist countries – over an extended period of time. Thus the argument is dependent on a trend towards equality in these countries. As I have pointed out above, however, in at

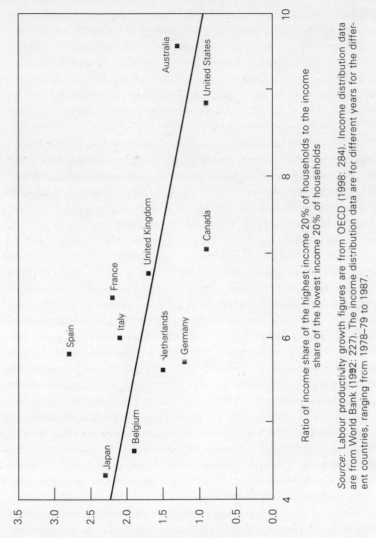

Source: Labour productivity growth figures are from OECD (1998: 284). Income distribution data are from World Bank (1992: 227). The income distribution data are for different years for the different countries, ranging from 1978–79 to 1987.

FIGURE 3.1 Income inequality and labour productivity growth 1979–96, selected countries

least some of these countries – the USA and a few others – the trend of
recent decades (since Kuznets's analyses) is in the other direction. The
inverted U may be turning into an S that has flipped around backwards
and fallen on its face. It is perhaps too early to tell whether these recent
experiences constitute a new direction of change or are simply blips in the
long-run move towards greater equality, but they certainly weaken the
empirical foundation of Kuznets's argument. In this regard, the variation
(noted above) in the income distribution experience of countries during
recent decades is also important. This variation of experience suggests, at
least at the upper levels of national income, that one should be wary of
generalizations about the relationship between income distribution and
growth.

With regard to the lower-income countries, lack of income distribution
data over long periods of time makes it difficult to determine the extent
to which experience may or may not confirm Kuznets's speculations. Those
data that do exist suggest that, as with the advanced countries, there is no
basis for generalization. Sundrum (1990: 120–1), for example, looks at
experience in sixteen countries in recent decades and finds no discernible
general connection among the levels of inequality, the levels of income
and the trends in inequality.[3]

Because of the paucity of historical data on income distribution, much
of the 'verification' of the Kuznets Curve has been based not on comparing
the situations in individual countries at different points of time, but on
'cross-country' analyses comparing different countries at the same point of
time. To use cross-country data to infer what happens to a country over
time involves the assumption that each country will develop as the countries
before it have developed. This is a heroic assumption which ignores the
fact that the previous success of the now economically advanced countries
has altered the economic environment in which development might take
place. For example, the existence of the advanced economies leads many
poorer countries along the raw material exporting path, a path that appears
to generate a high degree of inequality (see below). Also, the role of
multinational firms based in the advanced countries is likely to shape
political and social structures in today's poor countries in ways that contribute to continuing inequality. It is possible that the existence of the
already advanced economies could also push the low-income countries
towards greater equality – though I am hard pressed to think of examples.
Yet regardless of the difficulties in figuring out the ways that the prior
development of the advanced countries has impacts on the pattern of
development in poor countries today, it is hardly legitimate to assume no
impact at all.

In any case, in the cross-country analyses, an initial examination of the situation of the many countries for which we have income level and income distribution data at a point in time appears to support the accuracy of Kuznets's speculation. Countries with very low levels of per capita income tend to have more equal distributions of income than do somewhat higher-income countries. The economically advanced countries (the rich countries) generally have more equal distributions of income than do the middle-income countries. India, with an average per capita income (in 1993) of about $300, is an example of a very low-income country with a relatively low level of inequality; in India, the ratio of the income of the richest 20 per cent of the population to that of the poorest 20 per cent of the population is only 4.7 to 1. Brazil illustrates (in an extreme way) the great inequality in the middle income countries; with a per capita income of about $3,000, Brazil shows a ratio of the income of the top 20 per cent to that of the bottom 20 per cent of 32 to 1. Japan fills out the pattern, with a per capita income of over $30,000 and an income distribution ratio of 4.3 to 1 (World Bank 1995). (While this India–Brazil–Japan triplet appears to be consistent with the Kuznets Curve, it should be noted that this example would not lead many people to accept the neo-liberal argument that countries should abjure political and social action to equalize income and wait for the Curve to turn downwards. Few people in India, for example, would set aside political and social action if told that they must endure the extreme inequality of a Brazil on their way to reasonable economic conditions; they would likely all be dead long before those reasonable conditions were attained.)

Few groups of three countries, however, would illustrate the supposed relationship as well as India, Brazil and Japan. Even if an inverted U does provide an accurate general description of the relationship, it is clear that changes in the level of income account for only a small part of the changes in countries' income distributions. For example, consider Nigeria, South Korea and the United Kingdom, with 1993 per capita income levels of $300, $7,660 and $18,060 respectively. Nigeria and the UK have roughly the same degree of inequality, with the ratio of the income received by the highest 20 per cent to the lowest 20 per cent of about 9.6 to 1 for both countries. Yet, for South Korea, the ratio is 6 to 1. These three countries seem to fit the pattern of a right-side-up U. This is not to say that the Nigeria–South Korea–UK relationship is as typical as the India–Brazil–Japan relationship. It is not. Nevertheless, these data indicate that in cross-country comparisons the inverted U is not such a strong relationship. Thus we cannot have much confidence that rising inequality in the early stages of development will be offset by greater equality in the later stages of development.

The point is that there are other differences between countries in addition to differences in the levels of income, and these other differences sometimes explain more of the variation in inequality. For example, whether or not a country is a raw material exporter appears to have a substantial impact on the distribution of income; in general raw material exporting countries are more unequal at any level of income. If lower-income countries are divided into raw material exporters and 'others', then within neither group does there appear to be a clear relationship between income distribution and the level of income (Papanek 1978: 265). The extensive study undertaken by Irma Adelman and Cynthia Taft Morris (1973) does find a pattern among lower-income countries that is roughly consistent with Kuznets's inverted U. Adelman and Morris (1973: 183) conclude, however, that it is not primarily changes in the level of income that bring about changes of income distribution; instead: 'The most important variables affecting income distribution are ecological, socioeconomic, and political.' This, it turns out, is a conclusion that is consistent with Kuznets's argument.

For in spite of the way Kuznets's original speculations have been used to justify a rejection of political and social action to bring about income equality, Kuznets himself saw such action as an important means by which the distribution of income became more equal in later stages of development. Following his remarks (quoted above) to the effect that the people born in cities would likely have 'a better chance for organization and adaptation, a better basis for securing greater income shares', Kuznets goes on to say:

> Furthermore, in democratic societies the growing political power of the urban lower-income groups led to a variety of protective and supporting legislation, much of it aimed to counteract the worst effects of rapid industrialization and urbanization and to support the claims of the broad masses for more adequate shares of the growing income of the country.

We are left with the recognition that the pattern described by Kuznets's inverted U is at most only a very rough relationship. There is no economic 'law' by which very poor countries must become more unequal as they begin to develop and by which they can expect to become more equal as they attain some substantial growth success. Whatever general pattern does exist, it appears to be shaped as much by political and social intervention in markets as by the operation of markets per se.

Why is Relative Income Equality Good for Economic Growth?

The classical and neo-liberal argument that there is a positive connection between inequality in the distribution of income and a higher rate of economic growth is wrong because it ignores the multiple ways that the distribution of income affects social and economic relations. The argument focuses on the ways that inequality is likely to raise the personal savings rate and generate stronger incentives. Yet this focus obscures a complex of other effects that, on the basis of the evidence reviewed above, appear in aggregate to have a more powerful influence on economic growth.

In particular, the focus on savings and the level of investment obscures the role of technological change in economic development. Investment is certainly an important factor affecting the rate of economic expansion, but it is not the sole factor and, of special importance, it is not independent of technological change. There are a number of ways in which greater equality in the distribution of income can induce technological change that is favourable to a higher rate of economic growth. Rapid technological advance, in turn, is likely to induce a higher rate of investment.

In addition, savings is not simply a function of the level and distribution of income. If a higher rate of economic expansion is established – for example, through rapid technological advance or the stable expansion of aggregate demand – it will create opportunities that will in turn alter savings behaviour. This is all the more true when, as is always the case, savings does not only come from private individuals within a country, but also from corporations, government and foreign sources. In addition, savings will be affected by the broad economic environment, including a country's overall economic and political stability. If a more equal distribution of income favourably affects either technological change or the stability of the economy, it will also bring about a higher rate of savings.

On the matter of the incentive role of inequality, different sorts of inequality are likely to have very different, perhaps opposite, impacts. For example, the economic inequality of South Africa's apartheid system hardly gave an incentive to the country's black population. Whenever people are discriminated against because of factors over which they have no control – race, ethnicity, sex, the income or position of one's parents – the resulting income inequalities are not likely to generate positive incentives. In fact, in so far as people perceive that their economic position is determined by such factors beyond their control, the resulting inequality may operate as a disincentive. Also, while moderate inequalities, when perceived as legitimately connected to people's efforts, may serve as incentives to greater production, extreme inequalities – perhaps because they will almost necessarily be seen as unconnected, or only distantly connected, to people's efforts – may serve to discourage effort.

These general speculations suggest that there are numerous reasons why relative equality in the distribution of income tends to enhance economic growth. Beyond general speculations, however, there are some more specific explanations of the apparent positive influence of equality on growth. These are presented below under five headings: (1) education and social investment; (2) incentives; (3) innovation; (4) aggregate demand; and (5) fairness. The different explanations, it will become apparent, intersect and overlap with one another; also, issues of technological change arise in numerous places.[4]

Education and social investment The importance of formal education and other forms of social investment for economic growth have been recognized at least since Adam Smith and especially during the last few decades, following the formulation of 'human capital' theory in the 1960s. Yet, while economists have argued that, in general, higher expenditures on education cause higher rates of economic growth, there has been relatively little attention paid to the question of what are the factors that yield higher expenditures on education. Once we ask this question part of the answer is quickly evident: relative equality in the distribution of income is likely to lead to higher levels of educational expenditure. Thus, part of the equality–growth link is an equality–education–growth link.

The various causal links that establish the equality–education–growth link are examined by Nancy Birdsall et al. (1995) who emphasize the experience of East Asian countries as compared to low-income countries in general. The empirical relationship is fairly clear: the East Asian countries stand out among low-income countries on all three measures. Birdsall and her colleagues focus on two 'virtuous circles', involving 'a process of cumulative causation, in which education contributed to economic growth, which, in turn, stimulated investment in education ... [and in which] education contributed to low levels of income inequality which, in turn, stimulated investment in education' (1995: 482). (They also argue, parallel to the discussion below, that there are mechanisms other than the education connection by which equality may contribute to more rapid economic growth.)

There are a number of explanations for the association between education and rapid economic growth, not all of which involve a direct causal connection. For example, in South Korea the land reform that took place in the 1950s undermined the power and position of a rural class of large landowners, a group that appears to have played a role of limiting the extent of education in many low-income countries (Bowles, 1978; Alesina and Rodrik, 1994). This change in the country's class structure, a result of particular historical factors and political events (Cumings 1989), had multiple economic impacts, including: a more equal distribution of income; the elimination of barriers to the development of the educational system; and opportunities for the implementation of policies that would support rapid industrial expansion and economic growth. Thus, the relative income equality in South Korea, the growth of the educational system and the acceleration of economic growth all had common roots in social change. Though they continued to have mutually supporting impacts, the original causative factor lay in the country's history and politics.

Also, there are more direct links between relative equality in a country's distribution of income and an expansion of a people's educational attainment. In so far as educational expenditures are determined by private decisions and paid by the individuals obtaining education (or by their families), equality is likely to raise expenditures on education because in conditions of inequality the very poor would not be able to finance their education. They would not have sufficient personal savings to cover the costs of education – neither the direct costs nor the lost income – and the credit system would almost certainly not meet their needs. In a situation of relative equality, more people would be in a position either to finance their own education or obtain the necessary credit through the financial system. Even when the direct costs of education are covered by the state in a public system, the poor still have to bear the costs of lost income, which can be substantial. (The lack of funds to finance the education of the poor is sometimes explained as a result of 'imperfect' capital markets because, presumably, if capital markets were 'perfect', then finance would be available for activities that have a high rate of return – as is the case with education of the poor. In this way of explaining things, the problem lies not with the market per se, but with alleged imperfections of the market. In reality, however, the market is always imperfect when it comes to providing financial support for the poor. Moreover, even if capital markets were in some sense 'perfect', the inability of the poor to provide collateral would present them with very high interest rates and thus limit their educational investments. In any case, regardless of the ideological paraphernalia with which one approaches the problem, making sure that finance is available to the poor always requires some form of political intervention.)

Moreover, under conditions of relative equality, the state is likely to provide more support for education. Popular pressure for state support of education will tend to carry weight when some degree of equality has already been attained and a smaller proportion of the population is alienated from politics by its poverty. On the other side of the political process, with relative equality, elite resistance to the growth of educational expenditures would not be substantial because state spending on education would not involve a major redistribution of income (the very rich paying for the education of the poor). Also, in so far as the equality is connected to a declining power of a landlord class and a rising power of industrial capitalists (as in South Korea or Taiwan, for example), elite groups are likely to see their own economic needs served by having a more educated workforce.

One way to interpret the economic growth gains that come with the expansion of education is to see that education as enhancing technological change. A more educated workforce allows changes in the way production is organized (that is, changes in technology) that enhance growth. This technological advance would tend to offset any loss of growth due to a lower savings rate that might (or might not) come with more equality. However, another way to understand the gains from education is to note that expenditures on education directly augment the rate of savings. National accounting practices count all educational expenditures as 'consumption', when in fact a large share of those expenditures is investment; and the financing of those expenditures is savings. If a proper portion of educational expenditures were counted as savings and investment, we could view equality and education as contributing to growth by raising society's rate of savings.

What is true of expenditures on education is probably true of other forms of social spending – health-care and training programmes almost certainly and probably various social welfare programmes as well. Studies of a broad range of social services in high-income countries suggest that they have a positive impact on economic growth because they improve the conditions of life of the recipients of services and thereby raise their productivity. In addition, a failure to spend on social services exacerbates social alienation and political instability, which can have growth-retarding impacts. There is every reason to believe that in low-income countries, the same mechanisms are at work connecting social spending to improved growth, and in all circumstances it is probably appropriate to count a large share of social spending as social investment. Likewise, the same sorts of causal connections that appear to exist between equality and educational expenditures are likely to apply more generally to social investment (Glyn and Miliband 1994; Strauss and Thomas 1998).

Incentives However true it may be that some inequality is useful in establishing incentives, it is also quite clear that equality can generate incentives that raise labour productivity and thus generate more rapid growth. The positive incentive impact of equality can be seen in the way capitalist firms respond to labour markets. Because of the incomplete nature of the labour contract, employers, having hired labourers, are continually faced with the problem of how to extract the most actual work from the people they have employed. (This 'problem' also presents employers with the opportunity that is the foundation of their profits.) They have a wide variety of mechanisms by which to accomplish this task, not the least of which is the negative incentive of dismissal. Yet, available evidence indicates that, in a great variety of production activities, the positive incentive of 'good' wages and working conditions (including a role for workers in decision-making) can be especially important (Leibenstein 1966; Buchele and Christiansen 1992; Green 1988).

A capitalist firm, of course, is not concerned with the maximization of productivity, but with the maximization of profits, and to ensure the long-run maximization of profits the employer must maintain control of essential decision-making (Braverman 1974). Higher wages in and of themselves conflict with higher profits, and better working conditions – especially when they involve an extension of workers' role in decision-making – can threaten employers' control. As a consequence, these positive incentives will be used to a limited extent, only in so far as their positive contribution to productivity outweighs their negative impact on profits. The result is that employers will, to the extent they have the choice, operate in a manner that does not maximize productivity growth, choosing methods of work organization that maximize profits rather than productivity growth whenever the two come in conflict.

However, under conditions of relatively high wages, which we can take as a proxy for relative equality, the structure of the labour market is likely to limit the choices open to employers. Relative equality implies that wages will be generally 'good' and that the power of workers will be sufficient to force employers to offer 'good' working conditions. In effect, relative equality may force firms to use a system of positive incentives and thus engender a more rapid growth of productivity than otherwise.

Samuel Bowles and Herbert Gintis (1993; 1995) develop a similar sort of argument, using the relationship between landlords and sharecropping tenants – a relationship of some significance in low-income countries – to illustrate the issues. The landlords are, like the capitalist employers, faced with the problem of getting the most effort and output from the tenants. The arrangement of share tenancy partially solves this problem by giving the tenants a stake in increasing output. Because the tenants' stake is only partial, however, their effort is likely not to be as great as it would be if they had full claims on additional output. If ownership of the land were then transferred to the tenants through an agrarian reform, the result would be both greater equality and greater productivity, since the now former tenants would have full claim on additions to production and thus a stronger incentive to raise output.

It would not be reasonable to argue that higher wages or a land reform *necessarily* leads to greater productivity growth and a more rapid rate of growth. It is possible, for example, that higher wages would cut into profits so severely as to undermine savings or even lead to capital flight; a land reform could lead the peasants to work less since it could raise their incomes and reduce the coercive effects of poverty. My purpose here – and with other points offered in this section to explain the apparent positive association between equality and growth – is not to argue that all effects are in the direction of a positive equality–growth relationship. I simply want to establish that there are a wide range of effects that work in this direction.

Innovation The story of economic expansion in the United States during the nineteenth century suggests an aspect of the equality–growth link that operates through the structure and rate of technological change. In efforts to account for the relatively rapid US industrial expansion in the last century, some historians have argued that relatively high wages, as compared particularly with England, induced rapid technological change (Habakkuk 1962).

Largely because the availability of land led to a relative scarcity of urban labour, employers in the United States were forced to pay high wages. In order to make a profit when paying these high wages, the employers had to find ways to raise productivity; this led them to innovate, especially in labour-saving technology but also in all sorts of organizational and mechanical processes that raised labour productivity. If we again take high wages as a proxy for equality, then this analysis provides one explanation of the way equality yields more rapid growth. (It is important to bear in mind that the argument about wages and technological change applies only to the capitalist sector of the US economy; the slave South presents a rather different story. Also, the issue of slavery indicates the problem with taking high wages as a proxy for equality. As in the USA during the nineteenth century, in some low-income countries today relatively high wages in an industrial setting can coexist with poverty-stricken agricultural labour.)

In discussions of economic growth in low-income countries, the issue of choice of technology has received considerable attention. Many people have argued, consistent with the experience in the advanced countries, that there are great advantages to be obtained from the adoption of capital-intensive, labour-saving technologies, and those advantages are not reflected simply in the private economic calculations that determine firms' choices of technique. In particular, the use of machinery – and, today, computers, other electronic devices, chemical processes, and bio-technology – engenders the development of skills in the workforce. These skills are created through training, experience, formal education and learning-by-doing, but they would not occur independently of the adoption of 'modern' methods of production. (In this sense, certain types of technologies have extensive externalities.) Recognizing the advantages of 'modern' technology, governments in some low-income countries have established incentives (subsidies on imports of machinery, for example) that encourage their adoption. These actions have spawned a debate over 'appropriate technology', with critics of these government actions pointing out that capital-intensive technologies, whatever their benefits, are inconsistent with the needs of the countries' populations. They do not provide employment; they generate greater inequality among workers; and they waste a country's scarce capital resources.

This appropriate technology debate, however, tends to miss the lesson of historical experience in the United States and other advanced countries and takes the issue of technology out of its social context. On the one hand, historically and in the current era, the adoption of capital-intensive technologies has generated wider development of skills in the workforce, and that skill development has been an important foundation for continuing growth. On the other hand, this wider development of skills – the externalities derived from adopting 'modern' technology – has occurred within the context of relative social and economic equality and in a context where the different sectors of the economy are relatively well connected (articulated) with one another.

Consider, however, many low-income countries of the current era that are characterized by dramatic inequalities; Brazil, South Africa (particularly in the apartheid era), and several other countries of Latin America and Africa would serve as examples. In these countries, the inequalities between urban and rural segments of the population are especially large, and there are only weak connections (disarticulation) between the 'modern' urban sector and the 'backward' rural sector. Agriculture may be a source of foreign exchange earnings for industrial expansion. However, agriculture is not an important supplier of industrial inputs and is not a dynamic source of demand for the products of industry either for consumer products (because of low-incomes in the countryside) or for inputs to agricultural production (because of the 'backwardness' of agriculture). Under these conditions, the adoption of 'modern' production techniques in industry is unlikely to transmit positive impacts to the rest of the society; the 'external' impacts on skills will be limited because of the great inequalities. Several countries in East Asia – as usual, particularly South Korea and Taiwan – provide the positive examples. In these countries, broad relative income equality has been associated with limited rural–urban differences, and agriculture has progressed along with industry.

These different experiences suggest that it is not technology per se that is the key to development, and there may be no 'appropriate technology' that, in itself, can change the course of a country's development. For technological changes in one sector of the economy to have broad, positive impacts, they probably have to be based within a wider social and economic equality.

Aggregate demand Classical arguments regarding the centrality of savings in long-term economic growth paid little attention to the role of aggregate demand. The development of Keynesian economics after the 1930s – to say nothing of the reality of the great depression of the 1930s – led economists to recognize the importance of aggregate demand, but primarily in the examination of short-run variations in the level of economic activity. Economists have by and large continued to view long-run economic growth as determined by the capacity of the economy to produce – that is, by the amount of capital stock in existence and the technological capacity of people to use that capital stock to produce goods and services. Since the problem of economic development is essentially a long-run problem, the rate of savings, which determines the rate of growth of the capital stock, has continued to have a central role in most analyses, and certainly in the neo-liberal argument.

This traditional approach of giving minimal attention to demand conditions has several problems that are relevant to understanding the role of income distribution in affecting economic growth. One of these problems is that there is a connection between short-run stability and long-run growth. Insufficient aggregate demand in the short run, which would be aggravated by the weak consumer spending that would be associated with a high degree of inequality and a consequently high savings rate (following the classical assumption), would inhibit investment and thereby reduce long-run economic growth. Greater equality, however, would tend to spur stronger consumer demand, reduce the severity of short-run instability, and thus encourage investment and long-run growth. This general argument follows readily from Keynes's basic insight that insufficient aggregate demand can generate recurring recession. Recurring recessions, even if they are not system-destroying, are bad for long-term growth. If insufficient aggregate demand is indeed the problem, then there are several solutions for an individual country. One is the principal Keynesian solution of government deficits to stimulate demand. Another is finding demand in the expansion of export markets. A third is greater equality, which would stimulate aggregate demand through a higher level of consumer spending.

This sort of 'under consumptionist' argument has been roundly criticized as giving insufficient attention to the roles of investment and consumption by the wealthy in bolstering aggregate demand. Even when – because of inequality or whatever other reasons – consumer demand by the majority of the population is weak, aggregate demand can be maintained by the consumption of the rich and by their investments; they must spend their money on one or the other, and from the point of view of simply maintaining aggregate demand, it does not matter which.

This claim that inequality does not undermine aggregate demand has some plausibility in a relatively closed economy (though see A. K. Dutt 1984). In the real world of international interdependence, however, inequality is likely to have a more deleterious impact on aggregate demand and growth. In many poor countries, the rich have a third choice in disposing of their incomes: they can send it abroad. Whether they spend their money on consumption that has a large imported component or invest their money abroad (capital flight), the depressing impact on domestic aggregate demand is the same. When the rich have an international option, then it seems relatively clear that an unequal distribution of income can undermine domestic demand and constrain long-term growth. (When the rich buy goods or assets abroad, this will have a tendency to drive down the value of the national currency and thus stimulate the demand for a country's exports. It is possible that the resulting increase in the demand for exports will offset the decline in demand resulting from the foreign spending of the rich. However, even under favourable circumstances such an adjustment is likely to take considerable time, and weak demand in the interim can have long-run consequences – and 'favourable circumstances' will often not exist.)

The question of how the rich spend their money leads to another explanation of the way inequality can undermine a country's economic expansion through its impact on the structure of demand. In poor countries, a relatively large proportion of consumption expenditures by the rich is on imported and hand-made (customized) luxury goods. If income were more equally distributed, the structure of demand would be different in a way that would create a stronger market for mass-produced industrial goods. A larger market for mass-produced goods could create a basis for a wider development of domestic industry because firms could produce in sufficient volume to take advantage of economies of scale (Murphy et al. 1989) The development of industry, in turn, can hasten the pace of technological change in a country, both directly and through its longer-term impacts on the skills and general qualities of the labour force.

The substantial inequalities that exist in many Latin American countries have often been cited as a limit to economic expansion based on import substitution. Because inequality limits the size of the domestic market for many manufactured goods, import substituting manufacturers operate at relatively inefficient levels, and they cannot compete with foreign producers or survive only because of import restrictions (Barkin 1990; Furtado 1976).

As the costs of this inefficiency become more and more burdensome, economic expansion can be maintained only by an income redistribution that enlarges the domestic market or by an enlargement of export markets. The structure of political power generally rules on the first option, and so many governments have turned to export promotion as a means to maintain economic expansion. The success of export promotion, however, often depends on suppressing wages, and thus a policy born of inequality can generate worsening inequality.

Kevin Murphy et al. (1989: 539) cite the experience of Colombia with coffee production around the beginning of the twentieth century to illustrate the potential positive impact of equality on growth. Colombian coffee production in that era was undertaken on small family farms, and thus the rising income from the coffee boom was relatively widely distributed. The resulting impact on Colombian industrialization was substantial. Fifty years earlier, however, a boom in Colombian tobacco production had had minimal impact on domestic industry. Tobacco production had been concentrated on large plantations, and the income gains from the boom had accrued to a small segment of the population. Harbison (1970, as cited by Murphy et al. 1989) provides the details of this comparison:

> The lion's share of increased prosperity generated by coffee production was enjoyed by the large poor *mestizo campesino* class, not the small group of rich white urban landlords. These peasants, in turn, certainly did not buy for themselves or their children foreign travel and foreign education or other luxury imports ... Since such items could not be produced in Colombia, the use of tobacco-generated incomes to purchase these luxury imports had resulted in a long-term depression and decline in Colombian artisan manufacture without compensating growth in another domestic sector. But coffee generated incomes in the hands of the Antioqueno farmers who spend precisely on those necessities ... The rapid expansion of coffee production redistributed income toward that segment of the population most likely to spend the incremental income on items characterized by high potential for generating domestic income – i.e., on domestic goods whose large-scale production could utilize modern low-cost technology – not imports.

More generally, the great success of a system based on mass production and high wages (Fordism) in the United States suggests the importance of the structure of demand in establishing an industrial foundation for long-term growth. The rising wages of the working class in the United States was the outgrowth of mass-production techniques and also, by widening the market for consumer goods, made those mass-production techniques possible. Even earlier in US history, the large consumer market that came with the country's relative equality was a stimulus to early industrial growth. Thus in the history of the United States it appears that relative equality contributed to growth through both its impact on the choice of technology (as discussed above) and its effect on the structure of demand. The point is illustrated by a paragraph from the catalogue for the 1851 London Crystal Palace exhibition:

> The absence in the United States of those vast accumulations of wealth which favour the expenditure of large sums on articles of mere luxury, and the general distribution of the means of procuring the more substantial conveniences of life, impart to the productions of American industry a character distinct from that of many other countries. The expenditure of months or years of labour upon a single article, not to increase its intrinsic value, but solely to augment its cost and its estimation as the object of *virtu*, is not common in the United States. On the contrary, both manual and mechanical labour are applied with direct reference to increasing the number of the quantity of articles suited for the wants of a whole people, and adapted to promote the enjoyment of that moderate competency that prevails upon them. (Rosenberg 1972: 50; as cited by Murphy et al. 1989: 538)

Fairness The impact of income inequalities on economic growth undoubtedly depends in part on the nature and origin of those inequalities. I have already pointed out above that when income inequalities arise because people are discriminated against on the basis of race, sex or other factors over which they have no control, the resulting inequalities may serve as a disincentive. On the other hand, if inequalities reflect actual differentials in work effort, they may serve as an effective positive incentive. Another way to say roughly the same thing is that the impact of inequalities depends in large part on whether or not they are perceived as 'fair'.

The importance of fairness, moreover, goes well beyond the incentive effect of inequalities. When inequalities are unfair, that inequity sometimes means that people with various capabilities are denied the opportunity fully to develop and use those capabilities. This is the case with various forms of discrimination. For example, on top of the human horror that was involved in South African apartheid (and continues to affect life in the country today) and beyond the negative incentives that the system generated, it undoubtedly involved huge economic waste as millions of people were denied opportunities to exercise their productive capacities. South African blacks could not obtain land, were extremely restricted in their operation of businesses, could seldom obtain quality education, had very limited access to credit – it was, on top of everything else, a horribly inefficient system. In many other countries, discrimination on the basis of race, ethnicity and social class background has accounted for similar, if less blatant, inefficiency and waste, and has surely retarded economic growth. (I might note in passing that the huge inefficiencies in South Africa's system did not prevent the IMF from providing loans to the country's racist government even while it justified its refusal to give loans to leftist governments by their supposed inefficient practices of state intervention in economic affairs.)

Likewise, gender discrimination the world over has been and continues to be a very wasteful, as well as a very nasty, form of inequality. Diane Elson (1995) reports findings of the relationship between gender and equality that illustrate in that particular context the sorts of general arguments suggested here. She points out, for example, that when discriminatory limitations on women's access to resources are eliminated, the consequent productivity increases contribute to overall economic growth. In addition, she cites evidence suggesting that the elimination of gender discrimination in patterns of occupation and pay not only improves women's relative position, but also tends to increase total output.[5]

Also, some studies have implicitly given an additional role to a lack of fairness in explaining the negative impact of inequality on economic growth. When inequalities are perceived as unfair, they may have significant impacts on social and political stability. The studies (cited above) by Persson and Tabellini (1994) and Alesina and Rodrik (1994) both argue that inequality has a negative impact on growth because it tends to undermine social and political stability, and instability depresses savings and investment rates. Great inequality is likely to generate various efforts, ranging from rebellion to tax legislation, that threaten to disrupt the existing distribution of income. These threats and the conflicts surrounding them create an economic environment that is unfavourable to growth. (Neither of these studies gives explicit emphasis to the issue of fairness, but it is almost self-evident that inequalities that are perceived as fair will not generate conflict to nearly the same degree as inequalities that are perceived as unfair.) The authors of these studies accept the classical connection between savings and growth and also the proposition that the rich tend to save at higher rates than the poor. They depart from the classical argument, however, in recognizing another mechanism – the social and political instability mechanism – by which inequality affects the level of savings.

Income Distribution and Growth: What are the Lessons?

Even in the face of considerable contradictory evidence, the durability of conventional wisdom about economic growth and inequality is not particularly hard to understand. The notions that inequality is good for growth and that growth will eventually bring about equality are important pillars of an ideology that supports the status quo of privilege and power. The status quo has a great deal of inertia, not because of some abstract law of social stability, but because those who benefit from the existing arrangement use their resources to preserve things as they are. One important part of this task is preserving the ideology that legitimizes the current state of affairs.

The conventional wisdom embodied in the neo-liberal position on income distribution and growth continues to be very powerful. It plays an important role in justifying much of the activity of the IMF and the World Bank; it is a buttress for much of US foreign economic policy, especially with regard to foreign aid programmes; and it continues to reign in elementary economics courses. Yet in recent years, cracks have begun to appear in the foundation of the neo-liberal edifice. The evidence that has been cited above, particularly the evidence suggesting that income equality has been good for economic growth, is hard to ignore. The experience in East Asia has been especially disruptive to conventional thinking. Even while the IMF, the World Bank, and the US government have continued to formulate policy that can be justified only by the now discredited assertions about distribution and growth, they have been forced to acknowledge reality. For example, in a March 1995 speech in Bombay, Stanley Fischer, the first deputy managing director of the IMF stated:

> both East Asia's dramatic progress over the past two decades and further research have made it clear that there is nothing inevitable in the relationship between growth and income distribution. What happens to poverty and income distribution during growth is determined in large part by policy. More important, the evidence suggests that rapid growth is not only compatible with, but is likely to be enhanced by, policies that also improve income distribution and reduce poverty. (Fischer 1995)

Confronted by the fact that relative equality often provides a sound foundation for economic growth, some neo-liberals have struggled to maintain the essence of their position by arguing that glaring inequalities in low-income countries are the result of government actions, and the solution is to give greater scope to the market. For example, the *World Development Report 1991* argues:

> Industrial protection and discriminatory taxes on farming help to explain why income inequality is more severe in Latin America than in Asia. The bulk of developing countries' revenues generally consist of indirect taxes, which are generally less progressive than income taxes. Subsidies for capital (in the form of tax incentives, subsidized credit, or currency over-valuation) invariably lead to more capital-intensive modes of production and thus

worsen distribution ... When markets work well, greater equity often comes naturally. (World Bank 1991a: 137–8)

At many times government regulations are the proximate source of socially destructive monopolistic gains as well as other inefficiencies and downright corruption. This line of defence for neo-liberalism fails, however, because it is based on the myth that there are such things as markets that work independently of government. As I will argue at length in Chapter 4, markets are always deeply embedded in social relations, and government is a central part of social relations. The choice is not whether we will have government involvement in markets, but *how* we will have such involvement.

Also, attributing responsibility to government for the creation of economic inequalities begs the question of why government acts as it does. When markets work well, to borrow the World Bank's phrase, they create winners and losers; this is the very nature of competition. Winners in the market use their economic power to bring about government policies that will further enhance that power. This power can be confronted and constrained by democratic movements, but only if those movements direct their actions at establishing alternative state policies (or perhaps alternative states!). It is not an option to eliminate state policies and thus allow markets to operate on their own (as I will explain in Chapter 4). In any case, if it were somehow possible to have markets operate 'on their own', they would simply re-create the conditions through which powerful groups could reassert and enhance their power.

Certainly we have no experience suggesting that an economy organized on neo-liberal lines would 'naturally' generate fairness (unless we define 'fairness' in a rather peculiar manner that excludes relative income equality). In recent decades, neo-liberalism has probably been strongest in Latin America, and, as discussed above, the era of neo-liberalism in Latin America has been an era of increasing inequality. Within the region, Chile is often touted as the neo-liberal showcase. In the era of Chile's neo-liberalism, income distribution has become substantially more unequal: in 1968, the highest income 20 per cent of the population in Chile received 11.7 times as much income as the lowest income 20 per cent; in 1992, the figure had risen to 18.3 (World Bank 1982; 1995). Without any basis in historical experience, the World Bank's claim about how markets 'naturally' operate becomes a crude ideological statement of faith.

As Kuznets suggests in his 1955 article, when equality does come about in the course of economic development, it is the result of popular groups having gained sufficient power to achieve 'a variety of protective and supporting legislation'. That is, equality depends upon democratic action, on using government to shape the operation of markets. In this way of looking at things, the distribution of income becomes a question of social power. Various groups contend for power in a capitalist society, both directly through the market and through those institutions, particularly political institutions, that shape markets. These struggles take on many different forms and have many different points of focus: union struggles over wages and workers' rights; community efforts to expand public education and other services; national political conflicts over the control of foreign trade and investment; and many more struggles in many more arenas. In all of these conflicts, in one way or another the issue is whether or not democratic action will be able to limit and weaken the traditional forms of privilege and power that operate both through the market and through the political system.

The evidence and analyses reviewed in this chapter imply that such democratic action is needed because there is no 'natural' sequence of events by which markets generate greater equality as economies grow. Also, the discussion presented here indicates that such action can bring about both more equality *and* more growth. Yet the equality–growth connection is not a simple one. It operates in a variety of ways, and it does not operate in only one direction. The evidence thoroughly destroys the neo-liberal position that equality is necessarily bad for growth, but it does not establish the converse that equality is necessarily good for growth. A lot depends on the way equality is established, on the particular policies that are pursued, and on the historical context.

These broad lessons provide part of a foundation for building alternative economic development programmes. Effective policies, for example, would do well to focus on education and other forms of social investment and on eliminating forms of discrimination that are widely perceived as unfair. Also, policies directed towards creating technological progress in industry may be most successful – in terms of both growth and equality – if they are combined with efforts to generate employment and raise incomes in agriculture. At the same time, effective policies cannot ignore the issue of savings; programmes must be financed, and if development programmes are not going to nurture and depend upon the wealthy, then they need to establish other sources of funds. These are the sorts of issues that will be integrated into the discussion of the chapters in Part II.

Notes

1. The moral issues surrounding income distribution are more complicated than they may appear at first blush. When we hold out 'equality' as a moral standard, for example, what do we mean? Should everyone receive the same amount of income? Should each person receive what he or she 'needs'? Do we mean 'equal pay for equal work', a principle which would, in some sense, have people remunerated in proportion to their

social contributions? And then how do we define 'social contributions'? Without answers to these questions, it is hard to define an ideal against which to evaluate our reality. Any reasonable answers to these sorts of questions would none the less give us an ideal very far from the current reality in most of the world. The questions are important, but, lacking answers, we can still form broad judgements about the status quo. For discussion of some of these sorts of issues, see Sen (1992)

2. Although their implications are at best limited, Sundrum's results are summarized as follows (with the figures in parentheses indicating the period of coverage): Rising Inequality – Argentina (1953–70), Bangladesh (1963–81), Brazil (1960–70), Colombia (1962–70), Mexico (1963–77), Philippines (1956–85), Thailand (1962–81); Mixed Trends – India (1953–75), Indonesia (1970–84), Malaysia (1957–67), S. Korea (1966–82), Sri Lanka (1953–81); Declining Inequality – Costa Rica (1961–71), Pakistan (1963–70), Peru (1961–72), Taiwan (1953–85).

3. The countries are those listed in the preceding note. Sundrum expresses scepticism about the reliability and comparability of these data.

4. The discussion that follows owes a good deal to Siddiqur Rahman Osmani (1996), though Osmani's classification is rather different from mine. Nancy Birdsall et al. (1995) also present a similar set of explanations of the equality–growth link, and Louis Putterman et al. (1998) provide a useful discussion and review of the literature. Although this list of several explanations of the same phenomenon may suggest a degree of vagueness about the actual causal connection between equality and growth, it would be better to understand the list as reflecting the fact that important social relationships are often 'over-determined' (Althusser 1970). Many of the analyses cited in the following pages focus their attention on one aspect of the link between equality and growth, and such focus often is useful in clarifying a point. When the focus implies an exclusion of parallel causal relationships, however, it is probably misleading. Different connections are probably of different importance at different times and at different places, but overall there is a whole set of forces that needs to be considered.

5. Elson refers to Ongaro (1988), Moock (1976) and Quisumbing (1993) on the issue of women's access to resources and to Tzannatos (1992) on the question of occupation and pay discrimination.

4

The Social Construction of Markets

My father used to enjoy telling a story about the young London labourer who, on his day off, decided to take a walk in the country. As he strolled through the woods, he came to a stone fence. Not seeing why this should limit his outing, the young Londoner hopped over the fence and continued on his way. Rounding a turn in the path, he found himself face to face with a country gentleman, who, upon seeing the young man, said indignantly:

> 'Sir, do you realize you are trespassing on my land?'
> To which the labourer replied: 'So this is your land, is it?'
> 'Yes, indeed it is!' answered the gentleman.
> 'Well,' the young man queried, 'where did you get this land?'
> 'I got it from my father.'
> 'And where', asked the worker, 'did your father get the land?'
> 'He got it from his father.'
> 'And where did he get it?'
> 'From his father,' answered the increasingly irritated gentleman.
> 'And where did he get it?' asked the young man one more time.
> 'Well, I suppose he fought for it!' proclaimed the gentleman, not without a hint of pride in his voice.
> 'All right, then,' said the worker, 'I'll fight you for it!'

Who owns what and *how they came to own it* are large elements in determining what will happen through markets. How do markets come to be as they are? How are they constructed? Where do they come from? What is the existing distribution of property rights and how has it been established? What are the laws, rules and customs by which markets operate and how have they been created? Without answers to these questions, we can say little about market outcomes and about the role of markets in economic development. Also, we can say little about the legitimacy of market outcomes or about how people, the participants in the market, will view the legitimacy of those outcomes. How people view the legitimacy of the market outcomes will affect how they respond to the markets and how they operate in those markets – in other words, people's view of the legitimacy of the outcomes will affect the outcomes themselves. So it is not only important to know how markets have been constructed, but also to know how participants believe they have been constructed. (Thus the importance of the debate over the original or primitive accumulation of capital. Was original accumulation the product of long years of hard work and abstinence? Or, as Karl Marx (1961 [1867]: 760) maintains, did capital come into the world 'dripping from head to foot, from every pore, with blood and dirt'? This dispute, which I will not go into here, is much more than an academic one. If Marx's position were widely believed, the ideological foundations of capitalism would be severely disrupted. Without wide acceptance of its legitimacy, any system becomes less stable.)

It turns out that, as the London worker in my father's story saw, property rights and markets come from history. To say that we should 'leave things to the market', is to say no more nor less than that we should leave things to history as it has come to us. The young man in the story saw no reason to take history as it had come to him, and it seems to me that is a good way to think about the role of markets in economic development.

The Construction of Markets: Illustrations

Let me illustrate some of the issues here with three examples: the labour market in the US South in the late nineteenth century; the market for land in Mexico during the twentieth century; and the international market for seeds as it has evolved during the last several decades. I have chosen these three examples because they are very different from one another and have arisen in very different circumstances. Yet they have common aspects that bring out issues of general importance.

The labour market in the US South in the nineteenth century As an outcome of the US Civil War, in 1865 black slaves in the southern part of the country obtained their freedom. 'Freedom,' however, turned out to have more than one definition. In the aspirations and demands of the slaves, freedom meant not only lack of obligations to any master, but also some land and capital. Their modest hopes were summed up in the slogan: 'Forty acres and a mule!' For the white authorities, in Washington and in the South, freedom meant simply lack of obligatory servitude.

Over time, the reality of freedom included a set of practices and legal structures that curtailed the economic options of African Americans. For example, southern planters contracted for labour by the year, with a large part of payment to workers coming due at the end of the season, and southern legislatures enacted 'anti-enticement' laws which prevented any employer from hiring a person whose previous contract with another employer had not ended by consent of the first employer. Combined with anti-vagrancy laws, to say nothing of extra-legal coercion, these practices and laws greatly restricted the job mobility of former slaves (Jaynes 1986: ch. 15).

One could say, along with Gerald Jaynes (1986: 15) and many others, that in the post-Civil War era 'the development of the southern economy and the black labour force would be largely left to the fluctuations of the market. The slave population was not to enter freedom as a yeomanry, nor, ironically, would their former masters receive the financial aid necessary to provide for a rebuilding of the economy upon firm capitalistic grounds.' To adopt this common language means that, at a given time, things are 'left to the market' if there is no immediate and overt government intervention at that time. Such language would be tenable only if we adopted the most myopic view of history, in this case speaking as though the history of the southern labour market began only in 1865. The creation and enforcement of slavery prior to the war and the war itself had been huge government interventions that defined labour relations for generations after the war (and, most would agree, still play a role 135 years later). Also, government and extra-government authorities after 1865 enforced a system – most notorious in the Jim Crow Laws – that organized political power in the South so as to disenfranchise black citizens. This disenfranchisement, in turn, greatly weakened the economic position of black workers and shaped the labour market.

It is at least conceivable, and certainly was conceived of by many former slaves, that things could have been different. Had African Americans been given the land and capital that they viewed as rightfully theirs after 250 years of forced servitude, the southern labour market would have operated very differently. Why do historians, of all people, say that, when slaves are forced to toil for generations and then set free without any compensation, things have been 'left to the market', but if they are forced to toil, set free and the state which enslaved them pays some minor compensation, things would then not have been 'left to the market'? The market under this latter set of circumstances would surely have operated differently, but it would still have been a market.

As history unfolded in the US South, southern planters and later industrial capitalists in the North as well as the South, had access to a cheaper labour supply than might have been the case. The southern labour market in the late nineteenth century was constructed so as to limit the options of African Americans, forcing down their wages relative to what they might have been. The impacts of this particular labour market structure can be seen in the wages of white workers, the structure of unions, technological choices of employers, and the entire history of racial inequality and conflict that has persisted up to the present day. All this has occurred as it has, not because the organization of the economy in the post-Civil War South was 'left to the market', but because that market was constructed – by events of that moment and by earlier historical events – in a particular way.

The land market in Mexico in the twentieth century In 1992, the Mexican government amended Article 27 of the country's constitution. Article 27 was one of the defining features of the 1917 constitution that was enacted in the wake of the Mexican Revolution. This article had provided for land reform, including land redistribution, and it established the rights of *ejido*. The *ejido* is the collective control of land by a village, similar to pre-capitalist practices in rural societies in much of the world. *Ejido* land was formally owned by the state but was controlled by the village as a whole, and each family of the village had the right to work segments of this collective property. *Ejido* land could not be sold. An individual family could not sell or rent the land it worked, and the community as a whole could not sell the entire property (Barry 1995: esp. ch. 7).

In practice, both the land reform of Article 27 and the *ejido* system had been very constrained. After 1917, Mexican peasants had been forced to engage in decades of struggle to obtain land redistribution, and even with their struggle redistribution had been limited and sporadic, with the period of most extensive and rapid success coming in the late 1930s. The rights of *ejido* were also limited, established somewhat sporadically in the central and southern parts of the country and hardly at all in the north. In general, *ejido* peasants and other Mexican peasants lacked capital and credit, access to water, adequate marketing systems and the support of agricultural extension networks on which they might have built a modicum of prosperity. As a result, rural poverty and rural–urban migration were much of the story of mid-twentieth-century Mexico. Also, as Barry (1995: 127) remarks: 'Clearly, the relationship between the state and the social sector [*ejidos* and other collective land holdings] needed a major overhaul. Decades of paternalism and corruption combined with the lack of a real commitment to make the *ejidos* productive made reform necessary.' The land reform and the *ejido* had none the less provided a small basis of security for some of Mexico's peasants. Also, whatever its limits, the Mexican land reform had resulted in substantial redistribution of land holdings and had been the basis for the country's achievement of food self-sufficiency (de Janvry 1981; Barkin 1990).

The constitutional changes of 1992 formally ended the land reform. While redistribution of land had been virtually halted for many years, as long as the right of land redistribution still existed in the constitution it had provided a basis for peasants' struggles. Also, the amendment severely undermined the *ejido* by facilitating land transfer by sale, rental and partnership arrangements (including with foreign investors). This important change in *ejido* rights was rationalized in the name of creating (or extending) a market for land in Mexico. The government claimed its actions would free the peasants from the constraints of the *ejido* system, allowing them to obtain credit by using their land as collateral (not an option when the peasants could not cede ownership of the land) or simply to sell the land. After the constitutional amendment, Mexican agricultural affairs would be more thoroughly 'left to the market'.

Although the Mexican government claimed that its actions would benefit the peasantry, there had been no movement among the peasantry itself to obtain 'freedom' from the *ejido* system. Instead, Mexican peasants appeared to want what they had always wanted: more land – that is, a fulfilment of the redistribution promise of the original Article 27 – and the support and resources they needed to farm the land. Aside from the larger argument over the desirability of a land market versus the efficacy of collective ownership, the demands of the peasantry suggest that if a market in land were to be extended in Mexico it could have been extended in a very different manner. Instead of building a land market in the 1990s on the basis of the distribution of land holdings that existed in 1992, the redistribution provision of Article 27 could have been fulfilled. Instead of a land market accompanied by a credit system, distribution facilities and water rights that could not sustain small scale farms in most of the country, the Mexican government could have built an institutional infrastructure to support peasant agriculture.

The land market that was created (or extended) in Mexico in 1992 was constructed on the basis of the rural poverty and the general inequality and insecurity that had characterized the Mexican economy for generations. Also, the reformulation of Article 27 was explicitly a component of the Mexican government's strategy to integrate the country's economy more thoroughly with world markets; it was presented as necessary groundwork for Mexico's move into the North American Free Trade Agreement (NAFTA). NAFTA was implemented at the beginning of 1994 and would progressively open the country's economy to imports of US and Canadian grain. In this context, the new land market is undoubtedly contributing further to inequality and insecurity and to migration out of rural Mexico, both to Mexican cities and to the United States. These results, and whatever other connected events ensue, will have been the result not of leaving things to *the* market, but of leaving things to *a* market constructed in a particular way, through a particular historical process, based on a particular distribution of income and wealth, and operating with a particular set of credit and marketing institutions.

The operation of agriculture-related markets in Mexico between 1917 and 1992 was in part shaped by the fact that many of Mexico's peasants did not accept the legitimacy of those markets. The 1917 constitution, in their minds, promised them land. While that promise was not fulfilled peasants responded with periodic land seizures and other acts of resistance that affected the operation and outcomes of markets. The amendment of Article 27 will probably not alter Mexican peasants' sense that they are entitled to the land, and at the same time the particular land market that this amendment created will probably yield an increasing concentration of landownership. Any calculation of the consequences should include the implications of the likely political conflict.

The market for seeds For several millennia, we are not quite sure how many, as human beings have practised agriculture, individual producers have provided themselves with seeds for the next year's crop by saving some of the seeds from this year's crop. This ability of farmers to produce their seed capital as part of the normal process of production, particularly in the cases of grain crops, meant that there was, for all practical purposes, no market in grain seeds until the twentieth century. (Markets for fruit and vegetable seeds, where the seed itself is distinct from or a very small part of the marketable product, did exist at least as early as the eighteenth century.)

The formation of a grain seed market depended in part on the emergence of the science of plant breeding, the ability to develop better strains of a plant through a focused breeding and selection process. The science of plant breeding alone, however, was not enough to bring forth the extensive development of a grain seed market. In addition, there had to be some mechanism by which the plant breeders (the seed companies) could control the use of their product and appropriate a profit. Otherwise farmers, once they had the better seed, could simply reproduce it for themselves from year to year as they always had with other strains.

Hybridization was the first key that opened the door to development of the seed market. Hybrid plants are obtained by cross-breeding two different inbred lines of a plant. Through hybrid breeding, as through any other focused breeding process, it is possible to obtain new plants that are more productive than the parent lines. The distinguishing feature of hybrids, however, is not their 'vigour', as is often claimed. For understanding their role in the emergence of the seed market, the crucial factor about hybrid plants is that they are less productive in the second generation. Farmers who use hybrid seeds, therefore, cannot obtain high-yield seeds for next year simply by saving some of this year's product; they must buy again from the seed company.[1]

The first major advances with hybrid crops came with the development of hybrid corn in the United States during the second quarter of the twentieth century. Through a large research and development programme under the auspices of the US Department of Agriculture (USDA) and including research at several public universities, hybrid corn virtually replaced traditional corn varieties throughout the United States by the 1950s. In subsequent decades, partly through the 'green revolution', the use of hybrid varieties of corn and some other crops spread through much of the world. For farmers to take advantage of the higher yield seeds developed through this breeding process, they had to use the hybrids; once they used the hybrids they were tied into the seed market. Technically, nothing prevented a farmer from growing his own hybrid seeds each year. Yet doing so on the small scale of an individual farm was not economically practical, and an individual farmer was not likely to keep abreast of the yield gains obtained by the seed companies.

It is not particularly important here to resolve the issue of why the USDA focused its corn research and development on hybrids instead of on non-hybrid forms of breeding and selection. All we need to do is reject the claim that this was a 'natural' line of work because hybrids are technologically superior. It is widely believed that hybrids have some special 'vigour'. This claim, however, does not have biological validity (though the genetic issues may not have been fully understood when the claim originated). Also, yield gains obtained in other, non-hybrid crops were as great as with corn; a good example is wheat, where the smaller number of seeds set on a plant makes hybridization unprofitable for the seed companies. Thus it appears to have been focused breeding and selection, rather than hybridization per se, that led to the increases in corn yields.

While hybridization was a first critical step in the construction of the seed market, in more recent decades the central issue has been the establishment of patent rights for seed varieties. With the development of 'genetic engineering', seed companies (and others) have claimed and begun to win the right to patent life forms. A firm's patent on a particular seed variety creates a legal structure that plays the same role as the biological–economic structure that exists with hybrids. It requires the farmer who wants to take advantage of the higher yielding varieties – which is to say the farmer who wants to be able to compete effectively – to enter the market to obtain the seeds.

In recent years, particularly with the efforts associated with the creation of the World Trade Organization to extend a uniform system (essentially the US system) of patent laws internationally, there has been considerable controversy over the ethical issues involved in strengthening patent rights, especially on life forms and pharmaceuticals. The controversy is important, but its substance need not detain us here. Suffice to point out that both the changes that have been taking place in patent laws and the controversy underscore the fact that the markets in question are very explicitly *constructed* markets, depending for their existence on conscious, political intervention in economic affairs. The fact that they are constructed makes it clear that they could be constructed in other ways. Those 'other ways' would lead to other outcomes, affecting levels of production and the distribution of benefits obtained in the operation of these markets. (Later in this chapter, I will take up more thoroughly the role of property rights in the construction of markets.)

In both the hybridization stage and the patent-of-life-forms stage of the construction of the world seed market, publicly sponsored research has played important roles, and in the latter stage the reshaping of legal codes has been essential. The seed companies and other firms with parallel interests have been able to use the state to establish a market that serves their interests fairly well. Their success in constructing such a market and then their success in 'leaving things to the market', this constructed market, have had far-reaching impacts on the level of production, the shape of technology and the distribution of income.

My point in discussing these three markets for labour, land and seeds has not been to show that something 'bad' was done, either from the perspective of ethical or economic growth considerations. My point has been simply to show that *something was done*. Also, things did not have to be done as they were; *alternatives were possible*.

Government and private interests took a series of actions that constructed these important markets. Some of those actions were intentional, conscious efforts to affect the shape of the market in question. Other actions were not immediately directed towards the formation of market structures, but they none the less played identifiable roles. The important point is that these markets did not just happen. They were not simply the 'natural' result of myriad unrelated and undirected human events nor could they be attributed to the nature of technology (as though technology were some abstract force independent of human events). These markets, like markets generally, were *historically constructed*.

The basic argument that markets are not in some sense 'natural' but have been created or constructed has, perhaps, been most thoroughly developed by Karl Polanyi (1944). Focusing on classical disputes about the development of free market liberalism in Britain during the nineteenth century, Polanyi writes:

> There was nothing natural about *laissez-faire*; free markets could never just have come into being merely by allowing things to take their course. Just as cotton manufactures – the leading free trade industry – were created by the help of protective tariffs, export bounties, and indirect wage subsidies, *laissez-faire* itself was enforced by the state ... The road to the free market was opened and kept open by an enormous increase in continuous, centrally organized and controlled interventionism. To make Adam Smith's 'simple and natural liberty' compatible with the needs of human society was a most complicated affair. (Polanyi 1944: 139–40)

Market Basics

The recognition that markets are historically constructed has considerable impact on how we might formulate an economic development programme. Any such effort is confronted with the question: What role should markets play in economic development? Or, alternatively: How should markets be constructed in economic development?

In the preceding chapters, by examining the roles of foreign commerce and income distribution in affecting economic growth, I have argued that the neo-liberal prescription of relying on unregulated markets is not an effective way to generate economic development. The arguments of those chapters provide partial answers to the questions I have posed here: the role of markets in economic development should not be an unregulated role; in so far as markets are to play a role in economic development, they should be constructed consciously, in ways that serve appropriate social goals.

In order to establish a context for formulating democratic development initiatives, however, it will be useful to go beyond this partial and general answer to the question of what role markets should play in economic development. Having begun this chapter by using particular examples to illustrate some very broad points, I now want to develop a more focused framework for understanding the role of markets in economic development. To do this, I need to begin by getting some definitions straight.

Markets and market systems

What is a market? The simplest and most concrete definition of a market is a site where people buy goods and services from one another. The buying and selling can take place by means of money, which is what we usually mean, but it can also take place through direct exchange.

In this simple sense of a site where people exchange goods and services, markets have existed throughout history and in a great variety of social systems. In feudal Europe, village markets existed for the exchange of basic foodstuffs, for example, and periodic markets or 'fairs' took place for the buying and selling of goods that came from distant locations. In ancient civilizations, markets of this sort also existed, as they do today in relatively remote, rural areas. In the communist societies of the twentieth century, goods and services have been bought and sold at particular sites. All of these markets have been defined not simply by the place they have operated and by the existence of exchange. They have also been defined by the sets of formal and informal rules that have regulated their operation. For example, village markets in rural societies sometimes operate only on certain days. In many markets, bargaining is an accepted part of the process, while in others exchange takes place or does not take place on the basis of the price set by the seller. In still other markets, some prices are set by a party not involved in the actual exchange – the government or, in medieval Europe, a guild.

By and large, however, when we speak of 'markets' we mean something broader and less tangible than 'a site where people buy goods and services from one another'. A market is also a set of arrangements by which exchange takes place, regardless of the location of the actual transaction. Markets as sets of 'arrangements' are fundamental economic institutions of society. Douglas North (1990: 3) offers the following relevant definition: 'Institutions are the rules of the game in society or, more formally, are the humanly devised constraints that shape human interaction.' (North's use of the phrase 'humanly devised' captures what I mean when I say that markets are 'constructed'.)

We might speak of the market for wheat, for example, and mean a whole system of connections among farmers, traders, millers, wholesalers and various users of flour. Or when we speak of the stock market, we do not mean simply Wall Street or the City of London, where many financial transactions actually take place. Instead, we mean the whole system of arrangements – the laws, conventions, physical and social infrastructure, and the distribution of wealth and property – on the basis of which shares of stock are exchanged.

One particularly important part of the arrangements that define a market is the nature of property rights. In order for people to exchange things, there needs to be clarity about what ownership means, what can be owned and how it can be disposed of. It is not possible, for example, to have a market in air because no one has yet figured out how to establish a property right over the air. Also, it is no longer possible to have a market (at least publicly) in human beings because most of the world's people accept the principle that slavery is illegitimate. Until quite recently, markets in life forms (for example, a seed variety) could not exist because it was not possible to own a life form, but this has changed dramatically in recent decades. The ownership of water rights and land rights have been continually evolving, and as they have evolved the nature of water markets and land markets has changed. (As will be evident in my argument below, in fact most of what we call 'government regulation', can be placed under the heading of 'the nature of property rights' because in the economic realm regulations are essentially limits on property rights.)

The set of arrangements forming the foundation of markets also includes society's physical and social infrastructure. Roads, other modes of transport, telecommunications and the media determine the geographic scope of markets, the spread of information and the degree of interaction among market participants. In order for people to exchange things, they must be in contact with one another. The existence of supermarkets, for example, depends on society's ability to transport both goods and people over substantial distances at relatively low cost. The existence of international markets similarly depends on the means of transport, and also decisively on the means of communication; knowledge about wheat production and prices in Australia affects the buying and selling of bread in Argentina. The impact of knowledge depends not simply on its existence, but on the capabilities of the population to use that knowledge. Those capabilities are in part a consequence of education, a central element of social infrastructure. Social infrastructure – by which I mean education, health-care and other formal and informal ways in which people's basic capacities are created and maintained – is virtually ubiquitous in shaping market arrangements, affecting tastes, workers' productivity, social stability and the distribution of income and wealth.

Another part of the arrangements defining a market is the existing distribution of ownership of the items traded in that market and the distribution of the buying power that operates in that market. For example, a market for medical services in which there are many independent providers (doctors) and in which the distribution of buying power (income) is fairly equally distributed will operate very differently and achieve different results than a market in which all the providers operate as a single unit – in a for-profit medical organization, for example – and buying power is very unequally distributed. These two situations will define two very different markets for medical services.

In any society, the state plays the central role in defining markets by virtue of its importance in determining property rights, establishing social and physical infrastructure, and affecting the distribution of income and wealth. Below, after having established the 'market basics', I will return to the role of the state in providing the foundations for markets.

Even in the broader and less tangible definition of a market as a set of arrangements, location is not irrelevant. For when we speak of a market, we have in mind a set of exchanges that have some relatively direct and immediate impact on one another. If, for example, hairdressers in Rio de Janeiro raise the price of their services, the price of similar services in Kuala Lumpur will be, for all practical purposes, unaffected; the market for hairdressing services is a relatively local market. If, however, sugar producers in the northeast of Brazil cut the price at which they are willing to sell their product, the price of sugar around the globe will be affected; the market for sugar is an international market. In defining a market, however, it is not location per se that is important, but interaction. Interaction, in turn, means that the terms of exchange – the relations between prices and quantities – in different transactions affect one another.

To say that the terms of exchange in different transactions affect one another is to say that there is variation in the terms of exchange. Moreover, this variation is determined within the markets themselves by the *choices and decisions* that people make when they engage in exchanges. Without choices and decisions there is no market. There was, for example, no market for labour on a slave plantation in the British West Indies, even though in some sense we might speak of a master 'exchanging' food and housing in return for services of the slaves. The slaves had no choice in the matter and made no meaningful decisions about the exchange.

Likewise, within a family, though different members of the family may perform different functions that in some sense are 'exchanged' for one another, usually family relations do not include the sorts of choices and decisions we associate with market exchange. Instead of involving decisions and choices based on prices, as in a market, actions in a family are based on social positions (which in turn are defined by a complex evolution of gender and generational power relations). Though practices within families vary a great deal across class, history and culture, in any particular situation people in families do what they do, give what they give, and receive what they receive largely on the basis of the positions they hold. I prepare food for my children not because I have calculated the return (in either love or money) and deemed the act worthwhile; I prepare the food because they are my children. In a market relation (at least in a pure market relation), the social positions of buyer and seller do not matter. In this sense, the market relationship is anonymous. The anonymity of the market relationship shrouds it in a veil of objectivity – a point to which I will return below.

As in a slave society or a family, in feudal society the central economic relationships were dominated by social position. A serf, because he was a serf, was required to render a certain number of labour days per year to the lord, and in 'exchange' the lord provided (at least in principle) protection for the serf. But in this situation we would not speak of a market for the labour of the serf because the parameters of the serf–lord relations were set by rules and traditions defined in terms of social positions; within the system, there was little scope for choice and decisions. If the serf disliked the terms of the arrangement between himself and the lord, he was not free to shift his operations to the lands of another lord who might offer better terms.

Today, in our relations with government, we might say that we 'exchange' our taxes for the set of services we receive – schools, roads, police and so on. Yet this relation between the citizenry and the government is not a market relation because it is determined by a political process. The immediate participants in the exchange cannot choose. The political process gives them rights and obligations because of their identities. If, for example, I do not believe that the police in my town do an adequate job for the taxes I pay, I cannot take my taxes and buy the services of another police force. (I can buy the services of a private security force, but this does not free me from the obligation to pay taxes; nor does it free the police from the obligation to protect my rights.)

In most societies today, individual firms interact with the rest of the world largely through markets. They buy goods and services. If they do not like the terms they are offered by any particular seller, they are free to look elsewhere. Likewise, they sell their products on a market, and if they cannot obtain the price they desire from a particular buyer, they can look for other buyers or even withhold their products from the market. Within firms, however, there are usually no markets. For example, the sales division of a large firm does not normally bargain with the production division in order to obtain goods at a lower price; it does not search around within the production division for the team that will provide it with the lowest-cost product. It takes what it is given, as determined by the higher executives in the firm. These intra-firm relations may be greatly affected by the firm's market relations with the outside world, but that does not make them market relations.

It is easy enough to see in the examples of the preceding paragraphs that many important economic relations are not market relations. Nevertheless, there is often no ready distinction between a market and a nonmarket exchange. There can be a good deal of room for confusion over the degree of choice and the extent of decisions that exist. In monopolistic situations, for example, the choices of buyers are limited by the power of the sellers. Short of an absolute monopoly (of which there are relatively few examples), the buyers are able to exercise some choice and make some decisions. Yet there is no neat line that tells us when we have a market and when we have an exchange so dominated by a single seller (or buyer) that there is in effect no market.

In general, we can say that for a market to exist there must be some price fluctuation in response to the choices and decisions of both the buyers and the sellers, and there must be some adjustment in the amount offered by sellers and the amount purchased by buyers in response to price changes. Virtually all societies have had markets in this sense. The amount of economic activity that takes place through markets has varied widely among different societies, and even in the most advanced capitalist societies a large segment of economic activity takes place outside the market – in families, in volunteer associations, among friends, between the citizens and the government, within firms and within governments. Still, it is useful to keep in mind, especially when formulating policy about the role of markets, that historically and in the current day the existence of markets has been very widespread.

What is a market system? Markets, however, are not the same thing as 'a market system'. A market system is a society where markets not only exist, but one in which market relations are the dominant determinant of economic affairs. In a market system, people make most of their economic decisions based on their judgements about how markets operate. Karl Polanyi provides a foundation for this concept of a market system by noting: 'The outstanding discovery of recent historical and anthropological research is that man's economy, as a rule [i.e., prior to or outside of a market system], is submerged in his social relationships' (Polanyi 1944: 46). But what is important about the development of society into a market system is that 'it means no less than the running of society as an adjunct to the market. Instead of the economy being embedded in social relations, social relations are embedded in the economic system' (Polanyi 1944: 57).

Up until the last few hundred years, while markets existed, market systems did not exist. For example, in many relatively self-sufficient peasant societies, where people met – and in a few cases still meet – the majority of their needs through their own production, markets were a secondary part of their lives. In such a relatively self-sufficient peasant society, a peasant family produced directly for its own needs; if it was able to produce goods that it did not need for itself, it would trade these through the market to obtain some extra goods or services. In such societies, for most people, the market has been simply a means by which to take some of the goods they produce and transform them into other goods, either directly or through the use of money, that would meet their own needs. In these circumstances, there have been people whose lives have been organized around the market itself. Non-market societies have had their traders, shopkeepers, money-lenders and others; for these people market activity has been the dominant determinant of economic affairs. Some of these people have become quite rich and powerful through the market. Yet, if most of the activity of most of the people takes place outside the market, the society is not a market society.

In a market system, producers decide what and how much to produce based on the returns they expect to obtain through trade. A peasant family in a market system may also produce for its own needs, but that production directly for use is secondary. Living in a market society, people generally make their economic decisions based on the 'signals' they receive through the market. Those signals come as prices. In the first half of the twentieth century, for example, many of the peasants of Bengal decided whether to produce rice or jute (a plant used to make burlap that can be produced with the same soil and weather conditions as rice) depending on the relative prices of these two goods in the market. Their actions were determined not directly by their own needs, but by a whole collection of events among people in many other places. Was there a good rice crop in East Asia? That would push down the price of rice, and lead the Bengali peasants to switch towards jute. Did rug-makers in America find a new backing for their rugs? That would push down the demand for burlap, lead to lower jute prices, and induce the Bengali peasants to switch towards rice.

While prices are signals in a market society, the prices themselves are adjusted by buyers and sellers in response to the amount of the goods or services available for sale and the desires of the purchasers (that is, the desires of the people with capacity to buy the goods). When we say that an increase in the amount of a good available will 'push down' the price, we mean that sellers of the good will compete with one another to dispose of their products on the market; one aspect of this competition will be price reductions. Conversely, when we say that a rise in the demand for a product will 'push up' the price, we mean that the buyers of the good (either because they have more purchasing power or because they are devoting a larger share of their purchasing power to the product in question) compete with one another for the existing supply; one aspect of this competition will be offers to pay a higher price for the good. These are the sorts of adjustments that dominate people's economic lives in a market system.

Competition, then, is an integral part of markets, and when market relations dominate, competition dominates. So in a market system, people's well-being depends not on how well they do in an absolute sense – how much of a particular product they produce, for example – but how well they do relative to the competition. If, for example, last year I produced ten tons of potatoes on my land, this may have provided me with enough income to purchase all I needed for a comfortable life. If this year I also produce ten tons of potatoes, it would seem that I would do just as well. Yet, if other producers of potatoes, near and far, find ways to increase the amount of potatoes they can produce on their land, then the price of potatoes will drop and I will not be able to purchase what I need for a comfortable life. Or things may work in just the opposite direction: a drought occurs in distant potato–producing lands; the resulting shortage leads to a substantial increase in the price of potatoes; and my ten tons of potatoes make me a rich man.

Through markets, people living in a market system are affected by the actions of many other people whom they never meet and with whom they never come into any direct contact. Events completely outside their control and often unknown to them will affect their livelihood and lead them to change their own economic operations. During the nineteenth century, for example, improvements in transportation greatly expanded the realm of supply for foodstuffs. Farmers in the Americas increased production, developed new technologies, and reaped large financial gains. Producers of basic food grains in Europe were placed in competition with lower-cost producers in the Americas (and elsewhere). Some of these European producers were forced out of business, some changed to the production of other crops, some found more efficient ways to continue to produce the same crops, and some successfully sought government protection from the new competition (for example, through import restrictions). These sorts of shocks and adjustments exist to one degree or another in all markets, but in a market society they are central aspects of people's lives.

A capitalist system is a particular form of a market system. Under capitalism, people are not only linked together through markets for goods and services. In addition, markets for land and capital are widespread, and the majority of people earn their living by working for wages and salaries. They exchange their capacity to work in return for money in a labour market. Corresponding to the fact that the majority of people sell their capacity to work, a smaller segment of society is made up of capitalists who hire others to produce products that they, the capitalists, will then sell in order to make a profit.

The development of capitalism greatly extends the degree to which people's lives are organized through markets. In pre-capitalist market societies – most of Western Europe and the United States at the beginning of the nineteenth century, and much of the so-called Third World up until the middle of the twentieth century – people's economic activity may have been dominated by markets, but, because land, labour and capital markets were not extensive, a significant part of their lives was insulated from markets. In pre-capitalist market societies, most people obtained their living from the land. If they were independent peasants, their access to land gave them options outside the market; whatever happened in the market, for better or for worse, they could meet most of their own needs from their own land. If they were in some way dependent – as sharecroppers or tenants – their access to the land was more confined, but it still provided them with alternatives to the market. In general, land was not bought and sold, and even dependent peasants had land-use rights, generally embodied in custom and sometimes in law. (For example, Russian serfs in the nineteenth century had the adage: 'We belong to the lord, but the land belongs to us'.) During the last two hundred years, as people have moved out of agriculture, they have moved off the land. The vast majority have entered the labour market. With their basic livelihoods obtained through their wages and salaries, they have lost much of their insulation from the market.

Even with the full development of capitalism, not all activity is subsumed in markets. As I have already noted, a great deal of activity continues to take place outside markets: in families, in volunteer associations, among friends, between the citizens and the government, within firms, and within governments. In addition, markets are limited by regulations; there are alternative sets of rules that can govern the operation of markets, and it makes a difference which rules are used. For example: sellers can be required to provide full information about the products they are selling; employers can be required to meet certain safety conditions when they buy people's capacity to work; executives with access to special knowledge of their company's plans can be barred from trading in the stock of the company; the owners of land through which a river flows may be limited in how they use that water; landowners may be prohibited from using their property in ways that create a public nuisance or otherwise harm the public interest. The role of the government, beyond enforcing the direct regulations of markets (of the sort just listed) is also an important part of the 'rules' that govern the operation of markets. For example: by providing an educational system, the government has impacts on labour markets; by its regulation of public health, the government has impacts on medical services and medical supplies markets; by its hiring practices, the government has impacts on the whole labour market; by its procurement policies, the government shapes markets for many goods and services; by all of these policies and by its tax policies, the government affects the distribution of wealth and income, which in turn has ubiquitous impacts on all markets.

All of this is to say that there is not one market system and there is not one capitalism. Once we recognize that we operate within a market system, which in today's world pretty much means that we are operating within a capitalist system, there are still a great many alternative ways of organizing our economic lives. These different alternatives have different immediate implications, and they have different implications about the ways in which our society will evolve. In the current ideological climate in much of the world, and especially in the former communist countries, people often speak of a market system as though there is only one thing that we can call a market system. Aside from the difference between modern capitalism and pre-capitalist market societies, there are different kinds of capitalist societies, each characterized by different sets of markets. (While we might reduce the differences between different capitalist societies to a question of the extent of the government's role, this would be misleading because the role of the government in relation to markets is not one-dimensional and cannot be reduced to a single quantitative relation. For example, the size of government purchases of goods and services in Japan is only about 10 per cent of gross domestic product, but in the United States the figure is almost 20 per cent; yet there are many ways in which the Japanese government plays a larger role in its country's markets than does the US government.)

Also, it should be evident from all of this definitional discussion that markets, market systems and capitalist societies do not just happen. They are created by people. In these acts of creation, people make choices. As in other realms of human endeavour, those choices will usually have socially better results when they are made in an open, explicit, fully informed and democratic manner. Yet, however they are made, they must be made. Because alternatives exist, it is not very meaningful to advocate 'for markets' or 'for a market system'. When people say they are 'for markets' or 'for a market system', they are primarily making an ideological statement and not giving a practical answer to the question of what roles markets should play in economic development. A practical answer to the question, even a very general practical answer, requires considerably more detail.

What happens through markets?

Markets and allocation In any market system, and, in particular in the capitalist system of today's world, people's decisions through markets are the immediate determinants of a wide variety of economic phenomena. To begin with, there are a whole set of phenomena that come under the rubric of 'allocation'.

Seeking to meet their needs, people with purchasing power (which we can think of as money) buy goods and services in markets. They buy food, housing, transportation, entertainment, clothes, banking services and so on. In so far as they have choices, they compare what is available with their desires and use their purchasing power to make themselves as well off as possible. If there is a good which no one or relatively few people will buy, then in so far as there is competition in the market, sellers are likely to lower the price in order to attract buyers. If, in order to sell their stocks of the product, producers must lower their price below the cost of production, then they will not produce any more of the good. Conversely, if there is a good which everyone, or a great many people, want to buy at the existing price, the competition among them is likely to lead sellers to raise the price. The higher price will tend to induce sellers to produce more of the good.

Through this sort of process, resources get allocated towards the production of some goods – those for which the demand is strong – and away from the production of other goods – those for which the demand is weak. Labour, land and capital get shifted around (reallocated) in response to what happens in the market. Also, the market process leads producers to organize production in the most profitable manner, that is to choose the most profitable technology. So labour, land and capital not only are reallocated so that more of some goods and less of others are produced, but also are reallocated among different ways of producing goods. (The most profitable technology is not necessarily the least-cost technology. While capitalists are concerned with costs, their primary overall concern is profits. An employer may be faced with a situation, for example, where costs would be reduced by introducing a production technique that gave workers more control, more decision-making authority, over their activities. Yet by giving the workers greater control, the employer might be placing her or his long-run authority in question, and this could undermine long-run profits. For discussion of such issues, see Braverman 1974; Marglin 1974.)

At the same time as the markets serve this allocation function, they also perform a second broad function, determining the distribution of income – an issue to which I will return in more detail shortly. Most immediately, people who make their income from the goods and services for which there is a strong demand will gain, and those who are dependent on the goods and services for which there is a weak demand will lose. Less directly, but no less important, people who own resources that are used in the production of the former will gain while those who own resources that are used in the production of the latter will lose. It is precisely this gain and loss that makes markets work to serve the allocation function. In order to obtain the gain and avoid the loss, people who have resources to sell will attempt to do things that meet the demands of the people who have purchasing power; *and* they will try to shape markets in ways that lead people with purchasing power to demand what they have to sell.

The allocation function of markets is no small marvel. In normal times, in most places in the world, people with purchasing power can meet their daily needs through markets, even when those needs are fulfilled by goods and services produced in distant parts of the world by people they will never know or see. Innumerable exchanges of innumerable products at innumerable sites generate a huge amount of information that gets used by people to make their economic decisions. Without any single guiding authority, decisions about investment, production and employment are made. By and large, the markets work to get products to people who want them *and* have the money to buy them. This is the 'magic' of the market.

While there is no 'single guiding authority' that directs market activity, markets do not operate 'on their own'. What happens in markets is the outcome of decisions made by people, and, what is more, the markets themselves, as I have already argued, are constructed by people. Markets are not constructed and then left to operate somehow on their own. People are continually reconstructing markets.

One obvious example of the way sellers reconstruct the markets for their products is advertising. By advertising and other aspects of marketing, sellers attempt to expand the demand for their product, increasing the amount that people will buy at any particular price; and, as Paul Auerbach (1994) points out, it may be necessary to expand the demand from zero – that is, to create the market. Related to (and including) advertising but a much larger and broader practice, firms construct and reconstruct their markets through the creation of sales and distribution networks. One of the great advantages of large size (at least in many industries – seeds, automobiles and books, for example) does not lie in the making of a product and delivering it to a market, but in expanding the market through sales and distribution strategies.

Many sellers also attempt to restrict the extent to which other, competing sellers can enter the market. For example, to sell their services doctors and electricians in most countries must have licences. In industries where production is based on a natural resource – oil or diamonds, for instance – firms go to great effort and expense to control those natural resources and thus control supply in their industries. (If firms are completely successful in structuring their markets so as to eliminate competition, they are effectively eliminating the market. As pure monopolists, or monopsonists, they would so dominate the situation as to eliminate the choice that is essential to the existence of a market.) Through unions, many groups of workers attempt to shape both demand and supply in the market for their services. Firms supplying inputs to agriculture have traditionally engaged in educational efforts ('agricultural extension') to get farmers to demand their products – or they have used the government to carry out this task on their behalf.

Indeed, in almost all markets, though much more so in some than in others, the actors, the buyers and sellers, attempt to use the government. Government is, first of all, a large buyer of goods and services. Firms or workers can therefore shape their markets by affecting the ways in which government makes its procurement decisions. Because of the volume of its purchases, moreover, the way in which the government operates has far-reaching impacts; the terms on which the government hires workers or buys paper, for example, will affect labour and paper sales in private markets. But the role of the government as buyer is only one of the many ways in which it structures markets. In addition, for example: government defines and secures the property rights that lie at the core of markets; government establishes and enforces (or does not enforce!) a gamut of rules defining markets, everything from health, safety and environmental regulations to disclosure rules in financial transactions; government defines the geographic scope of markets, setting the terms by which foreign goods, services, capital and labour enter the country, and affecting foreign sales opportunities for domestic actors; government sets tax policy, affecting both particular markets and, by shaping income distribution, the general operation of markets. In each of these realms of government activity – and this list is not exhaustive – market actors not only can but must seek to influence the structure of their markets by influencing the action of the political authorities.

So when markets serve their allocation functions, when they perform their 'magic', they do not do so in some independent or 'natural' way. Allocation of goods, services and resources through markets is not an alternative to conscious human intervention in economic affairs. Markets are the mechanism through which that intervention is organized.

Markets, wealth and power   This way of describing things makes it quickly evident that social power is at the centre of the market allocation process. Power, by which I simply mean people's ability to shape social situations to operate in their own favour, affects market allocation in two broad ways. First, there is the power to structure markets. The most obvious exercise of such power comes in the political arena, affecting government actions of the sorts I have just discussed. One factor creating such power is control over wealth. Wealth can be used directly to influence the political process, and, because political authorities are dependent on the actions of private wealth-holders to maintain economic well-being, wealth allows private individuals and groups (including corporate entities) indirectly to influence political decisions by indicating (implicitly or explicitly) how they will use their wealth in response to those decisions. Wealth can also be used to affect the construction of markets outside the formal political process, through, for example, advertising or gaining control of a natural resource. Power, especially with regard to the political arena, has other bases as well; for example, especially in political democracies, there is strength in numbers. It will become evident shortly, however, that with regard to understanding 'what happens through markets', a focus on wealth is particularly relevant.

The second way in which power affects market allocation is a matter of wealth, pure and simple. This is the power to affect outcomes within existing structures. Wealth is purchasing power. As I have tried to make clear, markets work so that suppliers deliver the goods that are desired by people who have the purchasing power, the money, to buy those goods. Desire without purchasing power is meaningless in a market. In so far as a person has wealth, that person has power to shape what is made available through the market, what gets produced, where labour and other resources are used. Furthermore, because actions at any given time affect the structures in which actions take place, in shaping what is made available now a person is affecting the development and future structure of markets. For example, when wealthy consumers in Brazil or South Africa use their purchasing power to buy meat today, agricultural producers are likely to shift from the production of food grains to the production of feed grains, affecting the availability and relative prices of goods tomorrow.

Markets and income distribution   Wealth is accumulated income. As I have noted, when they perform their allocation function, markets also necessarily determine the distribution of income. Consequently, within a market system there is an important circularity: existing wealth affects both the structure of markets and the operation of markets; at the same time, the structure and operation of markets, by affecting the distribution of income, affects the distribution of wealth.

Because of this circularity, markets tend to increase inequalities in the distribution of income and wealth. Differences (whatever their origin) in human abilities, in conditions prior to the operation of markets, and in what we call 'luck', mean that the operation of markets will produce differences in income. The differences in wealth that then exist become the power by which different actors restructure markets and affect the within-structure operation of markets in their own favour. Differences of income then become larger over time.

Markets, however, also create tendencies in the other direction, limiting this growing inequality. Success induces responses. One type of response is that of emulation and competition, as arises when a successful monopolist faces challenges from others entering the market. Another response is conflict from actors on the other side of a market, as occurs when sellers face resistance from buyers who attempt to develop other sources of supply, band together in boycotts or strikes, reshape their own needs (for example, by altering consumption patterns or changing production technology), or reconstruct the market, perhaps through the political arena.

On a purely theoretical level, there is no way to determine which of these tendencies will dominate, whether markets will generate more and more inequality or will limit the degree of inequality.[2] There is no technical formula that determines the distribution of income (though at any given time technical conditions play a role). This is especially clear when the role of politics is recognized, both in the construction of markets in ways that exacerbate inequalities and in their reconstruction in ways that attenuate inequalities. The political arena is organically connected to, if not part of, the distribution process of markets, and the outcome of conflict and struggle in the political arena is not determined by technical considerations; it is a social process (Bowles and Gintis 1982). Even within the relations of the market narrowly conceived, it is not possible to make a theoretical pre-determination of the balance of forces, the degree to which various actors will be able to affect the relative scarcities for the goods and resources through which they earn their income. (At any particular time in history, it is possible to make an appraisal of the balance of economic and political forces and on that basis foresee how the market will engender the evolution of the distribution of income. Experience of recent decades in much of the world suggests that, in general, at this time in history the balance is very much in favour of growing inequality.)

While we may not be able to determine what distribution of income will be generated through markets, we can take note of the fact that the extent to which markets generate inequality depends on the way they are structured, including the way they are affected by politics, as well as on the way politics separately operates. Markets tend to generate less inequality, for example, where public education in particular and the 'social wage' generally are large; where workers' rights to organize are relatively secure; where peasant farmers are secure in the rights to their land and where a large share of land is in the hands of small and medium-sized proprietors; and where political democracy limits the extent to which wealth controls politics. In short, it seems reasonable to conclude that (1) markets contain powerful forces tending to create a more unequal distribution of income and (2) the limitation of those forces, which can also take place through markets, is a social and political process, involving struggle to establish regulation – that is, struggle to reconstruct markets in a way that limits income inequality.

Markets and the world outside markets   A large part of the social impact of market activity can be understood in terms of allocation and distribution. Yet the story of what happens through markets is not simply a story of what happens within markets. As I have already noted, a great deal of economic activity takes place outside markets. In order to illustrate some of the ways in which markets affect the world outside markets, consider the relationships between markets and families.

Even in the most thoroughly developed capitalist societies, a great deal of production takes place within the family. Because these activities are outside the market and have no price directly associated with them, their magnitude is often not fully recognized. Recent efforts to take proper account of the economic role of women, who have traditionally carried out their economic activity in the home and outside the market, have begun to bring attention to the volume of this work. Some estimates suggest that if women's work in the home were valued at market prices, gross national product in the advanced capitalist countries would increase by at least one-third (UNDP 1995: ch. 4).[3]

Although the amount of this work is very large, it is declining. One of the fundamental features of markets is that they expand. The competition which is endemic to markets leads firms continually to seek new realms, new sources of supply and new sources of demand. Indeed, when economies of scale are present, as they generally are, firms have no choice but to seek to expand; they must become larger in order to cut costs and survive. The phenomenon of the growth imperative, affecting both the average size of firms and the overall volume of production, is a central and distinctive feature of market societies and particularly of capitalism. This dual expansion of the units and the system is 'accumulation' or the 'accumulation of capital'. Accumulation in part involves the creation of new goods and services and more goods and services. It also involves the replacement of non-market production of goods and services by market production, and one large part of this replacement during the last two centuries has been the shift from family production to market production.

Work in the home has traditionally included a wide range of activities: preparation of food; production of cloth, clothing and other goods; tending of children; and caring for adults, both physically and emotionally. Over time, and to different degrees in different countries, these activities have shifted from the home to the market. This shift has not simply been a physical relocation from home to workshop or office, but it has also been a shift in the social nature of the work. Things that were done individually, or by small family groups in an independent manner, are now done by wage labour under the supervision of authorities in capitalist firms. Both the markets for the goods and the labour markets have been reconstructed. Society has moved towards a 'universal market', towards a situation where all production takes place through markets for profit (Braverman 1974).

The history of the move towards a universal market is a tale of the construction and reconstruction of markets. As women have moved out of production in the home, new types of work have come into being, new laws have regulated and organized that work, technology has been altered, education has played new roles, and new organizations and conflicts have emerged. One way to tell this story would be to note the great expansion in the volume of production that has taken place as the universal market has been created. Even when we make allowances for the uncounted losses of home production, this expansion has been considerable – and is still of great importance in most parts of the world. The social and disciplined market production of capitalist firms has far surpassed home activity.

The development towards a universal market has also dramatically changed relations among people. Women have gained independence. Teen-aged girls who obtain work in the export processing factories of Manila, for example, leave behind the traditional bonds – sometimes oppressive, sometimes nurturing, sometimes both – of family life. Child-rearing practices have been altered. As peasant families have been displaced from the land in Central America, for example, many men have become migrant workers and women have focused their work on income-generating activity. Children can no longer be socialized by working with their parents, and parents have less time to deal with their children. Family life is irrevocably altered.

Yet the move *towards* a universal market is not a move *to* a universal market. Families continue to exist, playing important social and economic roles in all societies even while capitalism is a powerful and global system. The dynamic of markets on their own may drive towards the elimination of families, as family production is replaced by market production and more and more people are pulled into wage labour; but markets never operate 'on their own'. Markets operate within a social framework, and that social framework plays a large role in constraining and defining markets. Family-related property laws, income sharing within families, legal and social definitions of parental responsibility, and long-established social obligations of kinship are parts of the foundation on which markets operate. These are practices, moreover, that are created, and their construction is part of the construction as well as part of the limitation of markets.

Again, the point is not to argue that the changes involved in the operation and construction of markets are 'bad', though undoubtedly many people see these changes in traditional family life as bad. Instead, the point is, first, that the construction and reconstruction of markets, driven by the force of competition, bring huge changes in social relations, and in the self-expansion of markets the non-economic value (positive or negative) of these social changes plays no role. Second, and at the same time, the expansion of markets is not simply self-expansion, not simply the results of profit and income-maximizing decisions of firms and individuals operating under the pressures of competition. In decisions to alter the realm and structure of markets, people make conscious social and political choices; they exercise power.

The experience of families in relation to the market is illustrative of a phenomenon that affects all social groups held together by social bonds that are not defined in terms of income maximization (as they are and must be in markets). Communities, in particular, are subject to the same disruptive influence of the market and efforts to preserve community are part of the construction and reconstruction of markets. Also, the relationship between the state and the market is in part affected by the same dynamic. The widespread 'privatization' mania, for example, can be seen as an effort to construct a wider realm for the operation of markets. It would give greater rein to the self-expanding power of the markets.

One of the particularly important aspects of the general relation between markets and the world outside the market is the connection between markets and the physical environment, what we often call 'nature'. Market society, capitalism in particular, has achieved untold success in subordinating nature to the economic demands of human beings. Virtually entire continents have been cleared for cultivation; rivers have been redirected to provide irrigation and power for industry; vast mineral wealth has been mined from miles inside the earth and from beneath the seas; land, air, rivers, lakes and oceans have all accepted the waste of human industry.

Alongside these great accomplishments, as a necessary part of them, the natural environment has been severely despoiled. Private decision-makers operating in markets are forced by competition to find ways to reduce their costs. In so far as they fail to do so as effectively as their competitors, they will be forced out of business. One way to reduce costs is to externalize them, organize production so that the negative impacts occur outside the market relationship. For example, when oil tankers are flushed out at sea (a common practice), the market costs of cleaning are minimized. The consequent pollution of the ocean is a social cost, but it appears nowhere in the transactions of the oil transport industry. Or when rain forests are cleared by timber companies, cattle ranchers or land-poor peasants, the long-term social costs do not play a role in the calculations; they occur outside the market.

The destruction of nature by the economic advance of human beings is not a historically new process, nor is it peculiar to capitalism (Foster 1994). The tremendously expansionary force of market activity has, however, brought environmental destruction to a global level, as evidenced by global warming and the depletion of the ozone layer. In this way of looking at things, environmental destruction is not a product of greed or human indifference to nature. It is a product of accumulation, a consequence of the way competition works through markets.

Although the fundamental phenomenon of expansion and external-ization of costs is inherent in markets, the degree and manner in which a market economy affects nature depends on the ways in which markets are constructed. The nature of property rights is a particularly important issue. How far do the rights of a landowner extend? To what extent, for example, can private landowners cut down trees on their land, a practice which has impacts on society generally? To what extent can they use fertilizers, pesticides and herbicides that wash off into public waters? These are not questions that allow an absolute answer. (On the one hand, the answer of zero tolerance is not possible, because that would ban the ill person from exhaling. On the other hand, no one would claim that I have the unlimited right to shoot my gun on my own property if the bullet crosses the boundary and hits another person.) Yet if there is no absolute answer, then markets can be constructed in a variety of ways giving rise to a variety of outcomes. In this sense, social regulation is not something that happens separate from markets; it is an essential, unavoidable and omnipresent force in the construction and operation of markets.

Markets have a great expansionary power, and in their expansion they tend to devalue all non-market relationships and objects; families, communities, government and nature are all subordinated to the dictates of the market. At the same time, the actual histories of the relationship between markets and the rest of the world demonstrates that markets are differently constructed and constrained, and they can have different sorts of impacts. It would be folly to ignore the inherently destructive aspects of market expansion that accompany the creative increase in the volume and variety of the goods and services that define that expansion. Yet it would be similarly erroneous to claim that all market situations have the same impacts regardless of how they are constructed.

Where Markets Come from: the Role of the State

The controversy over the role of the market in economic development is often expressed in terms of the role of the state. Neo-liberal advocates of a large role for markets define their position as 'anti-statist'. In much of Africa, Asia and Latin America, according to neo-liberalism, incomes are low because the state has played an excessive role in the economy. Even more so in the former Soviet Union and in Eastern and Central Europe, economic problems are seen largely in terms of the excessive role of the state in the economy over the last several decades. Discussions of economic policy in all of these regions of the world, and often in the advanced capitalist countries as well, are represented in terms of the state versus the market. Much of the preceding argument should indicate, however, that this is a misleading way of thinking about economic policy. Instead of markets being an alternative to state intervention in the economy, the general existence of markets as well as the particular ways in which markets operate are defined and determined by state intervention in the economy.

The meaning of property: contested terrain The centrality of the state to the existence and operation of markets can be seen in a fundamental theoretical or conceptual issue, the meaning of 'property' or 'property rights'. Property rights lie at the foundation of markets. When people exchange things in a market, they are exchanging things that are their property, things over which they have rights of ownership, including the right to exclude their use by others and the right of disposal. Property is a social entity, and property rights are relations among people. Their particular nature and stable existence depends upon society, and, as the state is society's organized mechanism through which property is defined and protected, they depend upon the state.[4]

The social conception of property in itself might not bring the state into the economy as anything more than a neutral watchman, which is the classical liberal view of the state's appropriate role. Property and property rights, however, need to be defined and, as social circumstances change, redefined. This defining–redefining role can be played only by the state, and, because it involves reshaping social relations among people, it is a process in the exercise of power in which the state must go far beyond the role of neutral watchman. Also, simply in the protection of established property rights, the state as watchman is neutral only in so far as those established rights are generally accepted as legitimate and uncontested.

Legal history provides various examples indicating that in the course of economic development the state must intervene actively in defining property rights. An illustrative case is the experience with water rights during the early nineteenth century in the United States. (US historical experience is particularly relevant here because it is so frequently held out, explicitly or implicitly, as a model for market-based economic development. Also, Anglo–American economic and legal thought is important for my purposes because it has been at the centre of the ideological development of liberalism, classical and neo.)[5] English common law, which provided the basis for the US legal system, had grown out of the power of the landed classes and provided virtually absolute protection of the rights of landed property. Morton Horwitz explains:

> Two basic assumptions determined the approach of the common law to conflicts over water rights. First, since the flow of water in its natural channel was part of nature's plan, any interference with this flow was an 'artificial,'

and therefore impermissible, attempt to change the natural order of things. Second, since the right to the flow of a stream was derived from the ownership of adjacent land, any use of water that conflicted with the interests of any other proprietor on the stream was an unlawful invasion of his property ... The premise underlying the law ... was that land was not essentially an instrumental good or a productive asset but rather a private estate to be enjoyed for its own sake. (Horwitz (1977: 35–6)

This structure of property rights greatly restricted using land and water for profitable enterprise that might advance economic development. If, for example, one landowner wanted to dam up a river to create a fall to power a mill, he could be prevented from doing so by the upstream landowner, whose land would be flooded (even if that upstream land were not used for any productive activity) or by the downstream landowner whose flow of water would be impeded. The common law allowed only insignificant appropriations of the water's flow, consistent with traditional domestic and agricultural uses. In an era when water power was needed to drive industrial development, the law as it existed was a substantial impediment to change.

In their attempt to revise the law in a way that would allow the profitable use of water and water power, the courts were faced with a dilemma. On the one hand, they needed a principle that would allow the productive use of water power – to power a mill, for example – even when that use interfered with the traditional land rights of other property-owners; they needed a principle that would allow change. On the other hand, they needed a principle that would assure a landowner who had established a productive use of the water that his operations would not be undermined (or washed away, so to speak) by the later actions of a downstream or upstream owner; they needed a principle that would provide stability. Only by the middle of the nineteenth century did a clear principle emerge in the doctrine of 'reasonable use'.

'Reasonable use' was defined explicitly in terms of the economic development needs of the community and, in effect, gave a wide discretionary power to judges. The application of this doctrine allowed, for example, the establishment of large integrated cotton mills, which, once in existence, frequently precluded other uses of the same stream. Thus, the doctrine often overrode equal distribution of water rights, since it allowed judges to favour exclusive exploitation of streams if, by their judgement, this best served the larger economic interests of the community. 'Once the question of reasonableness of use became a question of efficiency, legal doctrine enabled common law judges to choose the direction of American economic development' (Horwitz 1977: 42).

This reconstruction of property rights, at least in its general outlines, was probably a necessary step in the advance of US capitalism. It was of immense importance in itself because of the very great role of water and water rights in the expansion of the US economy. It is also important as an illustration of the manner in which property rights, and thus markets, are shaped by the state in ways that are neither neutral nor natural.

The continuing history of conflicts over property rights in the United States further illustrates the general point that the state must play and does play an active, interventionist role in the construction of markets. It is particularly interesting to consider the interaction between state regulation and property rights.

The framers of the US constitution had been especially concerned with the protection of property rights, fearing the levelling power of the democratic political procedures that they were establishing. One of the ways in which they protected private property was to write into the constitution (actually, the Fifth Amendment) that private property could not be 'taken' by the state without 'due process of law' and 'just compensation'. This provision would allow the state to exercise its power of eminent domain by taking land that it needed for public uses, but would assure that property-owners would receive just compensation; the need to provide just compensation would, presumably, limit abuses by the state of its authority to take property.

However, as US industrialization accelerated in the last quarter of the nineteenth century and the structure of the economy shifted, the courts were increasingly confronted with the question of when a regulation on the use of property became a 'taking' of that property. The question existed with regard to land or other physical property, but it became especially acute with the growth in importance of commercial and intangible property. The expanding definition of property forced the acknowledgement of the fact – explicitly recognized by the US Supreme Court in an 1880 case – that property is not simply a physical thing with value determined by its possession and use. Property is anything that has value in the market, that can be exchanged for other things. This shift from a physicalist 'use-value' definition of property to a broader 'exchange-value' definition had far-reaching implications (Commons 1974 [1924]: ch. 2).

If the government takes an action that reduces the exchange value or market value of a person's property, then this could be interpreted as constituting a 'taking' of that property. As Horwitz points out, the market value theory of property brought a major legal contradiction to the fore: 'How does one avoid the conclusion that any governmental activity that changes expectations and hence lowers the value of property constitutes a taking?' (Horwitz 1992: 149–51). How could one accept the market value theory and the ban on government taking of property, and still manage 'to avoid the absurd conclusion that every governmental action that interferes with settled expectations is unconstitutional?' As this theory of property took shape in the late nineteenth century, 'American courts came as close as they ever had to saying that one had a property right to an unchanging world.'

In the twentieth century, the USA was able to promulgate numerous and far-reaching regulations that affect property values. The courts, the legislatures and the executive found ways to circumvent the apparent dilemmas embodied in legal principles, accepted theories of property and the US constitution. Yet no stable set of principles has been established by which conflicts between property rights and state regulation can be consistently adjudicated in a generally accepted manner. At the end of the twentieth century, disputes in the United States over environmental regulation illustrated that the conflict between property rights and state regulation remains one of contested terrain.

This brief review of some issues in the legal history of property in the United States should establish, first of all, that property and therefore markets do not exist independently of an active state. Indeed, when the economy is growing rapidly and substantial structural change is therefore occurring, then in all probability the state must play an increasingly active role in redefining property rights. Secondly, the very fact of continuing change in the definition of property undermines any appeal to a 'natural' state of affairs as the foundation for the operation of markets. If property does not exist outside conscious state intervention, then neither do markets.

The creation of infrastructure What is true of the state's role in establishing the legal infrastructure for economic activity is also more broadly true of the state's role in creating a social and physical infrastructure on which economic development can progress. In its actions to establish means of transport and communications and in its operation of an educational system (and other institutions for the expansion and alteration of people's basic capacities), the state is continually constructing and reconstructing markets. These actions are not those of a neutral watchman. They can be carried out in a variety of ways; there are options. How they are carried out has far-reaching implications for multiple aspects of economic development.

In most countries, railways have been a state-sponsored project, established either as government enterprises or with substantial government subsidies. (Britain's original railway development seems to be a significant exception.) The justification generally offered for state involvement has been precisely that railways play such an important role in shaping the development of markets. Yet there are different ways to form rail systems.

For example, in colonial Africa, rail systems were designed to facilitate the connection of the export-producing regions of the colonies to the world market. In southern Africa, British colonial authorities made sure that railways were built to connect the Rhodesian mines to port facilities. In East Africa, railways would bring the produce of Ugandan and Kenyan agricultural regions into international trade. Aside from the fact that state decisions to construct railways in a particular way often bring large income transfers to certain groups (in these cases, to Rhodesian mine-owners and to traders and white settler farmers in East Africa), the shape of rail networks can determine the long-run orientation of trade which, in turn, has long-run impacts on the rate and form of economic development. In the Rhodesian and East African examples, as in many other colonial regions, the railway structure contributed to the continuing external orientation and internal disarticulation of the economies.[6]

Successful economic development, on the contrary, has generally been built upon a physical infrastructure that connects the national economy to international commerce and, at the same time, ties a national economy together. In examining the economic history of Europe, J. H. Clapham (1961: esp. chs 7 and 12) illustrates the point well. Consider, for example, Clapham's discussion of Belgium:

> after discussion in Parliament, during the autumn of 1833, it was decided, partly for the glory of the young state, partly because the government was resolute that the whole work must be carried out systematically, that the projected Belgian railways should be a national undertaking ... Belgium wanted to exploit the advantages of her position as a land of passage. Her railway system should begin with a cross, linking, north and south, Antwerp, Malines, Brussels, Mons and France; east and west, Ostend, Bruges, Ghent, Malines, Louvain, Liege and Germany ... There were to be branches, on the western arm, from Ghent towards Lille via Courtrai, and from Ghent northwards to Antwerp; on the eastern arm, from Tirlemont to St. Trond; and on the southern from Braine-le-Comte to Charleroi and eventually to Namur. So Belgium would link up England, France, Germany and Holland, by 347 miles of railway, and draw across her territory the trade of all ... It was a brilliant plan ... By 1844 the original plan was approximately complete. (Clapham 1961: 141)

The point here as elsewhere in this chapter, is not so much that one set of state actions is 'good' while another set is 'bad' but that state actions are in fact taken and that they determine the nature of markets. 'Leaving things to the market' means, in part, leaving things to the existing state-sponsored (if not state-built and -owned) infrastructure. At any given time, for the state to create new infrastructure may or may not be a socially and economically desirable policy, but to refrain from doing so would not be to 'leave things to the market'; it would be to leave things to past state intervention.

In the realm of education, a central component of any society's social infrastructure, similar issues arise. Aside from 'law and order', there is perhaps no other activity that is so widely accepted as legitimately within the public sphere of responsibility (though dispute is intense over the way in which the state should carry out its educational role). Milton Friedman (1962: 86), for example, one of the twentieth century's leading politically conservative and economically liberal economists, acknowledges that the social value of education is greater than the private value of education and allows 'there can be much honest difference of judgment about how extensive a subsidy is justified. Most of us, however, would probably conclude that the gains are sufficiently important to justify the government subsidy' (Friedman 1962: 88). (Friedman, I should emphasize, was not accepting a public educational system, but only state subsidies for education that would be best provided privately. Yet it would be thoroughly unrealistic and naive to suppose that state subsidies could exist without state regulation, and it is state regulation that is the foundation of a public system.) The acceptance by economic liberals of the state's role in providing education can be traced back to Adam Smith and on to John Stuart Mill who writes:

> [The government] should ... be capable of offering better education and better instruction to the people, than the greater number of them would spontaneously demand. Education, therefore, is one of those things which it is admissible in principle that a government should provide for the people. The case is one to which the reasons of the non-interference principle do not necessarily or universally apply ... [It is] an allowable exercise of the powers of government to impose on parents the legal obligation of giving elementary instruction to children. This, however, cannot fairly be done, without taking measures to insure that such instruction shall be always accessible to them, either gratuitously or at a trifling expense. (Mill 1976 [1848]: 953–4)

Yet there are very different ways to shape educational systems. In several East Asian countries, relative economic success has been associated with relatively high levels of educational expenditure and attainment. Low-income countries generally, however, have relatively low levels of educational funding (which can be characterized as 'underfunding' in the sense that rates of return to educational expenditures remain quite high). Also, in countries with comparatively low levels of educational expenditure, a dual educational structure often exists: a relatively brief and poorly funded education, essentially primary education, for most of the population and a small but relatively well-funded secondary and higher educational system for elite social groups and the upper echelons of the working class. One of the important features affecting both different levels and structures of funding appears to be the extent to which landed classes and traditional elites continue to play substantial roles in determining state policy (Bowles 1978). Higher funding and a less dualist structure seem to emerge when a national capitalist class or a developmental state or both dominate state policy, as in South Korea and Taiwan, for example.

Likewise, more well-funded and more uniform educational systems are typical of the economically advanced countries. Yet among the advanced countries, there are also substantial differences in education. Germany, for example, has a much more extensive programme for the development of technical skills than does the United States. In Japan, students are in school for significantly more hours than in the United States, and maths skills are taught at an earlier age. The United States has a far more extensive higher education system than do most other advanced countries, and the research training in its elite universities is especially extensive.

So while it is tempting to look at some of the broad differences in educational policies and pronounce that more education is good for economic growth and probably good for income equality as well, there is every reason to believe that the impacts of different educational systems on economic life are far more complex. Education has ubiquitous effects on the structure of the labour force, patterns of consumption, and on social and political practices. Different forms of education, as well as different quantities of education, affect different industries differently. Broadly speaking, more education favours industry over agriculture. More specifically, for example, emphasis on maths and science skills in a country's educational system can be seen as a subsidy to 'high-tech' activities, and emphasis on technical craft skills is likely to favour the advance of engineering industries.

In these ways, even the most basic and widely agreed upon government intervention in economic affairs has far-reaching impacts on shaping markets. These impacts are not neutral. They are not natural. They are not the impacts of a watchman. Once the advocates of economic liberalism have accepted the responsibility of the government to provide a social and physical infrastructure, or simply education, they have given up the principles on which they might oppose an active role for the state in shaping the economy. For it is not possible to create infrastructure – railways and schools, telecommunications and health systems – in a neutral manner. Once the state undertakes to sponsor social and physical infrastructure it becomes actively engaged in constructing markets, and it is impossible then for the state to 'leave things to the market'.

Having thus implicitly accepted the legitimacy of state intervention in ways that affect the direction of economic change through the mechanism of infrastructure investment, economic liberals cede any principles on which they might oppose the intervention of the government through tariffs, direct subsidies, tax policy or even state industry. There may remain quite reasonable pragmatic grounds on which to oppose a tariff or some other form of state intervention; but the principle of avoiding state intervention and leaving things to the market is gone. (The defenders of liberalism would probably respond that their principle is summed up in the adage: that government is best which governs least. Then, they would maintain, in accepting that 'least' does not mean 'none', they do not void the principle. Yet it seems to me that the principle is voided when it becomes clear that this 'least' intervention in fact has very extensive impacts that can in no manner be seen as 'neutral', either with regard to the structure of economic activity or income distribution. To rescue economic liberalism on this point, it is necessary to come up with a principle – not simply a pragmatic argument – by which it is acceptable, for example, to promote the development of the metallurgy industry by educational expenditures that support the development of engineering and technical craft skills, but not acceptable to do so via a tariff or direct subsidy.)

The distribution of income The impact of education on the structure of markets is so important in part because of its role in affecting the distribution of income. One of the widely accepted justifications of state spending on education is that it is a means to reduce the extent by which the inequalities of one generation are passed on to the next.[7] Similarly, much of what we call 'social welfare' expenditures (not so widely accepted) is justified on the grounds that the state has a legitimate role to play in reducing at least the most egregious income inequalities. Also, certain aspects of countries' tax systems are explicitly designed to bring about changes in the distribution of income. Were these explicitly redistributional policies the only ways in which the state brought about changes in the distribution of income, the resulting impact on markets would be extensive. In reality, however, the state's impact on the distribution of income goes far beyond these explicit policies.

It is conceptually difficult, if not impossible, to determine the overall impact of state activity on the distribution of income because there is no reasonable way to determine what the distribution of income would be like in the absence of state activity (Reynolds and Smolensky 1977). My purpose here, however, is not to make any quantitative determination of the distributional role of the state nor even to specify the direction of the state's impact (which, presumably, has been different at different times in different places). I can underscore my point that state action constructs markets through affecting the distribution of income simply by pointing out several ways in which government policies, regardless of their explicit intent, have widespread distributional implications.

• When the state maintains law and order it protects the existing distribution of wealth and income. While law and order has other meanings beyond the protection of property, the protection of property is surely its most basic and extensive meaning. One can easily raise questions about the legitimacy of protecting the status quo in property relations. For example, in post-apartheid South Africa the Government of National Unity came into being on the premise that the pre-existing social order – and thus necessarily the distribution of property rights that lay at its foundation – had been fundamentally illegitimate. Yet the government 'felt compelled to clamp down hard on grassroots protest in situations where wildcat strikes or land invasions or occupation of vacant housing or inner-city buildings threatened the sanctity of private property' (Mayekiso 1996: 277). Presumably the government justified these actions on the pragmatic basis that if it failed to protect private property, the ensuing economic instability (to say nothing of political instability) would have severe negative consequences. Legitimacy and pragmatism aside, however, these actions will affect the shape of markets in South Africa for years to come: where wildcat strikes have been beaten and where workers remain unable to obtain secure housing, wage levels will be held down; maintenance of the historic two-tier income structure will preserve the meat–millet pattern of consumption and thus the operation of markets for consumer commodities; with capital protected, funds are less likely to flee the country, which will be reflected in capital markets as lower interest rates. In South Africa and elsewhere, it is impossible for the state simply to maintain law and order and leave economic affairs to the market, for maintaining law and order gives a particular shape to markets.

• In virtually all of its regulatory activity, the state brings about shifts in the distribution of income relative to what it would be in the absence of any particular regulation. It has, for example, become widely recognized that controversies over environmental regulation are often predominantly distributional controversies, and the case of deforestation in many low-income countries provides a useful particular illustration.[8] In South Asia, for instance, decades of deforestation combined with the privatization of public lands have deprived the rural poor of one of their main sources of fuel. According to Bina Agarwal:

In the Himalayan foothills of Nepal, a journey to gather firewood and fodder took an hour or two a generation ago – today it takes the whole day … In some villages of Gujarat [state of India] where the surrounding forests have been completely denuded, women spend long hours collecting weeds and shrubs and digging out the roots of trees … Fuel shortages are driving villagers in several regions of South Asia to shift to foods that require less fuel but are of lower nutritional value, or to miss some meals altogether and go hungry. (Agarwal 1991: 93–4)

The source of this fuel crisis for the poor has multiple origins, but in part it can be traced to the history of government regulation in the subcontinent, dating back to at least 1864 when the colonial Forestry Department was created, forest users were deprived of traditional rights, and the government promoted the use of forests and forest land for commercial purposes. The post-colonial governments continued to regulate the use, and devastation, of forests in ways that favoured commerce over the needs of the rural poor. These distributional shifts brought about by the state's environmental regulation (or, formally, sometimes a lack of regulation) have had one of their largest impacts on labour markets; as the rural poor are deprived of an essential aspect of their traditional livelihood, they are forced to seek new forms of employment, often through migration.

- Macroeconomic policy directed towards growth and price stability always embodies immediate distributional implications. The general phenomenon is illustrated by governments that adopt structural adjustment programmes (SAPs). The SAPs give highest priority to price stability and prescribe cutbacks in government spending (a fiscal policy of austerity) as the route to price stability. Such policies are supposed to reduce inflation by cutting aggregate demand, and thus they are also supposed to raise unemployment. The higher levels of unemployment quickly translate into greater income inequality because those at the bottom of the income hierarchy directly lose incomes as they become unemployed and others near the bottom are negatively affected by the greater competition for the remaining jobs. (Also, the austerity programmes usually affect the poor further by a reduction of social services.) In Argentina during the early 1990s, for example, the neo-liberal government tied the quantity (and thus the value) of the country's currency to its dollar reserves as a means to stave off inflation. At the beginning of 1994, in the wake of Mexico's financial crisis, Argentina saw a massive outflow of dollars which led immediately to general deflationary pressure; the resulting record levels of unemployment were accompanied by looting and rioting in some provinces (Fainaru 1995). A graphic indicator of the effect of SAPs on markets in Argentina and elsewhere appears in the rapid growth of the 'informal' sector, an illustration of the general reshaping of markets brought about by macro-economic policy.

• The international trade policies that have been essential foundations for virtually all cases of successful economic development (see Chapter 2) have entailed substantial income redistribution. Most frequently, protection of manufacturing from foreign competition has involved a large sectoral income transfer, from agriculture to industry. It has thus often been associated with a decline in the political power of land-based social classes. For example, in South Korea, at the beginning of the 1950s, a combination of pressures that derived from landlord collaboration during the era of Japanese colonialism and then from the Korean War resulted in a substantial redistribution of agricultural land. The 'redistribution created a vast mass of small-holding peasants and quieted the country-side, while land lords received state bonds convertible to industrial wealth' (Cumings 1989: 12). In subsequent years it was then possible for the South Korean government to follow trade policies – import-substituting industrialization, promotion of manufactured exports, and large imports of low-priced grains – that often worked against the immediate interests of the agricultural sector without facing substantial political resistance. (Because of the extremely high rate of economic growth in subsequent decades, South Korea did not generate the sort of rural poverty that has often been the result of trade policies favouring the manufacturing sector. Yet the country did experience massive rural–urban migration and a huge increase in the debt of rural households.) The agriculture-to-industry income transfer generated by the South Korean government's trade policy has reshaped markets in ways that have contributed to the country's extremely rapid economic expansion. In the 1980s, for example, by keeping the country's market open for US agricultural goods, to the continuing detriment of South Korean farmers, the government was able to maintain access to US markets for its industrial products (Bello and Rosenfeld 1990: ch. 4). The South Korean experience is unusual for its success in generating rapid growth, but the income transfer and reconstruction of markets associated with its trade policy is typical of the experience of many countries.

The Role of Markets in Economic Development

The discussion in this chapter has a number of implications for the role of markets in economic development. These implications will receive more complete elaboration in Part II where I will give attention to the meaning of 'economic development'. There I will offer specific proposals for moving towards a situation where democratic authority could dominate economic development. Here I simply want to bring together and summarize a few of the broad points discussed in this chapter.

The most general point that I have tried to establish is that markets do not simply exist. Economic development, therefore, cannot be 'left to markets' as though they are natural and neutral arbitrators of social affairs. Instead, markets are continually being constructed and reconstructed by governments, firms, social movements and individuals. Therefore, in determining the role for markets in economic development, the central issue is not how to use markets but how to construct them.[9] To a large degree, this means that the central issue is how to use the state to construct markets, for, although markets are constructed in various ways, the state is the principal mechanism we have for collectively affecting the social structures in which we live. Instead of framing ideological conflicts over economic development in terms of the state versus the market, the problem is one of finding ways in which society can effectively use both state and market. An emphasis on the fact that markets are constructed is a step towards solving that problem.

Markets in general or 'the market' are rather abstract concepts, however, and it is difficult to conceive of constructing an abstraction. Also, if our definition of the market remains an abstract one, then it is difficult to recognize the array of possible alternatives. So I have tried to provide a definition of markets that will facilitate a recognition of the various ways that they can be constructed. If markets are 'a set of arrangements by which exchange takes place', then it is possible to focus on alternatives by focusing on the particular arrangements and the particular alternatives that are possible. Property rights, physical and social infrastructure, the distribution of income and wealth, the myriad regulations that govern economic affairs – all these things that define markets are products of human decisions. What is more, when we think of markets in terms of these things, it is possible to trace the relationships between particular decisions and their impacts. It becomes relatively easy to recognize not only that markets are constructed but also to see how they are constructed. Then it is all the easier to begin to conceive of alternatives.

Any attempt to construct markets in alternative ways – that is, as compared to the general way they are constructed in most places today – would best begin by accepting the widespread existence of markets in time and space, across history and across different social systems. Markets are very widespread, moreover, because they perform various necessary social functions. They are a very effective mechanism for allocating goods and resources, and they serve to distribute income. Also of considerable importance, markets accomplish these tasks in a way that appears to be independent of direct human intervention. The market, that is, casts an aura of anonymity and neutrality over these extremely important social processes. I have tried to provide a description of markets here that shows these processes are not at all independent of human intervention, and they are certainly not neutral. Nevertheless, it is important to recognize that they appear that way, and this appearance has a lot to do with their social acceptability.

So if we set out to construct markets in alternative ways or to limit the role of markets, we had better make sure that our alternatives are going to perform the allocation and distribution functions in a reasonable manner. We also had better make sure that our alternatives are going to accomplish these goals in ways that are socially acceptable. Otherwise we will have no alternatives at all.

At this stage in history (or under foreseeable future circumstances), there is no reason to believe that it is possible to pursue economic development by generally doing away with markets. Non-market attempts to allocate goods in any but the most simple societies (that is, societies with only very few members and very few goods) have generally been plagued by severe problems, as the many volumes written about Soviet-type economies attest. While some advocates of 'democratic planning' avow the possibility of collective decision-making as the universal means to organize allocation for both goods and services generally as well as for labour and capital (for example, Albert and Hahnel 1991), it is difficult to maintain this argument in the context of today's real world with its multitude of commodities – even if the difficulties were partially reduced by moving towards local self-sufficiency. In addition, efforts to eliminate markets, however well intended, are likely to remove some of the constraints on state power. It seems to me that whatever lessons history holds for the desirability of limiting markets, it also suggests that it is a good idea to maintain some limits on state power.

Yet to accept the existence of markets as a practical matter does not mean that they should be either the universal or even the dominant mechanisms by which to organize economic development. It certainly does not mean that markets should be unlimited, unregulated or constructed as they generally are today. I have pointed out several times in this chapter that a great deal of economic activity takes place outside markets, on the one hand in small family and community units and on the other hand in large firms and governments. These experiences make it clear that a great deal of economic activity can be organized outside markets (which, however, is not the same thing as organizing economic activity without markets). Having things outside the market is neither good nor bad in itself: families and communities, for example, can be nurturing and supportive institutions, and they can be violent and oppressive; firms and governments can be effective organizers of resources, and they can be bureaucratic and corrupt. Yet the existence of these activities outside the market demonstrates the possibility and potential desirability of alternatives that limit the sphere of the market.

All this amounts to saying that in economic development we should use markets rather than allow ourselves to be used by markets. This approach, the very idea that we would make conscious, collective, democratic political decisions about the organization of markets, even when those markets are very extensive, violates the principles upon which a market system operates. In a market system, as I have defined it here, market relations are the dominant determinant of economic affairs. This is not compatible with a system where political decisions dominate markets.

The dual existence of extensive markets and their domination by political decisions implies tension. Markets, as I have explained above, tend to expand. The existence of markets creates interests that will try to reshape markets in ways that expand their realm. So if the primary position of democratic authority is to be maintained over markets, there will be continuing conflict and struggle. This is certainly not a fatal flaw of such a dual structure, nor is it even a criticism. Economic development, after all, is a process of social change, and social change never takes place without conflict. We are better off, I suspect, if we recognize the conflict and find ways to deal with it rather than if we pretend it is possible to construct systems – state-run, market-run, community-run or whatever – that eliminate tension and conflict.

Notes

1. This discussion of hybrid corn is based on a set of papers by Jean-Pierre Berlan and Richard Lewontin, including Berlan and Lewontin (1986; 1995) and Lewontin and Berlan (1986; 1990). Breeding of hybrids is accomplished by, first, creating two true breeding self-pollinated lines from a plant population (for example, corn). These two inbred lines are then crossed to produce the hybrid, making each hybrid a cross between two lines. By searching among all the possible combinations of pairs of lines, it is possible for the plant breeders to find one cross that has a yield superior to the original population from which the lines were made. Recently, genetic engineering has moved to a level that will allow the same ends for the seed companies to be accomplished by genetic engineering instead of hybridization: 'It was announced on March 3, 1998 that a patent had been granted for a genetic manipulation that would allow plants to set a seed and therefore make a crop, *but which would render those seeds unable to germinate*' (Lewontin 1998: 80). While hybridization made seeds 'economically sterile' in the second generation, this new 'terminator gene' makes them biologically sterile. This new technique should have far wider application in expanding seed markets than hybridization, for with many crops, as pointed out below, hybridization can not be used effectively.

2. In Marxist economic theory, it is generally maintained that the power of capitalists to determine the organization of production (the technology) is a central factor leading to growing inequality in the distribution of income between capital and labour. When labour succeeds in pushing up the wage, capitalists have a greater incentive to replace workers through labour-saving technology. When capitalists as a group take such action, the demand for labour falls, the supply of unemployed workers (the reserve army of labour) grows, the wage falls, and the distribution of income becomes more unequal. Yet in reality the extent to which these processes dominate depends on the way markets are constructed at any particular time: for example, the extent to which capitalists' decisions regarding technology are constrained by law, the degree of union power, and a gamut of factors, other than technology, that affect changes in the reserve army of labour. The Marxist argument is an accurate account of a powerful tendency, but it is not a universal description of reality.

3. Work outside the market and outside national accounts is not confined to women, and any full accounting would include a great volume of the activity of men and children as well. According to the estimates in the *Human Development Report 1995*:

> Clearly the value of non-SNA [System of National Accounts] production in industrial countries is considerable, whatever the standard. *It is at least half of gross domestic product, and it accounts for more than half of private consumption* ... On a global level, some rough estimates can also be made ... If these unpaid activities were treated as market transactions at the prevailing wages, they would yield huge monetary valuations – a staggering $16 trillion, or about 70% more than the officially estimated $23 trillion of global output. This estimate includes the value of *unpaid* work performed by women and men as well as the value of the *underpayment* of women's work in the market at prevailing wages. Of this $16 trillion, $11 trillion is the non-monetized, 'invisible' contribution of women. (UNDP 1995: 97)

4. This definition of property rights as a social relationship is developed by Morris Cohen:

> Any one who frees himself from the crudest materialism readily recognizes that as a legal term 'property' denotes not material things but certain rights. In the world of nature apart from more or less organized society, there are things but clearly no property rights ... [A] property right is a relation not between an owner and a thing, but between the owner and other individuals in reference to things. A right is always against one or more individuals. This becomes unmistakably clear if we take specifically modern forms of property such as franchises, patents, goodwill, etc., which constitute such a large part of the capitalized assets of our industrial and commercial enterprises. (Cohen 1982 [1927]: 45)

The state is not the only mechanism by which society can enforce its rules regarding property. Douglas North points out: 'we think of life and the economy as being ordered by formal laws and property rights. Yet formal rules, in even the most developed economy, make up a small (though very important) part of the sum of constraints that shape choices' (North 1990: 36). I focus on the state not simply because it is 'very important', but also because it is the instrument of conscious enforcement and change of the rules.

5. The discussion that follows is based on Horwitz (1977: esp. 34–42).

6. African colonial experience, and in particular the experience with the East African railways, also provides striking examples of the role of the state in the construction of labour markets. On these issues, see Mamdani (1976: esp. chs 2 and 3).

7. In reality, in spite of this widely accepted justification, it is not clear that education

works to reduce inequalities. It may do just the reverse, providing the foundation and rationale for the maintenance of inequalities. Regarding this issue in US education, see, for example, Kozol (1991) and Bowles (1972). I will discuss this issue further in Chapter 7.

8. The following comments are based on Agarwal (1991). Agarwal's essay appears as one of a set of essays collected by Sontheimer (1991). The set brings out the point that the distributional impacts of environmental policy are not simply those that affect the size distribution of income, but also those that affect the relative positions and well-being of men and women.

9. Dealing with the complementary problem of how to explain different countries' historical development experience, North (1991) poses the question more broadly, not simply as a question of how markets have been constructed but of how economic institutions have been constructed. In so far as 'the market' is the central economic institution, the ways of approaching the question are very similar. Nevertheless, the market is not the only economic institution. (Also see North 1990.)

Part II

A Strategy for Democratic Economic Development

5

The Bases of a Democratic Alternative: Definitions and Context

Many years ago, I think when I was a teenager, I heard a radio comedy routine that involved an argument between a young man and his father. While disputes between fathers and sons are commonplace, this one had a special character because the father and son were members of a society that practised cannibalism. The argument had arisen because the son did not approve of eating other people. I recall particularly his lines: 'Eating people is wrong!' and 'I won't let another man pass my lips!' The father, in exasperation, kept saying, 'But people have *always* eaten other people!'

As best as I can recall, the pro-cannibalism father did not make the argument that is today frequently offered in defence of the status quo. The father did not confront his son with the rhetorical question: 'Well, if you don't like cannibalism, what's your alternative?' He might have buttressed the argument implicit in this question by pointing out that human flesh is a particularly good source of protein. If the anti-cannibalism son really cared about his fellow human beings (as something other than food), then, the father might have argued, he had better make sure he was well fed. One cannot carry out social justice campaigns on an empty stomach or on a protein-deficient diet. The son would just have to face up to the fact that some people would have to be sacrificed – quite literally! – in order that more would be saved. 'There really is', the father might have said, 'no alternative to cannibalism.'

In many countries where neo-liberal economic policies have been implemented, usually as Structural Adjustment Programmes (SAPs) formulated by governments under the guidance of the World Bank and the International Monetary Fund (IMF), the ensuing disruptions of economic life have involved considerable sacrifice. As far as I know, no one has claimed that cannibalism has been involved, but the human suffering associated with neo-liberal SAPs has been substantial. The first step in the standard SAP is fiscal and monetary contraction designed quite explicitly to bring a recession, and recessions invariably have considerable social costs. The recession, so the argument goes, is the necessary first step in creating economic stability; with stability, it will then be possible to implement structural changes that are supposed to be a foundation for long-run growth. In this neo-liberal scenario, the SAP is the immediate cause of human suffering, but the fundamental cause is the economic mismanagement that made it necessary to impose the SAP. What is more, the extent of human suffering would, according to the argument, be even greater were the adjustment programme not implemented. There is no viable alternative to the SAP; sacrifice is necessary in order that more might be saved.

There are, it seems to me, three ways to develop a counter-argument. One of these is a direct critique of neo-liberalism, establishing that its claims are false in that the sacrifices in fact do not lead to the desirable ends. There is considerable evidence that the neo-liberal programmes, and SAPs in particular, are not effective in bringing about economic development, either when economic development is defined narrowly in terms of economic growth or when it is defined more broadly to include other aspects of social well-being. Part I of this book includes important elements of a direct critique of neo-liberalism, but a direct critique is not my focus here in Part II.[1]

A second counter-argument rejects the neo-liberal position on ethical grounds by maintaining that the creation of human suffering is an immoral means that cannot be justified by an appeal to desirable ends. Most of us, for example, might well reject cannibalism even if we could be shown that through cannibalism some greater good might be obtained. If we were to take this line of argument, then we could dismiss the neo-liberal position out of hand. The there-is-no-alternative claim could be rejected by pointing out that the SAP itself is an unacceptable alternative because in imposing human suffering it is immoral. This sort of argument has considerable appeal, but I do not accept it and I expect most other people also do not accept it; most of us are willing to do some damage if we think that the end results will be desirable and outweigh that damage. In any case, it is a philosophic argument that is outside my boundaries in this book. (I should add, however, that in rejecting this line of argument, we should not forget it. Great crimes against humanity have been committed by people claiming that the horrors they are generating are necessary in order to achieve some laudatory end.)

The third line of argument, the third way to rebut the neo-liberal claims both as they apply specifically to SAPs and more generally to the entire development process, is to provide a response to the rhetorical question: what is the alternative? Of course, if neo-liberalism and SAPs do not work in their own terms, then it is not really necessary to present alternatives in order to reject them. They themselves do not provide a reasonable alternative for people attempting to bring about economic development. There is, furthermore, no shortage of historical examples that provide alternatives to neo-liberalism. Today's advanced and advancing economies did not get where they are by liberal economic policies. The state has played large, though varying, roles in the experiences of the United States, Western Europe and Japan, to say nothing of the recent East Asian successes (financial crises of the late 1990s notwithstanding).

Nevertheless, even if all participants in the economic development debates were to accept the proposition that neo-liberalism does not provide reasonable prescriptions, it would still be necessary to define an appropriate set of alternative policies. Instead of facing the what-is-the-alternative question as a rhetorical device, we can accept it as a starting point for discussion of how economic development might be organized.

In this chapter and in the following three chapters, I will develop some of the basic elements of an alternative economic development strategy that would define a general path for economic progress in many countries. It is a strategy for *democratic* economic development, and in this chapter I will define the sort of economic development I am dealing with, and I will explain the political assumptions I make when discussing alternatives. The central features of a democratic strategy include:

- *A non-regressive expansion of taxes combined with a reallocation of existing government spending towards social programmes (made possible by reduction of military spending and of corruption and waste).* One of the first steps in arguing that an alternative development strategy exists is to establish that such an egalitarian macroeconomic policy is possible, and this is what I will do in Chapter 6. Such a macroeconomic policy necessarily includes *some form of controls on the financial connections to the international economy.*

- *A defining emphasis on the expansion of social programmes, especially education, health and environmental preservation programmes.* Although these programmes would be financed by the state and would be formally state programmes, they would incorporate extensive community participation in their planning, development, and operation. In Chapter 7, I will explain the way the social programmes of a democratic strategy might be constructed, and I will focus in particular on the role of education (schooling).

- *The use of incentives for private investors that would push firms towards a 'technological high road'.* Such incentives would focus on the expansion of training programmes and skill development among the workforce. In Chapter 8, I will develop the basis for a programme of regulating the private sector. One of the principal aspects of the programme will be a description of incentives that could be constructed in ways that are consistent with the broad social goals of a democratic strategy.

- *A recognition of the value of local production.* Local production of many goods and services can have substantial social, technological or environmental benefits, but these benefits often do not appear in the accounting on which private decisions are based. These considerations apply to both emerging industrial activity *and* traditional rural production. In fact, the importance of the condition of the peasantry, a very substantial portion of the population in many parts of the world even at the beginning of the twenty-first century, demands a clear recognition of the social value of their productive roles. A system of subsidies, taxes and regulations is necessary to ensure that the benefits of local production are taken into account in private decisions. At the same time, while it is essential to regulate foreign trade and the flow of investment in and out of the nation, it is also necessary to avoid those forms of protectionism that both disrupt economic growth by breeding severe inefficiency and undermine the broader goals of democratic development by generating greater inequalities in the distribution of income and political power. These issues relating to the value of local production will be addressed in Chapter 8 as part of the programme for regulating private activity.

- *Land reform* is also an essential part of any democratic programme in most of the world's low-income countries. Land reform is needed for several reasons: social stability, expansion of production, income distribution, environmental preservation and, perhaps most essential, to destroy the political power of traditional agricultural elites. Nevertheless, I will not give any serious attention to land reform in this book. This lack of attention does not imply a lack of importance of land reform. On the contrary: I have excluded it in part because it is too important to deal with in the summary manner that would be necessary here. Any prescription for land reform would require a consideration of rural social structures and land tenure systems that would go well beyond the scope of this book. The reader should keep in mind, however, that land reform is a part of the package, a major element in a democratic strategy. (Hiding behind irony, perhaps I can cover this omission of the land reform issue by using a ploy commonly adopted by economists in such matters: Let us assume land reform!)

Democratic Economic Development

It is widely agreed that economic growth, in the sense of a rise in the per capita income of a country (or region), is a central part of 'economic development'. The economic growth that is associated with economic development involves a change in the way production takes place – a change of technology – that allows greater output per amount of labour time. This rise of productivity is generally accompanied by a shift in the composition of output, with agriculture accounting for a smaller and smaller share of total production. A definition of economic development simply in terms of rising per capita income and technological progress has long dominated the discussion of economic policy in low-income countries. In practice, this narrow definition of economic development has provided the central rationale for policy at the World Bank and the IMF (though, as I pointed out in Chapter 1, the rhetoric of these institutions has used an increasingly broad definition of economic development in recent years).[2]

Yet there have been many criticisms of the development-equals-growth approach. The first of these criticisms came from a 'basic needs' perspective and arose from the observation that economic growth often did little, if anything, to improve the material conditions of the very poor or to spread basic education and health care (Seers 1972; Hicks and Streeten 1979.). As a result of this basic needs criticism, the meaning of economic development has increasingly come to include a *widespread* improvement in people's material well being. Growth of average income would generally not be viewed as development if the distribution of that income were highly skewed so that only a small segment of the population gained. Often, therefore, economic development is measured in terms of improvements in a variety of indicators such as infant mortality rates and literacy rates that show the extent to which the basic needs of the population at large are being met. The *Human Development Report* of the United Nations Development Programme, with its annual calculation of a *human development index*, emphasizes this concept of economic development.

The basic needs argument seldom confronts directly the issue of the *distribution of income*. To a degree, it may be possible to define basic needs in absolute terms, using some minimal standards of nutrition and shelter. In the context of analysing famines, for example, basic needs might be understood in these absolute terms, independent of the distribution of income (Sen 1981). Yet in most circumstances the separation of basic needs from distributional issues is not meaningful. Beyond minimal biological needs, our needs are socially determined, which is to say they can be defined only in relative terms. Our standards of literacy and medical care, for example, cannot be defined without reference to the general levels of education and health facilities in society. The same is true of our standards of shelter, transportation, clothing and, indeed, virtually all of our basic needs – they can only be defined relative to the standards of the society in which we live. A society with a highly unequal distribution of income, therefore, can never meet the basic needs of many of its people. So to include basic needs in the definition of economic development requires that relative equality in the distribution of income be part of the definition as well. (There are other reasons why relative income equality is an important component of the development definition, and I will come to these shortly.)

Environmental *sustainability* has also become a component in the definition of economic development, as in recent years many people have become more and more concerned about the impact of economic change upon the natural environment. Economic growth that destroys the natural environment, either through the depletion of natural resources or pollution of various sorts, undermines its foundation, cannot therefore be maintained, and does not constitute economic development. As Kenneth Arrow et al. (1995) point out, 'all economic activity ultimately depends' on the 'environmental resource base'. Economic growth that negatively affects that resource base, 'may irreversibly reduce the capacity for generating material production in the future'. Today, virtually everyone embraces the concept of sustainability and incorporates it as part of the definition of economic development, but there is much less agreement on either what sustainability means or on what should be done to attain sustainability (Daly and Cobb 1989).

Just as economic change that destroys the natural environment could hardly be viewed as progress, change that would destroy social bonds among people and undermine the bases of their security would not be consistent with any positive concept of economic development. Thus another amendment to the traditional definition is needed to include the *maintenance of community* in the concept of economic development. Unlike the concepts of basic needs and environmental sustainability, community has not generally become an element in definitions of economic development. Indeed, when community is considered at all in discussions of economic development, it is often taken for granted that economic growth will almost necessarily mean the destruction of traditional community.

Yet the social bonds that tie people together in communities are an essential part of human well-being, particularly in that they are such an important foundation for economic security. This is so directly because strong community is in itself a guarantor of security. The community is what people turn to when they need help, when their lives have been disrupted. Also, maintaining the community requires that security-threatening disruptions be limited, so a high value on community necessarily places a high value on security. The maintenance of community is not necessarily an unmitigated blessing, unless we fully adopt cultural relativism; and the destruction of traditional community sometimes means, for example, overcoming the traditional and oppressive position of women. While we may dispute the desirability of maintaining particular aspects of particular communities, we should none the less be able to recognize the general value and many benefits of community. (If we include democracy as a component of economic development, as I shall do shortly, the importance of community is increased because economic development cannot be democratic if it undermines the social bonds that allow people to act together politically. Nevertheless, in suggesting that community is a foundation for common political action and therefore a foundation for democracy, I recognize that many communities are not at all democratic. I am simply asserting that the social bonds of community are a *necessary* basis for democracy, not that they are a *sufficient* basis.)

Regardless of the particular elements that are included in the definition, economic development is almost always defined in terms of goals, in terms of the direction in which a process is moving. The nature of that process itself is generally not an issue. In particular, the extent to which the organization of material life can be characterized as 'democratic' is not an issue in most definitions of economic development. To be sure, sometimes democracy is seen as an outcome or goal of economic development. One of the leading economic development textbooks, for example, includes expansion of 'the range of economic and social choices' as one of the main objectives of economic development (Todaro 1997). Also, neo-liberals and others often argue that development generally, and perhaps necessarily, leads to the emergence of political democracy. Yet the extent to which the process itself is democratic is not an element in the common definitions of economic development. Thus Indonesian and Chinese experiences of recent decades and experiences in South Korea, Brazil and Chile during eras of military dictatorship are all generally viewed as successful economic development in spite of the authoritarian political circumstances of these situations. Likewise, few people see any conflict between economic development and the authoritarian organization of capitalist workplaces.

There are, however, compelling reasons to avoid the separation of democracy from economic development, whether the issue is analysis or formulation of policy. Perhaps most important, the degree of political participation and popular control of social processes will surely affect the ultimate outcome of those processes. Economic change that is democratically directed will not be the same as change that is designed and controlled through some authoritarian mechanism. The latter, for example, would almost surely give less emphasis over the long run to the provision of basic needs and perhaps also to issues of environmental preservation. A lack of emphasis on basic needs, it is important to note, does not necessarily translate into more rapid economic growth (that is, as discussed in Chapter 3, there is no automatic growth–equity trade-off); often an expansion of basic needs is an important foundation for more rapid growth, as with literacy and nutrition. The point, however, is not that democratic economic development would involve more rapid or slower economic growth than development controlled by an authoritarian regime, but simply that it would be different.

Also, it is almost true by definition that a democratic economic development would more likely and more rapidly lead to the expansion of democracy than would economic development under authoritarian conditions, even if we were to assume – as is often argued by supporters of neo-liberal programmes – that economic growth will ultimately generate political democracy (and there is no clear indication from the empirical record that economic growth yields democracy). Though the connection between means and ends is seldom simple and direct, it is generally the case that the nature of a social process carries over into the outcome of that process. Undemocratic processes tend to yield undemocratic outcomes. The more thoroughly economic change is undemocratically structured, the more difficult it is likely to be for a democratic transition to occur. So if one of the reasons to pursue economic development is to attain political and social democracy, it seems desirable to organize economic development democratically.

These considerations lead me to focus attention on what I will call *democratic economic development* or, alternatively, to include in the definition of economic development that it is *a process of change that is democratic in its nature and moves society towards an expansion of democracy*. In this way of looking at things, popular participation in social affairs, along with the political rights on which meaningful popular participation depends, becomes a component of economic development. 'Political participation' means elections, the rights of opposition, and institutionalized mechanisms of consultation by which people can have direct input to government actions that affect them – for example, environmental impact hearings at which people can comment upon public projects and on private projects requiring government approval.

Yet, while these procedures of democracy are essential, they are not sufficient to assure meaningful popular participation. Democracy depends, in addition, on a reasonable degree of income equality and a broad realm for political authority. The importance of income equality for democracy should be relatively obvious: when large gaps exist between the rich and the poor, the power of the former will so dominate political affairs as to vitiate the procedures of democracy (Vilas 1997). The point is illustrated by Jean Dreze and Amartya Sen (1995). Explaining the 'inadequacies of local governance in rural India', a country often described as the world's largest democracy, they note that, among other factors:

> local democracy has often been undermined by acute social inequalities. The low involvement of women in local representative institutions such as village panchayats is a clear illustration of this problem. In large parts of the country, local governance is in the hands of upper-caste men from privileged classes, who are only weakly accountable to the community and often end up using local public services as instruments of patronage. In some cases, the rural elite has been known not only to be indifferent to the general promotion of local public services but even to *obstruct* their expansion, to prevent the empowerment of disadvantaged groups. (Dreze and Sen 1995: 107)

As to the realm of political authority, if private property rights are such as to prevent the political process from having extensive influence over economic affairs, then the procedures of democracy are hollow. If democracy is to be meaningful in the sense of allowing people to assure their own economic and social well-being, then private property rights cannot, for example, prevent the state from implementing land reform, regulating health and safety on farms and in factories and offices, restricting environmental degradation, establishing minimum wages, or limiting the movement of capital.

The concept of economic development I am using here, democratic economic development, includes widespread political participation in social and political affairs as one of its defining features – not simply as a goal but as an aspect of the process itself. In addition, my definition includes economic growth and rising productivity, the widespread provision of basic needs and relative income equality, environmental sustainability, and the preservation (and creation) of community.

This definition of economic development shares a problem that exists in any multi-dimensional definition of social progress: to what extent are the defining features of democratic economic development in conflict with one another? For example, it has been widely believed among economists that there is a trade-off between equality and growth, and it often appears that preservation of the natural environment is in conflict with economic growth. Likewise, many authoritarian regimes justify their suppression of democracy on the grounds that economic growth is in the general interest, growth requires social stability, and democracy undermines stability. In the case of community, the conflict with growth appears almost tautological, as growth means change and community is often taken to mean stability. If these conflicts, or trade-offs, are real, then to establish a multi-dimensional concept of economic development may be to advance an unattainable goal. Would it be better to return to the simple, one-dimensional definition of development as economic growth and let the other goals wait until some future date – supposedly after development has been attained?

Yet the avowal of necessary trade-offs among the components of democratic economic development may be more an ideological construct, reflecting the interests of dominant social groups and the philosophic underpinnings of modern economics, than a real phenomenon resulting from constants, or laws, of economic behaviour. Nowhere is this clearer than with regard to the equality–growth relationship, as recent research has thoroughly debunked the idea of an essential trade-off (as discussed in Chapter 3). Likewise, the growth–environment relationship is probably not so hostile as it is often portrayed. Certainly there are real environmental limits to economic growth, and the idea that growth itself will solve society's environmental problems is little more than a fantasy. Yet not all growth must be organized so as to be waste-intensive and heavily dependent on carbon-based energy. As to the democracy–growth conflict, while it may provide a convenient apologia for elites who run their societies through authoritarian regimes, it does not stand up to scrutiny. In fact, the empirical evidence can be interpreted to support the conclusion that democracy supports growth (Pastor and Sung 1995). It seems likely that even the community–growth connection need not be one of antagonism. In all of these cases, the relationship between economic growth and the other dimensions of democratic economic development depends on the way economic change is organized. What are the institutions by which economic growth is organized? How are markets constructed and regulated? What kinds of programmes are pursued and given priority by the government? How is civil society structured and what is its role in development? Answers to these sorts of questions will determine the relationships among the various components of democratic economic development and, indeed, determine whether or not democratic economic development can be attained.

Finally, in so far as there *are* necessary, real trade-offs in my definition of democratic economic development, their existence need not lead to a rejection of this definition of social progress. Social change is full of tensions, conflicts and the economist's trade-offs. They cannot be eliminated by the semantics of a definition. Better, when they are really there, to recognize and deal with them explicitly, rather than to ignore the conflicts and implicitly suppress one goal in the name of achieving another (Sutcliffe 1995).

This is the challenge that will be addressed in chapters 6, 7 and 8: How can economic change be structured so as to promote democratic economic development? What is a strategy, or policy, of democratic economic development?

The Context for Alternatives

Most discussions of economic development policy are severely constrained by the way 'policy' is defined and by the desire of participants in the discussions to be 'realistic'. Policy generally refers to the actions of governments. When we ask the question, What should the policy be?, we generally mean, What should the government do? Governments operate within the existing set of social relations; their role is to administer the existing society, not to change those social relations. The question of 'policy' is a question of what the government should do to achieve its goals, not a question of what those goals should be. Being realistic, then, usually boils down to the problem of how we can get the government – which is to say either the existing government or a government that might come into power without some major disruption – to administer things 'better'.

So being realistic means confining oneself to options that do not challenge the status quo of power relations. Many options, many alternatives, are very quickly eliminated from the discussion even though they would make positive contributions to economic development; because they would challenge the goals of government and alter existing power relations, they are not politically realistic. The Economic Commission for Latin America (ECLA), for example, has developed for the region a design for public policy reforms that are directed towards a multi-dimensional set of goals, including equity, sustainability and political participation along with growth and 'competitiveness' (Lahera et al. 1995). Yet the ECLA strategy falls within the traditional 'realistic' policy framework, and is largely a programme for how to manage the existing system 'better'. Many of the proposals in the ECLA programme would make positive contributions to democratic development, but, in an apparent effort to remain 'realistic', it avoids the sorts of proposals that would involve substantial social change. (In terms of the way I will approach the problem, the ECLA programme is unrealistic because it fails to grapple with the issue of social change.)

My discussion of democratic economic development policy will be set within a rather different context, one in which *policy is defined more broadly and in which realistic is defined very differently*. My meaning of policy will include the actions of governments, but it will also include the actions of other organized groups, such as labour unions, social movements and community organizations. One reason for this definition of policy is to escape, at least partially, the slide into statism that can plague anti-neo-liberal arguments. There are certain realms of policy where action must be undertaken by the state and implemented by governments, but there are other effective steps towards economic development that can be taken outside the state apparatus by organized groups in civil society. The implementation of policy outside the sphere of the state serves to limit state authority directly and, by building the power of civil society, indirectly.

A second reason to define policy as including the actions of labour unions, social movements, community organizations, and perhaps other groups is to underscore the idea that the correct prescription for economic development is not only a matter of substance but is also an issue of democratic process. *What is done* is important, but it is also important *how it is done.* States can do good things (as well as bad things), and, to the extent that those states are democratically controlled, those good things might both express and enhance democracy. Yet democracy is carried a step further and given deeper roots when broad social groups formulate and implement economic development programmes. In addition, as I shall suggest latter, in at least some realms of policy good things can be accomplished most effectively only when they are accomplished in such a participatory manner.

Also, in defining policy in this way, I am trying to say something about my constituency, about the people whom I am trying to reach, however indirectly. I would argue (though space does not permit me to do so here) that most important social changes come about as a result of broad, popular social action. My hope is to give some support and assistance to groups that are engaged in this action. So when I talk about policy, I am to a large extent talking about what these groups might do. One part of what they might do involves the direct implementation of economic development projects.

Another part of what might be done by groups pressing for social change is the articulation of actions that should be undertaken by government. So part of the problem of formulating policy for social groups is formulating policies that these groups could demand be undertaken by a government. While this part of the problem appears at first to be the same as the traditional policy formulation problem, it is in fact rather different because it begins from the question of how to bring about social change rather than from the question of how to administer the existing set of social relations.

If we begin the formulation of economic development policy with the goal of bringing about social change, then we alter the meaning of what is realistic. For if the goal is social change, it is thoroughly unrealistic to confine the discussion to alternatives that are acceptable to those who administer and benefit from the status quo. As I explained in Chapter 1, when we talk about social change, at least about social change that is meaningful, we are talking about 'structural' reforms or, to use the term coined by Andre Gorz (1964), 'non-reformist reforms'. Such reforms in themselves can never be embraced by those who hold power because that power is derived from and dependent upon the structures, the social relations, that are the object of change. It would be unrealistic to think otherwise.

This is not to say that structural reforms or social changes are impossible while those in power remain in power. For while they will not embrace the reforms or accept the reforms as a better way to achieve their own goals, they can be forced to accept change. Structural reforms do not require a prior change of power – a prior 'revolution' – but they do require a degree of popular support and action that can demand their implementation, that can force their adoption by government (or their tolerance by government, in the case of those programmes undertaken by civil society). In this aspect, my approach differs from that of Ciro Gomes and Roberto Manga-beira Unger (1996). Gomes and Unger propose a progressive alternative to neo-liberalism for Brazil that overlaps in important ways with the strategy I develop here (see Chapter 6). Yet they suggest that there are only two possible options for a programme of democratic development in Brazil, as a programme of 'national unity' or as some sort of insurrection. They then opt for finding a way to achieve a 'national' programme that would build on a broad social base, including big business. I am suggesting, however, that national unity and insurrection are not the only options, that there is the additional option of political struggle and structural reforms as a means for implementing a democratic strategy. (This difference in approach is, I think, connected to some of the further particular differences that I have with Gomes and Unger on which I will comment in the next chapter. Their argument and much of the programme they offer for Brazil is none the less similar to my own.)

Implementation, however, is only a first step. In order that the reforms be effective, their operation cannot be immediately vitiated by the economic responses of private actors. For example, it may be feasible to force a government to implement a highly progressive tax system; but, if this tax system is unaccompanied by other changes (of the sort that will be discussed in the next chapter), it may result in capital flight, economic decline and a substantial loss of income by the poor. Or, as another example, a government might be forced to undertake large social spending programmes; yet if the spending were based on deficit finance it could generate inflation and general economic instability, which would bring about severe recession.

These various considerations mean that an alternative economic development policy directed towards egalitarian, democratic social change is realistic if:

1. *It is realistic in its promise of social change.* It challenges the status quo social relations, the existing relations of power, by extending democratic authority in some manner. To be realistic in this sense, a programme will generally be unrealistic in the sense that it would not be acceptable to the existing authorities as a better way to achieve their own goals; it can only be achieved by popular pressure.

2. *It is politically realistic in that it can gain the popular support* necessary to force its implementation by government or to assure that government will tolerate its independent implementation. To meet this test of political realism, an alternative programme must offer clear and intelligible gains to a wide segment of the population, and generally it cannot demand that a large number of people accept substantial sacrifices. (Neoliberal programmes, by contrast, generally demand very substantial sacrifices in the name of distant, unclear gains. Not surprisingly, they are often imposed by governments on the population, rather than the other way around.)

3. *It is economically realistic in that its implementation is feasible without a prior change of the economic system.* An alternative economic programme, while extending democratic authority, cannot ignore the structures of organization and economic power that are characteristic of market societies. It must be technically feasible. We are dealing with the process of changing market societies, moving in the direction of reducing the extent to which the market dominates people's economic lives; we are not dealing with programmes that might be implemented after that change has been fully accomplished. (In an effort to build support for change, it may be very useful to talk about the types of programmes that could be put in place in a different economic system. Such a discussion could both underscore the limitations of the existing system and be an inspiration for action. But a discussion of 'post-change programmes', however useful as a political device, is something different from the task that I have set here.)

Although the core of any alternative economic development programme directed towards social change would be to a large degree in conflict with the interests of those who currently govern, not every element of such an alternative would be an issue of conflict. For example, in the realm of macroeconomic policy, most of the time neither those who advocate a democratic alternative nor those who attempt to preserve the status quo have an interest in a programme that would likely generate a high rate of inflation – though different groups will surely differ on the appropriate mechanisms for preventing the emergence of inflation. I state this caveat because particular aspects of the alternative programme that I will offer in the following chapters will appear to share common ground with more conservative agendas. It is necessary to set out these particular aspects to make it clear that an alternative programme does not eschew 'common sense'. An alternative programme must be based on a cognizance of the importance, for example, of fiscal and monetary balances, even while it would advance new ways to attain these balances.

One final word on context before proceeding. *All the discussion here is intended for countries where some degree of political democracy or a certain amount of flux or both allows the political space for opposition activity.* It must be possible not only to talk about alternative programmes – democratic initiatives, structural reforms but also to engage in some public organ izational work to advance these programmes. This includes many parts of today's world. It also means that the discussion is irrelevant or of questionable relevance for several countries, including some large countries – China, in particular, comes to mind, for example. Nevertheless, there are plenty of situations where we can talk about and even advance meaningful alternatives.[3]

Notes

1. I have also developed a direct critique in various essays; see MacEwan (1992; 1994; 1995). Lance Taylor has perhaps done the most extensive debunking of SAPs. A very useful overview of the issues appears in Pieper and Taylor (1998). Also see Taylor and Pieper (1996) and Taylor (1988).

2. When economic development emerged as a special field of inquiry in the post-Second World War years, the defining policy question was how to raise productivity and per capita income. See, for example, the writings of Rosenstein-Rodan (1943), Nurkse (1953) and Hirschman (1958), none of whom, incidentally, falls under the neo-liberal rubric. In recent years at the World Bank, there has been considerable effort to resolve the apparent contradiction between the focus on growth in practice and a rhetorical recognition of other development goals. In general, the Bank has argued that these other goals – equality, basic needs, democracy, environmental protection – will all follow from the proper economic growth policies. This argument has, for example, called upon the Kuznets Curve and has also asserted the existence of 'an environmental Kuznets Curve' – that is, as countries become richer, their environmental problems may become worse at first, but then, as income grows to higher levels, those problems diminish (World Bank 1992). I have dealt with the equality–growth relation in Chapter 3; on the lack of a general validity for the environmental Kuznets Curve, see Arrow et al. (1995) and Stern and Common (1996).

3. Dealing with a situation where a certain amount of democratic space exists and where political power is in flux, James Boyce (1996) and his colleagues offer a set of proposals for El Salvador following that country's 1992 peace agreement. Their work is a good example of the way a democratic programme can be formulated so that it is 'realistic' as I have defined the term here.

6

Macroeconomic Foundations of a Democratic Strategy

Inflation and the economic instability it represents can halt economic and social progress as effectively as a military coup. In many parts of the world, particularly in Latin America, experience with inflation has pushed the populace to accede to neo-liberal policies. Brazil provides the best example, with price increases ranging up over 2,000 per cent a year for periods in the late 1980s and early 1990s. High rates of inflation not only cause dire hardships and disrupt people's lives, but they also undermine economic growth as businesses are reluctant to invest when dramatic price changes create severe uncertainty.

A democratic economic development strategy – or, for that matter, any other sort of economic development strategy – would undermine itself if it generated substantial instability and inflation. I will argue in the next chapter that democratic development is defined by the content of its social programmes. Nevertheless, the central issue in establishing the viability of a democratic strategy is its macroeconomic framework. The contention that 'there is no alternative' to neo-liberalism rests on the claim that efforts to push development in a more egalitarian direction would create macro-economic instability through deficit financing (and regulatory disincentives to investment) and thereby undermine economic growth; the lack of growth, in addition to being a problem in itself, would then undermine any egalitarian programmes. This charge that democratic development would generate instability through deficit financing is a central macro-economic issue in the development debate.

Where Can the Money Come from?

Democratic development would require substantial amounts of public finance because it rests on extensive social programmes. Social programmes are, by their very nature, programmes that do not generate revenue directly and must be financed by public funds. There are only three possible sources of increasing funds for social programmes: diverting public funds from other uses (for example, from the military), raising taxes, and borrowing funds (that is, deficit finance). The contention that democratic development would generate macroeconomic instability rests on three corresponding assumptions: that the potential for diverting public funds from other sources is very limited, either because there are not sufficient such funds or because their diversion is not politically possible, or both; that the potential for raising taxes is very limited, partly by political reality but, leaving aside the politics of taxes, also by the negative incentive impact of taxes on investment and by the possibilities for tax avoidance and tax evasion; and that deficit finance will generate instability and undermine growth. So when governments try to implement social programmes, unable to divert sufficient funds from other uses or to raise sufficient taxes, they will turn to deficit finance, and the result will be instability and slower economic growth.

There are many countries where the large size of military spending suggests that as a technical solution (leaving aside political possibilities) diverting funds from other uses could make a substantial contribution to the financing of social programmes. Were a country to follow a path of democratic development, the need for a military would not be eliminated, but, in almost all circumstances, it would be substantially reduced. Nevertheless, generally the diversion of funds from other uses is not a realistic option for greatly expanding social spending. Table 6.1 shows central government military (defence) and social spending for a diverse set of countries. Because virtually all military spending is part of the central government budget but substantial portions of social spending are often at lower levels of government, the relative size of military spending is probably overstated in Table 6.1. Yet in the great majority of countries, military spending is less than half as large as social spending, and in some cases – Brazil, Chile, Ghana – it is only about 10 per cent as large as central government social spending. (Myanmar stands out as a grotesque exception in Table 6.1, with military spending more than three times as large as social spending in the central government budget.) These data suggest that in most countries even fairly substantial percentage reductions of military spending, entirely diverted to social spending, would not have large percentage impacts on social spending. For example, for Malaysia (the median country in the table in terms of military spending as percentage of social spending), a 25 per cent decrease in military spending would release only enough funds to raise social spending by 7.5 per cent.

The reduction of military spending would often be a good thing in itself, and in some countries such reductions could release substantial funds for social programmes. In addition, reductions of inefficiencies and

TABLE 6.1 Central government defence and social spending, selected countries, 1994

	Spending as a percentage of central government budget		Defence spending as a percentage of social spending	Social spending as a percentage of GNP
	Defence	Social		
Kenya	6.1	25.7	24	8.1
Ghana	4.8	38.5	12	8.1
Cameroon	9.3	25.5	36	4.5
Egypt	8.2	29.7	28	12.0
Myanmar	39.1	24.6	159	2.5
Indonesia	6.2	14.4	43	2.4
Philippines	10.2	23.1	44	4.1
Morocco	13.9	27.2	51	8.5
Guatemala	15.2	25.5	60	2.3
Romania	7.3	46.9	16	15.1
Colombia	8.1	31.5	26	4.7
Thailand	17.0	35.4	48	5.4
Turkey	9.5	21.7	44	5.1
Russia	14.5	54.1	27	14.9
Iran	6.5	37.4	17	9.5
Brazil	2.5	36.7	7	12.8
Malaysia	12.0	39.5	30	10.4
Chile	8.8	64.9	14	13.8
Rep. of Korea	18.7	32.0	58	6.0

NB: These countries were chosen among those for which data were available. They are not a systematic, well-defined sample, but were chosen simply to obtain a reasonably diverse set of countries by region and historical experience. Small countries were generally excluded. China and India were not included because the very small share of expenditures going to social services suggests that in these two countries most of the social spending budget is not at the central government level.

Source: World Bank (1996a: Table 14).

corruption in government programmes are desirable in their own right and in some countries could provide significant funds for social programmes. (I will suggest in the next chapter that democratic development establishes a foundation for reducing inefficiency and corruption.) Yet it would be hard to make the case that diversion of funds from other uses would by itself be sufficient to support the expansion of social programmes that would be the foundation of democratic economic development.

Deficit spending is also unlikely to be a sufficient means for funding democratic development, though moderate deficits may be a useful part of any economic development strategy. One need not accept the widespread anti-deficit mania to recognize that prolonged, substantial budget deficits tend to generate macroeconomic instability and harm growth. When governments run large budget deficits, they are caught between the horns of a dilemma. On the one hand, they can turn to private financial markets to raise funds. Yet, unless the savings rate rises to meet this new demand for capital, interest rates are likely to rise and hamper private investment (the 'crowding out' phenomenon). On the other hand, the monetary authorities can follow a policy of accommodation, buying up the rising government debt by issuing new money. Yet this increase of the money supply is likely to contribute to rising rates of inflation. Inflation, in turn, largely by the uncertainty it generates, will undermine private investment and growth. Simply the reasonable likelihood of these sorts of negative impacts of a persistent deficit can itself have negative impacts, as investors interpret a rising deficit to be a sign that the government is losing control of its macroeconomic policy and defer action until the situation has resolved itself (Fischer 1993).

Latin American structuralists have argued that deficits and the inflation that goes with them can create favourable circumstances for economic growth (Furtado 1976). In the face of supply inelasticities in resource markets and limited infrastructure, substantial government spending may be needed to support growth. Yet, the structuralists point out, political circumstances do not allow a rapid expansion of taxes, and thus the only way for government to play its necessary growth role is through deficit finance. This argument, however, is only a rationale for limited deficits. If deficits are large and persistent the instability they generate will almost surely undermine the positive growth impact. The structuralist insights, however, are a good antidote to extreme anti-deficit mania. (George Akerlof et al. [1996] provide more recent evidence suggesting support for the traditional structuralist position that low levels of inflation can be associated with improved economic performance.)

Various sets of evidence tend to substantiate the position that, while limited deficits and moderate inflation (in the one-digit or low two-digit range) are consistent with strong economic expansion, large and persistent budgetary deficits contribute to an instability that harms growth (Bruno and Easterly 1996). Most of the East Asian 'success stories' were characterized – up until 1997 – by macroeconomic stability, for example, while in Latin America when growth has been supported by large deficits it has generally led to accelerating inflation and sharp disruption. These anecdotal observations are supported by more sophisticated cross-country statistical analyses. There are exceptions where growth has continued for a period in spite of macroeconomic instability, and certainly macroeconomic stability in itself does not guarantee rapid economic growth. The association between instability and poor growth performance is none the less strong, and deficits are a central factor generating instability. (Stanley Fischer [1993] provides much of the basis for the discussion here. Fischer does recognize that causation can be in the other direction – that is, poor economic performance may be the cause of deficits, rather than the other way around. He interprets the evidence to indicate, however, that 'the causation runs significantly, but not exclusively, from inflation to growth'.)[1]

Thus, although diverting funds from other uses and deficit finance may provide part of the funding for a democratic programme in many countries and may be very substantial in some cases, in most countries these sources of revenue are probably insufficient over the long run. Ultimately, the viability of a democratic programme depends on a tax system that can raise the necessary funds.

The Feasibility of Higher Taxes

There is, it turns out, little evidence that the potential for raising taxes is severely limited by the negative impact on investment, though the claim continues to be part of the 'accepted wisdom' among economists. In their examination of the connections between fiscal policy and economic growth, for example, William Easterly and Sergio Rebelo note that economists' growth models usually

> link certain taxes to the rate of growth. Increases in income taxes, for example, lower the rate of return to private investment, making investment activities less attractive and lowering the rate of growth. It is hard to think of an influence on the private real rate of return and on the growth rate that is more direct than that of income taxes. If these do not affect the growth rate, what does? (Easterly and Rebelo 1993)

Yet Easterly and Rebelo go on to acknowledge: 'Unfortunately, the empirical evidence that is currently available to shed light on the importance of fiscal policy in determining growth is sparse.' They then suggest that the sparsity of evidence is explained by problems in measuring the variables that the theory specifies as important determinants of growth. More likely, the claim of economic theory that higher taxes harm economic growth is, if not simply wrong, insufficient.

The impact of taxes on economic growth cannot be meaningfully separated from the impact of government spending on economic growth. For example, Easterly and Rebelo's own study shows a clear positive relationship between growth and the share of public investment that goes to transport and communications, suggesting that higher taxes dedicated to such infrastructure investment may make a net positive contribution to growth. Likewise, it is widely agreed that public investment in schools contributes to growth, and this investment too depends, ultimately, on taxes. The issue here is most usefully understood by considering the total impact of government fiscal activity. If tax revenues are spent in ways that raise the rate of economic growth, then any reduction of the rate of return due to the taxes is balanced by an increase in the rate of return due to more rapid growth. (The absurdity of looking at taxes in isolation from spending can be illustrated by consideration of one of the results that Easterly and Rebelo report from their study: 'The government's budget surplus is also consistently correlated with growth and private investment in our cross-section.' One might infer from this that raising taxes and spending them on nothing – that is, simply using the taxes to increase the government surplus – would contribute to growth!)

The claim that tax revenues cannot be raised to finance the social programmes of democratic development seems to be given credence by the apparent rising international mobility of capital. Were a government to raise its country's tax rates above those in other countries with easily accessible capital markets, its actions would tend to generate capital flight, reduce investment and undermine growth. In earlier decades, rapid response to changes in government fiscal policy may have been attenuated by limits on information and lack of financial instruments. In today's world, however, such impediments to mobility are clearly declining.[2] In recent decades, there has in fact been a widespread trend towards lower tax rates, a trend that became especially marked in the 1980s (G. Jenkins 1991). One of the standard explanations of this trend has been that governments are increasingly constrained by the increasing international mobility of capital and, once some governments lower tax rates in order to maintain an internationally competitive position (with regard to attracting to or keeping capital in their countries), others are forced to do likewise (Lee and McKenzie 1989).

There are, however, several problems with the argument that the rising international mobility of capital eliminates the tax increase option as a means for funding democratic development. To begin with, the premise of the argument, the assertion of a dramatic increase in international capital mobility, is usually overstated. Things have changed, but the world has not shifted in a few short years from being a collection of sharply separated national economies to a seamless single capital market (see Chapter 2 and also, for example, MacEwan 1991; Glyn and Sutcliffe 1992; Sutcliffe and Glyn 1999; and Cable 1995).

The tax reforms of the 1980s were significant, with many governments substantially lowering maximum statutory income tax rates. Yet these reforms cannot be attributed simply to rising competition brought about by increased international capital mobility. In large part the reforms re-

TABLE 6.2 Reductions in top marginal tax rates, selected countries, 1984–90 (percentages)

Country	Individuals		Corporations	
	Before changes	After changes	Before changes	After changes
Australia	57	47	46	39
Austria	62	50	55	30
Bangladesh	60	55	60	55
Barbados	60	50	45	35
Belgium	72	55	45	43
Bolivia	40	10	30	2
Botswana	75	50	35	40
Canada	34	29	36	28
Colombia	49	31	40	30
Denmark	45	40	50	40
El Salvador	60	35	30	35
Finland	51	43	33	25
France	65	57	45	37
Gambia	75	35	47	47
Germany (FR)	56	53	56	50
Ghana	65	55	60	45
Greece	63	50	49	46
Guatemala	42	34	48	34
Hong Kong	17	15	18.5	16.5
Iceland	38	33	51	50
India	62	50	55/60	50/55
Indonesia	45	35	45	35
Ireland	58	53	50	40
Italy	62	50	36	36
Jamaica	58	33	45	33
Japan	70	50	43	37
Kenya	65	45	45	42.5
Kiribati	50	40	35	35
Luxembourg	57	56	40	34
Malawi	50	45	50	45
Malaysia	55	40	40	35
Mauritius	70	35	66	35
Netherlands	72	60	42	40
New Zealand	57	33	45	33
Nigeria	70	55	45	40
Norway	40	20	28	28
Papua New Guinea	50	45	36.5	30
Portugal	41/48	37	47	36
Saint Lucia	60	30	45	33.3
Singapore	45	33	40	33
Spain	66	56	35	35

TABLE 6.2 Continued

Country	Individuals		Corporations	
	Before changes	After changes	Before changes	After changes
Sri Lanka	55	40	50	50
Sweden	50	20	52	52
Tanzania	75	55	50	50
Trinidad & Tobago	70	45	49.5	45
United Kingdom	60	40	52	35
United States	50	28	46	34
Western Samoa	60	50	42	39
Zambia	80	35	50	35/45

Source: G. Jenkins (1991: Table 1).

flected an accumulation of experience indicating that high marginal rates were ineffective, as they created strong incentives for tax avoidance (finding loopholes) and tax evasion (hiding income) (G. Jenkins 1991; and Gillis 1989). Also, the reforms were in part a result of the growing leverage of aid donors – both directly and through the IMF and World Bank – that resulted from the debt crisis of the early 1980s; the donor governments and the powerful private interests that shape their international economic policies pushed strongly for these sorts of reforms. Not surprisingly, as with other reforms of the neo-liberal agenda, the donors found strong allies within the low-income countries (MacEwan 1990).

Even the lower individual income tax rates established in many countries during the 1980s show a considerable variation, indicating the substantial leeway that continues to exist in establishing tax policy. As to corporate tax rates, while they too were lowered in the 1980s, the variation among the top rates applied by different countries appears to have risen. Glenn Jenkins (1991) reports reductions in individual and corporate top marginal rates after 1984 for forty-nine countries; Jenkins's data are reproduced here as Table 6.2. The average top individual rate fell from 57.1 per cent to 41.7 per cent and the average top corporate rate fell from 44.7 per cent to 37.7 per cent. For the individual rates, the standard deviation fell only slightly, from 12.1 to 11.6, while the standard deviation of the corporate rates rose from 8.9 to 9.4. (Excluding Japan, Western European countries, the United States and Canada from Jenkins's list does not substantially change these figures, though the decline in the standard deviation for individual rates is slightly greater – from about 13 to about 11.) These data do not support the contention that the tax reforms of the 1980s were somehow forced on countries by a need to bring their top marginal rates in harmony with one another. (It should be emphasized that all of these rates are statutory, not effective rates, and no one should assume that they tell us very much about the taxes that the wealthy and corporations actually paid.)

Arguments about the impact of tax rates and other fiscal variables on the international mobility of capital, especially regarding fixed investment as opposed to financial flows, are often heavily dependent on case studies at best and anecdotes at worst. There seems to be little systematic evidence that would allow one to appraise the degree of sensitivity of business location decisions to tax rates (or other macroeconomic variables) in the international economy. Evidence about capital mobility within the United States, however, seems to be more fully developed. Because there are no regulatory restrictions on capital or goods movements among the fifty states while each of the state governments has considerable taxing and spending authority within its geographic jurisdiction, experience within the United States provides a good proxy from which to draw general inferences about the sensitivity of business location decisions to governments' taxation and spending policies. Broadly speaking, the evidence from US experience suggests that governments' macroeconomic policies certainly make a difference for business location decisions, but overall there remains a good deal of leeway for government action (Kenyon and Kincaid 1991; and NEER 1997).

Both studies of the US federal system and of capital mobility in the international economy, however, make it clear that generalizations obscure important variations in the relation between fiscal action and business decisions. The situation is very different for different types of industries. Manufacturing firms with relatively low fixed capital costs are fairly mobile, and they are relatively sensitive to tax changes – or, for that matter, changes in other local cost factors, especially labour costs. For a variety of reasons, manufacturing investment can play an especially important role in a country's or region's economic development, and therefore tax increases or other policies that might inhibit such investment could be detrimental. Thus, even if higher taxes did not have a large negative impact on overall investment, their impact on manufacturing investment could undermine development. These observations do not mean tax increases are ruled out or even severely curtailed, but that they are best adopted as a flexible tool and as part of a larger set of policies towards manufacturing investment (including the sorts of focused policies discussed in Chapter 8). When dealing with mobile industries, governments need to view their tax policy, and other policies, as part of a bargaining process.

Only when a country has nothing to offer an investor other than low tax rates will greater investment and higher taxes necessarily be in conflict with one another. As I discussed in Chapter 2, the bargaining position of governments *vis-à-vis* internationally mobile capital is influenced by a number of factors. Clearly, governments in countries with relatively large markets and a large pool of highly skilled labour will be in a stronger bargaining position than will governments in countries with small markets and a scant supply of skilled labour. Haiti is in a weaker position than is Brazil, as is Botswana compared to South Africa, or Laos compared to Thailand. These differences, however, are nothing new; perhaps things are more difficult in an era with greater mobility of capital, but things have long been difficult in very low-income countries.

In arguing that possibilities exist for tax policies that would raise significant additional revenue in low-income countries, I do not mean to suggest that the formulation of such policies is a simple task. There are better and worse tax policies. In the discussion of democratic development, a better tax policy is one that will increase revenues while also promoting – or at least not undermining – other development goals. In addition to the impact of taxes on investment and growth, the other most immediate impact of concern in tax policy is income distribution. Taxes that avoided any harm to investment incentives because their impact fell heavily on the poor would hardly have a place in a democratic programme. So once we have rejected the notion that tax revenues cannot be increased, the question becomes: *how* should tax revenues be increased?

One well-established part of a tax package is the income tax. While there are problems with raising income taxes substantially (on which, more below), higher income taxes would be one important part of revenue-raising policy in a democratic development strategy. In many low-income countries, income taxes can be highly progressive when they include a substantial personnel exemption – that is, they are a tax that is paid only by relatively high-income individuals. In this way the income tax becomes a focused tax, and the costs of administration are less severe. An income tax of this sort could raise significant funds and bring about some improvement in the distribution of income. Yet, increases of the income tax are limited by practical considerations, and they are unlikely to be sufficient to finance the social programmes of a democratic strategy. The purpose of a fiscal system is, in any case, not simply to redistribute income, but also to redistribute expenditure – that is, from private expenditure on private goods to social expenditure on public goods. Thus the tax programme of a democratic strategy needs to include more broadly based taxes, even though more broadly based taxes tend not to be progressive.

Formulating a democratic alternative to neo-liberalism for Brazil, Ciro Gomes and Roberto Mangabeira Unger (1996) contend that for an overall fiscal programme to be progressive it is not necessary that every tax which

composes it be progressive. They argue that a value added tax (VAT) can
be an effective tool of a democratic policy in spite of the fact that its direct
impact tends to be relatively regressive. A VAT is an attractive tool of
development policy because it is broadly based and relatively easy to collect;
it can therefore be an effective mechanism to raise state revenues. Also, a
VAT only taxes spending, and it thus makes savings relatively more attractive. In so far as economic growth is constrained by a lack of savings, a
VAT tends to enhance growth (relative to other types of taxes). In spite
of its effectiveness in terms of raising revenue and promoting savings, the
regressive nature of a VAT has generally undermined its support among
those forces that would favour a democratic programme. In this context,
Gomes and Unger's argument is insightful and provocative.

Nevertheless, Gomes and Unger's position is unsatisfactory in certain
respects. In suggesting that popular forces should accept a regressive VAT
because it would be part of an overall progressive set of government
policies, they are essentially asking the populace to make a sacrifice (tax
payments) in the present for an uncertain gain (the government programmes) in the future. Thus their programme, however reasonable in its
overall logic, is unlikely to be realistic in the sense that it could not gain
popular support. The overall logic of the programme is unlikely to overcome the weight of people's experience, especially in the case of a tax as
visible as the typical VAT.

A VAT, however, could still be a useful part of a democratic development programme if it were implemented in a way that would reduce its
regressive incidence. In particular, were food (and perhaps other necessities)
exempted from the tax, its incidence would be substantially altered. This
exemption would narrow the base of the tax, but it would still have a
relatively broad base and its (relative) ease of collection would not be
affected. VATs have been effective means of raising revenues in several
countries where they have been instituted (Gillis 1989). Implemented in
their standard form with regressive incidence, VATs would be inappropriate
and politically unrealistic as part of a democratic programme, but with the
exemption modification they could play an important role.

Also, as Gomes and Unger themselves suggest, a VAT could be introduced as part of a larger tax reform that would include more progressive
elements. In this context, as one part of a larger tax reform package that
included a progressive income tax, for example, a VAT could become
politically realistic. (Gomes and Unger, with their focus on Brazil, also
advocate the privatization of at least some substantial government-owned
industries as a mechanism for dealing with the short-run fiscal problems of
the state. As my concern here is not so much with short-run fiscal balance,
I do not take up this issue. However, Gomes and Unger are certainly correct

in arguing that privatization per se should not be ruled out of an alternative, democratic programme simply because it has long been anathema to progressive political forces. Within the context, as specified here, of attempting to formulate a democratic development programme within the constraints of the existing market framework, there is no good reason generally to proscribe privatizations of state industry – nor, for that matter, is there any reason generally to embrace them. Sometimes state-owned industries can play important and positive roles, but at other times they are wasteful, inefficient and corrupt bastions of special, privileged groups.)

The Need for Capital Controls

Still, there is considerable difficulty in the implementation of any set of taxes that redistributes income significantly. High tax rates, as noted above, induce strong efforts to avoid and evade taxes. Even when tax legislation is generally well crafted, wealthy individuals can often locate their income, particularly their capital income, in international tax havens. In so far as efforts to raise tax rates on high-income groups induce capital to move abroad, not only do the higher tax rates fail to generate more revenue; in addition, they generate a capital flight that harms private investment as well. I have already suggested that this problem is frequently overstated, but it is none the less real. It is probably not feasible to introduce substantial tax reform in a country, including redistributive taxes, without some constraints on the international movement of funds. Yet such capital controls are not themselves easy to implement.

One response to these problems associated with the implementation of redistributive taxes is to abandon redistributive taxes. As Gomes and Unger point out, this is not the same as abandoning a redistributive fiscal programme: if the government raises its revenues through, for example, a proportional tax and spends on projects that are disproportionately beneficial to the poor, then its overall fiscal programme would be progressive. I have argued above that a simply proportional tax would not be acceptable within a democratic programme because of the negative popular response it would tend to generate. Nevertheless, the implementation of the fiscal component of a democratic programme must be based on a recognition of the limits of redistributive taxes. Because of evasion and avoidance, including international movement of funds, highly progressive tax rates will generally not result in a highly progressive tax system. A democratic programme needs a degree of redistribution built into its tax system, but the bulk of the programme's redistribution must come through the spending projects and the larger structural relationships that it establishes.

Even if taxes are not steeply progressive, a democratic programme none the less requires regulations on the international movement of capital. The tax rates that would support a democratic development programme are necessarily higher than the rates that prevail in many countries, and the programme would always be under the threat of being undermined through capital flight. Moreover, the development of a democratic programme demands that society (through the government) have the capacity to adjust taxes, other aspects of its fiscal programme and regulations. Such adjustments could always lead to capital flight – because they actually threatened profit rates or were perceived to pose such a threat. In this context it is important to keep in mind that 'a threat to profits' is not an absolute matter, but arises only relatively. If any government is forced to ensure that, relative to all other countries, capital in its country never sees its income as 'threatened', it is in an impossible situation, virtually giving up all control of its economy.

A democratic development programme is necessarily a programme that to some degree does not accept the market as the guide to economic organization and decisions. Such a national programme is simply not viable without capital controls. This is not a new need, something created by late twentieth-century 'globalization'. It was an issue recognized by Keynes who argued in the first half of the century that 'government controls over the movement of goods and, especially, money across the nation's borders are an essential pre-condition for effective national economic planning' (Crotty 1989: 98).[3]

James Crotty and Gerald Epstein (1996) provide an extensive and useful defence of capital controls. While they consider a great many issues in their discussion, certain points deserve emphasis here:

- '[The] primary impediments to the successful use of capital controls are *political*, not technical. It is not support for capital controls, but the contrary belief that progressive economic restructuring can be achieved without at least the threat of successful controls that is utopian' (Crotty and Epstein 1996: 136). This conclusion rests in large part on the observation that governments of several countries – Crotty and Epstein cite Japan, South Korea and Sweden as prime examples – successfully employed capital controls for decades as foundation stones of their relatively egalitarian development policies. The financial woes of East Asia that emerged in 1997 and the longer-standing difficulties of social democracy in Sweden provide a basis for debate over various aspects of these countries' policies, but they do not undermine the conclusion that capital controls are technically feasible.
- One part of the argument that capital controls are not technically feasible in poor countries is that their imposition would reduce the inflow of capital that such countries need so badly. Crotty and Epstein

point out, however, that 'private capital markets are currently doing a poor job of transferring useful capital to most poor countries ... There are substantial two-way flows [in and out of poor countries], but little net transfer of funds [into poor countries]; and much of what does flow is short term and unstable' (Crotty and Epstein 1996: 142). Events in Mexico in 1994, which can be traced directly to the opening of the country's capital markets, and in East Asia in 1997 show the great damage that results when countries lack controls over the flow of funds in and out of their economies. Against the standard of these experiences, it would be difficult to argue that it is controls that represent the technically infeasible. Whatever problems are generated by the establishment of capital controls, they can make a substantial contribution to financial stability by reducing the amplitude of speculative swings. As the opponents of social spending are fond of pointing out, financial stability is an essential ingredient of economic expansion.

• Capital controls are not a simple, well-defined set of regulations. 'There is no single policy with respect to controls that is optimal in all countries under all circumstances' (Crotty and Epstein 1996: 136). Yet there are a number of general principles that serve as a guide and provide examples of policies that can be developed. Crotty and Epstein argue, in particular, that the first step is simply to halt the current trend toward liberalization, and they go on to point out various tax mechanisms that can be used to dampen speculation and inhibit capital flights. One example is a 'Keynes tax', a tax on the sale of any financial asset held less than some minimum length of time. Another example is the 'Tobin tax', a small percentage tax on all foreign exchange transactions (first suggested by the US economist James Tobin). Both these taxes are designed to discourage short-term speculation without harming longer-term capital flows. (The Tobin tax, however, has the distinct disadvantage that it could not be effectively administered by an individual government, but would require enforcement in all major financial centres.)

There are serious political obstacles to the establishment of capital control regulations, obstacles that are both internal to most countries and that are imposed by the most powerful actors in the international economy. The IMF and World Bank, the US government and the governments of other wealthy nations, and the largest private firms, both financial and non-financial, are all opponents of capital controls. Moreover, the trend of recent international economic agreements – in particular, that establishing the World Trade Organization – has been strongly towards deregulation. These forces are extremely difficult to overcome. (In the late 1990s, the financial crisis in East Asia led some officials at the World Bank to acknowledge the problems associated with unrestricted capital movements

[Stiglitz 1998a]. If history is a guide, however, it is unlikely that the acknowledgement will lead to any major policy changes at the Bank.)

Yet from a technical point of view, the *economic* argument against the higher tax rates and regulations on capital movements does not hold up, and economic considerations per se do not proscribe a tax system that would finance democratic programmes or the capital controls that would be an important foundation for macroeconomic stability. Even in the current era of globalization, there is no reason to believe that governments must cede all authority to 'the market'.

Notes

1. Fischer's work is part of the World Bank's Growth Project, and much of the other work he cites as supporting the same general conclusions are also connected to the Bank and the IMF. The work is certainly tainted by this association, for these institutions have a clear agenda that is best served by the sorts of results that Fischer obtains. One should never make the error of assuming that econometric work is unaffected by the biases of the researchers carrying out the work or by those of the sponsoring institutions. Nevertheless, on both theoretical and empirical grounds the case against large, prolonged deficit finance seems strong. In addition, many low-income countries run chronic deficits, and thus at the beginning of any democratic development a deficit would already exist. Thus financing an expansion of social programmes with deficit finance would often require not creating a deficit but increasing an already existing deficit.

2. Moreover, as tax rates have been lowered in the rich countries – most particularly in the United States – the downward pressure on tax rates in poorer countries is increased The problem for other governments of taxing the profits of US-based firms is aggravated by the US practice of allowing foreign income taxes to be taken as a credit against US taxes on income repatriated to the USA, but only up to the amount of tax payable at US rates. Under these circumstances, when another country raises its income tax rate above the US rate, the effective increase is substantially greater because the US income recipient will have to start paying US taxes as well. Were the US government to treat foreign income taxes as a cost of doing business, like any other cost, then the effective increase would, on the contrary, be less than the nominal increase. Similar problems arise from the tax practice in other high-income countries.

3. Crotty goes on to point out:

Of course the imposition of capital controls does not mean the elimination of international financial flows; it means, rather, their regulation. Under capital controls, the government has the authority to set the conditions under which money can lawfully enter and leave the country. For example, the government might permit unregulated *income* flows (as interest payments, dividends, or profits), controlling only the investment and repatriation of the original capital itself. And it might allow capital to be repatriated some months after the government has been notified of the owner's intention to withdraw the funds, a time period that could be altered in length depending on conditions in financial markets.

Crotty, I should note, is concerned with progressive policy in the United States and other advanced capitalist countries. The basic principles, however, are the same in a great variety of circumstances. For more on Keynes's argument, see Crotty (1983).

7

Social Programmes as the Core of a Democratic Strategy

In spite of the fact that around the world the twentieth century saw large gains in life expectancy and recent decades have seen significant reductions in illiteracy, the limits of health-care and education in many low-income countries are shocking by any reasonable standard. In Africa's most populous country, Nigeria, the infant mortality rate is over 100 per 1,000 live births, and the maternal mortality rate is 1 in a 100. In Brazil, less than half of the children of secondary school age are even enrolled in school. In relatively rich Argentina, about a third of the population does not have access to safe water, and in many countries of Africa the figure is around two-thirds. In India and Egypt, the adult illiteracy rate is 48 per cent; for the thirty-three countries other than India categorized as 'low human development' in the UN's *Human Development Report 1998*, adult illiteracy averages just over 50 per cent.

These sorts of figures on health and education betray a woeful lack of adequate social services in much of the world. Other measures of social well-being – measures of housing, environmental degradation, public transport and social security, for example – would tell a similar story. The need for social services is a starting point in the formation of a democratic economic development strategy. Although an effective macroeconomic framework, as I have discussed in the preceding chapter, is an essential foundation of any economic development strategy, the primary defining features of a *democratic* strategy lie in its social programmes.

The Core of Democratic Development

Social programmes are the central *democratic initiatives* of an alternative development strategy. These initiatives have a direct connection to people's lives, and their implications for social change are more readily apparent than is generally the case with macroeconomic policies. Social programmes can be implemented by government or by social groups working independently or with government.

Social programmes are a primary component in any democratic economic development programme because they meet real, basic needs of a wide spectrum of the population. Education and training, health-care, environmental repair and preservation, public transport, infrastructure, housing, social security programmes – these are good things in themselves. Social programmes are 'for the people', and they therefore make the programme *realistic* in the sense that they help make it possible for the programme to obtain wide popular support.

Also, social programmes are integral to democratic development because they can be foundations for effective popular political participation. This is most obviously true of education (that is, schooling); when it gives people knowledge, enhances their analytic capacities, and builds their confidence, it directly contributes to their political power. Other social programmes have parallel impacts, for as they provide people with basic needs they establish at least a limited foundation for political involvement. Furthermore, the expansion of social programmes, almost by definition, contributes to income equality because if the programmes are truly social – that is, if people's claims on these programmes derive from their existence as people rather than from their market power – their proportional impact on overall material well-being is inversely related to income. In so far as social programmes contribute to economic and social equality, they create a basis for democratic participation. When social programmes contribute to a more equal distribution of income, they also contribute to the more equal distribution of power that is essential for democracy. (The positive connection between extension of social programmes and an expansion of democratic power is by no means automatic. Schools, for example, can be used as a mechanism of control and as instruments for solidifying the inequalities of class hierarchy. I will return to this issue shortly.)

Perhaps most important, social programmes, financed and organized in the public sphere, offer the opportunity for *direct* popular participation – direct democracy – in their implementation. One of the central problems of democracy in any large, complex society is that the great majority of the population has no (or a very limited) direct political role in the operation of economic activity. The majority can (within constitutional limits) set government policy regulating private economic activity, but efforts to expand that role always run the risk of alienating business interests and undermining investment and economic growth. Yet public programmes can involve direct participation, direct democracy, without any such threat (or only minimal and indirect threat) to business. So the larger the sphere of public programmes, the larger the opportunity for democratic participation in economic activity. In so far as we value democracy for its own sake, this is a good thing. It is also a good thing because of its impact on the quality of the programmes; they can be pressured to be more effective and less corrupt. (Efforts to increase direct popular participation in private economic activity could also be part of a democratic programme, but they are a separate issue.)

More than this, however, the implementation of social programmes has broad potential implications in terms of the whole set of goals of democratic economic development. There is wide agreement, for example, that several social programmes are important components of successful economic growth. Education and health-care appear to raise people's productive capacity; public transport and infrastructure lubricate the labour market and provide a universal input to business; housing and social security can be important bases for the political stability that encourages private investment; programmes designed to protect and repair the natural environment, in addition to their direct benefits, establish the foundation for long-term development (and, not incidentally, can be important sources of employment). These links are not automatic. Public expenditure programmes can be plagued by corruption, and, corruption aside, they can be structured in ways that make them ineffective. My argument at this stage, however, is only one of potential. I will return shortly to the issue of how to shape the programmes effectively.

While social programmes can be important causal components of economic growth, economic growth can also be a foundation for the expansion of social programmes. This potential for positive circular causation deserves emphasis. Traditionally, the literature on poverty and economic development has focused on 'vicious circles', processes by which poverty itself creates a set of social relations, practices and institutions that create poverty (Myrdal 1957). For example, because a society is poor, it has a low savings rate; with a low savings rate, the rate of investment is low; without substantial investment, economic growth is very limited, and poverty is maintained or continually re-created. Or, to put the example in terms of social programmes: because a society is very poor, its spending on education and health-care (components of 'human capital') is low; children work in directly productive activity instead of going to school, and expenditure on clean water and sewerage systems – steps that would improve public health – are low; without the expansion of schooling and health-care, productivity does not rise, economic growth is very limited and, again, poverty is maintained or continually re-created. It is easy to make the vicious circle analysis both more relevant and more interesting by bringing inequality into the picture. Inequality, through a whole set of social mechanisms, can retard economic expansion, and the lack of economic expansion – the lack of change – can perpetuate the inequality. An escape from poverty and underdevelopment, then, requires some decisive break in this vicious circle of causation (Baran 1956).

Regardless of the political processes by which such a 'break' might take place (an important issue but outside the scope of this book), once any disruption of the vicious circle has occurred, the connections of the circle can work in exactly the opposition direction. A 'virtuous circle' of growth and development can drive the process of economic change. For example: economic expansion means higher levels of income, which can increase the savings and investment rates, increasing the rate of economic growth; likewise, growth can yield higher rates of expenditures on social programmes which, in turn, raise productivity and raise the rate of economic expansion.

The virtuous circle that appears to connect relative income equality and economic growth, especially as these two variables have been associated in the 'success stories' of East Asia, has received considerable attention (for example, Birdsall et al. 1995). In those situations, education has structured markets in ways that support both growth and equality. While analysts have offered various hypotheses to explain the apparent equality–growth connection (see Chapter 3), the analysis of immediate concern here is that which incorporates education and other social programmes as significant links in the circular causal chain. In this analysis, social programmes are not simply 'good things', nor are they simply generators of economic growth. They can also be an entry point into the virtuous circle, a key to the initiation of a democratic economic development strategy.

Education in a Democratic Development Strategy

In order to develop this line of argument, this position that a social-programmes-led development strategy could be an effective policy of economic development, I will focus on the connections between education – or, more precisely, schooling or formal education – and the complex of factors that define democratic economic development. In the previous section, dealing with fiscal policy, the essential argument was that the fiscal system *could* manage an expansion of social programmes. Here the essential argument is *how* those social programmes – in particular, education – could be expanded to enhance democratic development. In the subsequent section, I will offer some brief remarks on other social programmes.

Education and economic growth It is widely taken for granted that education enhances economic growth, and it therefore should be easy to argue that education could play a leading role in any economic development strategy, democratic or otherwise. There are, however, two problems. First, the connection between education and economic growth is not nearly so clear as is often assumed (Ashton and Green 1996). Second, and not unrelated to the lack of a clear education–growth connection, 'education' is not one thing of which a society or individual has more or less. So in order to figure out the role of education in a democratic strategy, it is necessary to examine the education–growth link more fully and to clarify what education actually is, and to this end it will be useful to begin by clarifying the distinction between education and schooling (or formal education).

In general, economic analysis of the role of education fails to make this distinction, equating education with schooling and, in fact, measuring education – of an individual or a society – by years of schooling. This is, in particular, characteristic of the approach of human capital theorists (Theodore Schultz [1961] is a classic statement). Without attention to the distinction between education and schooling, it seems easy – indeed, it is deceptively easy – to understand why education makes people more productive. Education means the transmission of *knowledge, information and understanding*, and, for many analysts, it appears obvious that people who have knowledge, information and understanding will be more capable producers. (This approach, not incidentally, embodies the common prejudices that equate lack of formal education with ignorance and also with stupidity, when in fact unschooled people often are well informed about many things – though not the same things as the social scientists who write about them – and as smart as anyone else.)

What appears obvious, however, is sometimes false. To begin with, people who have knowledge, information and understanding are not necessarily the most productive workers. Whether or not they are the most productive depends on the social organization of their work. David Ashton and Francis Green summarize their argument along these lines as follows: 'it is incorrect to assume a linear and automatic connection between skill formation and economic performance … [The] link between skills and performance has to be seen in its social context. The context both influences the strength of the link, and helps to determine the variables of interest, especially the nature of skill' (Ashton and Green 1996: 3).

When, in particular, work is organized so that it is most effectively carried out by unquestioning obedience to authority and involves little or no decision-making on the part of the workers, workers who have knowledge, information and understanding are of little use and may actually be a hindrance to the smooth operation of the workplace. Furthermore, since schooling is quite clearly not the only way in which people obtain knowledge, information and understanding, the special contribution of schooling to people's productive capacities would not be clear even in so far as these traits did make one more productive. In peasant societies, people who have never been to school have extensive knowledge, information and understanding about their work. They are in this sense well educated. If people who have been to school are more productive than the people in these peasant societies, it is not simply because they are more educated though it may be because they are more schooled.

Part of the problem here is that, as I have indicated, education cannot be viewed as one thing, of which people have more or less. People in peasant societies are educated, but they are educated differently – that is, both through a different process and with a different substance than are people who go through many years of formal schooling. At the same time, formal schooling is not the same for all people, and the differences are not random, individual differences. In virtually all parts of the world the schooling received by the poor is different from the schooling received by the rich. It is different not simply in that the rich receive a 'better education' – that is, more knowledge, information and understanding. It is different in terms of the nature of what is learned and how it is learned (Carnoy and Levin 1985: esp. ch. 5).

In addition, while education means knowledge, information and understanding, it also means *socialization* and, as part of socialization, *behaviour*. In recognizing that people learn in systematically different ways, we are also recognizing that they are socialized differently, that they are taught to behave differently. Different ways of behaving have different economic implications, different implications with regard to the productivity of the people who have been educated. Furthermore, the productivity implications of the behaviour that is obtained (learned) through the education process (whether schools, families or other mechanisms) depend on the social organization of the workplaces in which the educated people will work. Returning to the general example cited above, where work is organized so that it is most effectively carried out by unquestioning obedience to authority and involves little or no decision-making on the part of the workers, we might conclude that workers' productivity would not be enhanced by greater knowledge, information and understanding, but that it would be enhanced by greater adherence to certain behavioural characteristics that can, and often are, inculcated through schooling – characteristics including, most obviously, unquestioning obedience to authority, but also such traits as punctuality, following directions, and working for goals external to the job itself. On the other hand, were the social organization of work to emphasize, for example, cooperative group interaction, problem-solving and independent decisions by workers, then workers' productivity would be enhanced when they had had an education (however achieved) that would develop the behavioural traits that correspond to this form of work organization.[1]

I have intentionally drawn the dichotomy sharply here. The sharp dichotomy should make the point clear: a person who is educated, perhaps very well, in a way that would make her or him a productive worker in one set of circumstances (one type of social organization of work) is not necessarily productive in different circumstances. For education to be effective (in the sense of enhancing productivity), there must be a *correspondence* between (1) what people learn through their education and the *way* they learn it and (2) what they will do and the *way* they will do it when they enter the workplace.

This 'correspondence principle' is developed by Samuel Bowles and Herbert Gintis (1976) in the context of a general analysis of education and work in capitalist society. They argue that the very nature of the employer–employee relationship in capitalist society demands a particular type of education, one which is characterized, if not by unquestioning obedience, then at least by a general acceptance by the employee of the employer's authority, by a willingness to accept the employer's decisions about how the work will be done, what will be produced and how the product will be used. The education that effectively shapes people to fit in to this type of work arrangement – what Bowles and Gintis see as a typical capitalist work arrangement – is not consistent with what they and most other commentators see as the most effective way to develop knowledge, information and understanding (to say nothing of the most effective way to develop well-rounded, liberated human beings).

The logic behind the correspondence principle is widely accepted, even while many other commentators do not share the views of Bowles and Gintis regarding the nature of work in capitalist society. Richard Murnane and Frank Levy (1996), for example, argue that in the United States, the nature of work demands the teaching of 'new basic skills' in order for there to be a productive workforce. In their view, work increasingly requires such traits as the ability to work in groups and solve problems, as well as higher levels of maths and verbal skills than have not typically been required in the past, and they advocate that schools adjust accordingly. That is, they advocate that education – both in its content and form – *correspond* to the needs of the workplace.

The correspondence principle provides some insights into the distinction between education and schooling. Schooling is a particular kind of education, a kind in which society (or some segment of society) has considerable choice over the character of the education that is provided. Thus the education attained through schooling can be chosen to correspond to economic needs. Education provided outside schooling may correspond to economic needs; for example, in a traditional peasant society, the education that children receive by working alongside their parents corresponds to economic needs. However, in societies where most people work in large enterprises, where they usually work as employees, where they are required with some frequency to adjust the ways they work (that is, to adapt to changing technology), traditional mechanisms of education outside schools (usually the home) generally cannot educate people as effectively as schools (when the measure of effectiveness is productivity).

When economists and others aver that education enhances people's productivity, they usually mean that schooling enhances people's productivity. The general reason this is true, in so far as it is true, is that what goes on in schools, in terms of both content and forms of social relations, corresponds to what goes on in the workplace. Therefore, there is no single answer to the question, What makes schools productive?, just as there is no single answer to the question, How are workplaces organized? Thus:

- When work demands rapid adaptation to new technologies, the productivity of schools will lie in their capacity for preparing people to adjust to new situations; this is partly a matter of behaviour and partly a cognitive issue. In their study of Indian agriculture during an era of change associated with the 'green revolution', Andrew Foster and Mark Rosenzweig (1996) find evidence that schooling enhanced farmers' productivity because it facilitated their adaptability to change. Schooling by its very nature – as an institution away from and different from the home – almost necessarily creates such adapting abilities relative to no-schooling (though we can easily imagine schools that would do a better or worse job with regard to the augmentation of such capabilities).
- When work is organized in a thoroughly hierarchical manner and involves a high degree of division of labour – such as in the low-wage assembly operations typical of export manufacturing in many countries – the productivity of schools will lie in their ability to develop such traits as discipline, perseverance, punctuality and adherence to orders. The rigid format of education and the system of rote learning employed in some schools can thus be functional from the perspective of creating workers who will perform well in highly structured, mass-production factories and offices. Studies by Richard Edwards (1976; 1977) and Samuel Bowles, Herbert Gintis and Peter Meyer (1975) illustrate the correspondence between traits valued by supervisors of large offices and traits rewarded in schools; perseverance, dependability, punctuality and empathy with orders are all valued positively and rewarded, while creativity and independence turn out to be negative traits.

- When work is based on teams that are required to identify and solve problems in a cooperative manner and each team member is expected to perform a variety of tasks, the productivity of schools will lie in their ability to inculcate group social skills, imaginative thinking, capacities for adjustment, and a level of literacy and numeracy necessary for the solution of technical problems. (Traits such as punctuality and perseverance are also relevant in this context, but their *relative* importance is not the same as in the sort of work organization described in the previous paragraph.) Success in teaching these traits is most likely to be achieved when classrooms are loosely organized, emphasis is placed on processes and explanations instead of simply on outcomes, and group work is encouraged. Murnane and Levy (1996) combine a set of studies of schools and of 'best practice' firms – that is, firms relying on team work, problem-solving and rapid adjustment – to argue that the same principles that guide the firms can also be effectively used to guide progress in schools. (Murnane and Levy's five principles are: ensure that all frontline workers understand the problem; design jobs so that all frontline workers have both incentives and opportunities to contribute to solutions; provide all frontline workers with the training needed to pursue solutions effectively; measure progress on a regular basis; and persevere and learn from mistakes; there are no magic bullets.)

Two comments must accompany this set of examples involving the connections between different systems of work organization and different ways in which schooling can affect workers' productivity:

First, in any society, work is carried out in a variety of ways, and the examples of the preceding paragraphs can coexist in the same society at the same time. Even when the great majority of workers must follow orders and perform well-defined tasks in a hierarchical setting, there are still many jobs requiring problem-solving, adjustment and group co-operation. Schools reflect this pattern, with different schools or different 'tracks' within individual schools educating students in different ways for different roles in the economy. While some schools are preparing people for the high-level jobs and others are preparing people for the low-level jobs, they all may be doing well in creating the traits that will make their students most productive in the social settings where they will work. When education is organized in this manner, as it often is, it may positively affect productivity but it also reproduces the existing social hierarchy and economic inequalities.

Second, these different examples move from the organization of work to the need for a correspondence in the organization of education. There is, however, no reason to believe that the causation must go in only this one direction. The organization of the educational system can affect the way work is organized. That is, choices about the organization of schools are a means by which to structure (or re-create) labour markets. Private, profit-maximizing firms make their decisions about work organization within the context of the existing availability of workers of different kinds. The relative availability of obedient and punctual workers, on the one hand, and creative and independent workers, on the other hand, will presumably affect the returns to different choices by employers. While such choices may have their impact only over a relatively long period, their impact is none the less real. (Moreover, there are possibilities for pushing the private sector in a desired direction – see Chapter 8.)[2]

All of this has substantial implications for the formulation of education initiatives in a democratic development strategy. These include:

- Education can have positive impacts on worker productivity and economic growth in various different ways, but the productive impact of education cannot be appraised and understood independently of the organization of work. Policies for education initiatives need to be formulated in conjunction with policies for the development of the organization of work.
- While affecting productivity and economic growth, education also affects other variables that define democratic economic development, in particular economic and social equality. Education for equality and education for growth may not be, but they clearly can be, in conflict with one another; the conflict will be all the greater in so far as work is organized in a highly stratified manner.
- Because the organization of work is largely a private sector concern, it is easy to take it as a given in the formulation of public sector policy in general and the formulation of social programmes in particular. Yet a democratic strategy, even while respecting the autonomy of the private sector and the technical constraints imposed by the need to allow profitability in the private sector, has numerous mechanisms for affecting the organization of work. Some of these are incentives that can shape the direction of technological progress (the 'high road' versus the 'low road' choice that will be discussed in Chapter 8). In addition, the structure of the education system itself affects the organization of work through the way it structures labour markets.

Education and the multiple aspects of democratic development The emphasis on education in a democratic development strategy cannot simply be a quantitative matter, a policy of expanding the existing schooling system in a country. Such expansion is a necessary part of a democratic programme, but, as the preceding discussion has suggested, the impact of education depends on the structure (that is, the qualitative nature) of the education system. Having discussed the education–growth connection in the previous section, I will turn attention in this section to the way education can affect the other aspects of a democratic development strategy. My argument will be essentially the same: the expansion of education (schooling) can be an important factor supporting the multiple aspects of democratic development, but the impact of education depends as much on the structure of the education system as on its size.

Education, basic needs and equality Regardless of its larger economic impact, education in and of itself is often defined as a basic need. Education as a basic need follows from both the knowledge–information–understanding definition of education or from the socialization–behaviour definition. In order to function reasonably in any society, people need to be educated in both these senses of the term. As education has increasingly become a function of the school system, this means that schooling has become a basic need. It is easy to understand how this view of education as a basic need has been readily accepted in societies where illiteracy has prevailed and where large segments of the population, especially those on the bottom economic and social tiers, have been denied access to schooling. Certainly people who are literate are better off in some fundamental sense (in a basic needs sense) than people who are illiterate, and the schooling necessary to attain universal literacy is thus an essential component in any economic development strategy that is 'for the people'.

As I have pointed out earlier in this book, however, basic needs are closely bound up with economic and social equality, and a principal way by which a democratic strategy aims at meeting basic needs is through promoting equality. The belief that the spread of formal schooling reduces inequality is probably as widely accepted as the belief that the spread of formal schooling enhances economic growth. Indeed, the two beliefs are connected. In so far as a public investment endows individuals with greater productive capacities, it can raise both their earning power and total output. If the spread of formal schooling means greater equality of education, then it should follow that the spread of schooling will bring about greater equality of earnings.

Yet for some of the same reasons that the connection between schooling and economic growth is not clear and unequivocal, the equalizing impact of the spread of schooling is also not automatic. The problem is most apparent in the very different systems of schooling that are provided to the rich and poor in most countries, with the poor not only receiving a worse education by most standards but also a different sort of education.

(The usual procedure of using years of schooling to measure education becomes especially absurd in the light of this reality.) If the spread of education means that the children of the poor are schooled in a manner that prepares them for work in those jobs where the prime requisites are punctuality, obedience and perseverance while the children of the wealthy are prepared for the jobs involving creativity, independence and initiative, one hardly needs a sophisticated statistical analysis to recognize that the impact of schooling is unlikely to be greater income equality. Therefore, in a democratic development strategy, it is not enough to expand the schooling system as a means to promote equality; it is also necessary to equalize the educational system itself and eliminate the connection between family income and the quality and type of education that people receive.

It should not be very surprising to recognize that for education to be equalizing, the education itself must be equal. Yet this is a point that is generally ignored in most discussions of the role of schooling in economic development strategies.

This said, when education is organized so that it does generate equality, the promotion of education can provide an entry point on an important virtuous circle linking education, equality and economic growth. I pointed out in Chapter 3 that evidence from East Asia, where several countries stand out among low-income countries on all of these measures, suggests the existence of cumulative causation, where education (schooling), equality and economic growth have positive impacts on one another. Education can be an effective key to the ignition of these positive circular processes because policy-makers can readily take initiatives that affect education relatively quickly and directly, while such opportunities for quick, direct initiatives are generally not available with regard to either growth or income distribution. Furthermore, education offers special opportunities for groups outside the state to implement initiatives and affect the education–equality–growth relationship.

Education and democratic participation The connection between education and democratic participation can also be viewed in terms of virtuous circles, and it is relatively easy to envision a two-way causation between the expansion of democratic participation and the expansion of education. Although schooling is clearly not a sufficient condition to assure democratic participation, it is probably a necessary condition in all but the simplest forms of social organization. People's ability to participate effectively in democratic processes – that is, people's power in democratic societies – depends in part on the knowledge, information and understanding they possess. Moreover, in the same way that democracy depends on a reasonable degree of equality in the distribution of income, it depends on a reasonable degree of equality in the distribution of education. If groups or individuals have a relative monopoly on knowledge, information and understanding, there is no reason to believe that power would be widely distributed, whatever the extent of democratic forms of organization. Also, education, as I have pointed out, confers behavioural traits as well as cognitive skills. For education to serve democracy, it must be organized in a way that generates widespread independence, creativity and self-confidence, as opposed to, for example, the unquestioning obedience to authority.

Concerning causation in the other direction, the expansion of democratic participation would tend to favour the expansion of education. In virtually all modern societies, education is a primary demand of democratic movements, and the popularity of education is easy to understand. In the first place, education is – for the reasons cited in the previous paragraph – viewed as a route to a share of power. In addition, as I noted earlier, while the connection between education and economic growth may be complex and unclear, the connection for the individual between education and wage levels is clear and substantial. Thus, when democratic movements have sought power – for example, the anti-colonial movements of the mid-twentieth century – the expansion of education has been one of their primary goals.

One can easily extend the mutual causation link between education and democracy to include equality, making a more thorough 'circle' of causation. Education offers a particularly good entry point, but this circle of causation can start at any point: greater equality provides a foundation for democratic power which in turn leads to the expansion of education; greater democratic power leads to the expansion of education which in turn generates greater equality; the expansion of education generates greater equality which in turn provides a foundation for democratic power.

Again, however, as with the education–growth link and the education–equality link, it needs to be emphasized that education per se is not an automatic route to democratic participation. As education can instil in people characteristics appropriate to the regime of a hierarchical workplace, it can prepare them to accept a hierarchical political system as well. In the same way that, if education is going to prepare productive workers there must be a correspondence between the organization of the workplace and the organization of the schools, a similar correspondence must exist between the organization of the schools and the organization of political life. With regard to its preparation of citizens as with its preparation of workers, the school system is seldom uniform and without contradictions. I doubt that in a democratic development strategy there would be uniform practices in the schools or that contradictions would be eliminated. The point, however, is that the requisite of a democratic strategy is not simply for *more* education, but for education that is consistent with the other goals of the strategy: democracy, equality, growth.

The Cuban literacy campaign of the early 1960s provides an interesting and complex example of direct participation in an education programme oriented towards basic needs. The campaign involved a large number of people as teachers in its implementation, with many urban students working to teach peasants how to read and write. The popular participation on which the campaign was based had a profound impact upon Cuba's political culture (Fagen 1969). However, while large numbers of people were involved in implementation and necessarily in the day-to-day decisions of implementation, the basic design and organization of the campaign did not involve such extensive participation and its democratic impact was therefore less thorough than it might have been.

Education and community Similarly, the structure of education has important implications for the strengthening of community. This is widely recognized and supplies a basic justification for the existence of public education – as opposed to simply public funding of education, which could be justified by the existence of the economic externalities involved in education (Levin 1987). The schools in a public education system, as primary mechanisms of socialization, are widely viewed as developing citizenship and providing the values that are the basis of social cohesion. The socialization that is provided by the schools is a matter of both substance and form (or structure). For example, in the realm of substance, a community can be strengthened when the schools teach students their common history.

In the realm of form or structure, the impact of schools on community depends very much on how a school system is organized and the extent to which it is integrated with the community. The most immediate issue of integration with the community is the way a school draws its students – from, for example, the immediate geographic surroundings (the neighbourhood) or from a larger area. A school may be integrated with the community even when it draws from a larger geographic area, for 'community' is not defined simply by physical proximity.

Schools, in fact, are an important element in defining communities because they create connections (bonds) among people through common, shared experiences and the establishment of a common set of knowledge and social practices. Interesting examples – negative, positive and complicated – appear particularly clearly when community is defined by race. In Fiji, for instance, where the ethnic Fijians dominate political life, there are separate schools for the ethnic Fijians and for the ethnic South Asians. This separation of the schools serves to perpetuate the division of the country's ethnic communities. Similarly, in US history, racial segregation of the schools served to define separate communities, white and black. In this latter case, the detrimental impact of segregation on black schools and black students notwithstanding, black schools were often an important positive force in defining black communities in the US South (Cecelski 1994).

Another aspect of the schools–community link is the extent to which members of the community (however defined) are directly involved in the governance of the schools. Most school reformers believe that when students' parents and other members of the community take active roles in various aspects of the schools' operations, the quality of education is likely to be improved (Ascher et al. 1996). These active roles can include everything from curriculum planning and hiring of teachers to fund-raising and planning of school social affairs. Part of the reason such involvement may improve the quality of the schools is that parents and other community members have knowledge and understanding of the problems, needs and abilities of the students that they bring into the schools, facilitating the work of the teachers and administrators. Perhaps more important, such connections to the community create a sense among students that the school is theirs, and this sense of 'ownership' provides a strong motivating factor that enhances education. (There is at least a potential conflict between a close school–community link and equality. On the one hand, local control of schools can be associated with local financing of schools, which in turn often generates substantial inequalities between localities. On the other hand, when equality is established by centralized funding, it can be accompanied by a centralized and bureaucratic educational system that tends to preclude local involvement.)

As this school–community link might be developed in ways that both improve the schools and strengthen the communities, it also has connections to other elements in a democratic development strategy. Most immediately, the direct participation that builds this link can also strengthen democracy itself, as people exercise power through this participation and also learn from experience how to exercise power. Similarly, issues of economic growth and equality can readily be connected to the school–community link. Again, we have a relationship that can be seen in terms of a virtuous circle, and, again, the particular virtuous circle can be seen to encompass a wide set of elements.[3]

Other Social Programmes and Democratic Development

In the same way that education could serve as an effective policy entry point on virtuous circles of democratic economic development, health-care and other social programmes – from public transport and infrastructure to public housing, from environmental repair and preservation to social security – can play similar, if not so broad, roles in a democratic strategy. All social programmes have the common characteristic that they expand the social wage and therefore can be a bulwark of equality and security. While equality and security are desirable ends in themselves, they also enhance the options that people have in their political lives. Options are the basis of power, and thus when social programmes expand the social wage they expand the basis for democracy and provide support for attaining other goals of democratic development. In addition, like education, other social programmes provide opportunities for direct community involvement in a country's economic development strategy. Such involvement can enhance the effectiveness of the individual programmes and the general strategy, create opportunities for expanding democracy and build community.

The potential of health-care programmes, in particular, appears to have a great deal in common with that of educational programmes. Both improved health-care and better schooling have always been principal demands of democratic movements; both can make significant contributions to economic growth; and both offer extensive opportunities for popular involvement in their design and implementation.[4] The opportunities for popular involvement in health-care programmes warrant special emphasis. In many low-income countries dramatic health improvements can be, and have sometimes been, attained through public health measures such as inoculation campaigns, improvement of water supplies and sewage control. These sorts of programmes can be successful with the limited involvement of doctors and other highly trained (and costly) personnel. While these efforts require some technical support, they can be carried out by relatively unskilled personnel working at the community level, especially when the community itself is mobilized to define and deal with its own needs. In fact, beyond the health gains attained by such programmes, the benefits of popular mobilization itself are of substantial value as part of a democratic strategy.

Programmes to serve women's health needs are an example of special importance. Women's health presents severe problems in poor regions of the world because of maternal mortality, complications associated with pregnancy and discrimination against women. Also, women's lack of control over family resources can aggravate women's health problems. At the same time that women's health-care problems are often severe, relatively rudimentary actions can lead to substantial improvements, and thus gains can be obtained for relatively little cost. As with the expansion of health-care programmes generally, the improvement of health-care facilities for women is a desirable end in itself and a serious need in most poor parts of the world. In the context of a democratic strategy, moreover, public health-care directed towards women could make additional contributions. It could directly contribute to economic and social equality because the focus of its impact would be the most health-care-deprived group: poor women (and girls). Also, because women play important roles in creating and maintaining community stability, any programme that improves the condition of and mobilizes women could have amplified impacts through its impact on community security.

In Kerala, a relatively poor state of India, widely recognized for its extensive social reforms, the gains achieved by women stand out, and much of Kerala's activity towards women centres on health-care (Franke and Chasin 1994). Within India (and as compared to many low-income countries) Kerala is distinguished as the only state where females outnumber males, an indicator of the attention to women's health (Dreze and Sen 1995). Jean Dreze and Amartya Sen (1989: 222) point out that the role of public support in Kerala's achievements 'has partly taken the form of extensive medical coverage of the population through public health services, helped by the determination of the population – much more educated than elsewhere in India – to seek medical attention'. Kerala's experience is a good indicator of the mutually reinforcing nature of a package of social reforms as, for example, literacy and education support health-care, and Kerala compares extremely well with other parts of India on a variety of measures of social well-being. Kerala provides evidence that it is possible to exploit virtuous circles among social programmes. (Kerala's economic growth record, however, raises some problems that will be addressed shortly.)

With regard to the connection between health-care programmes and programmes to preserve and repair the environment, there is more than virtuous circles; there is also a significant overlap. Environmental problems are often health problems, from depletion of the ozone layer to ineffective garbage and sewage disposal (Broad and Cavanagh 1993), and environmental programmes and health programmes can be one and the same. In addition, the mutually supportive virtuous circle connection between environmental programmes (or environment/health programmes) and other goals of a democratic strategy are also extensive.

As with health-care programmes, there appears to be a mutually supportive relation between programmes to protect and repair the environment and community security. It is widely believed that poverty, in the sense of a low level of income, is a cause of environmental degradation (as put forth in the Brundtland Report, WCED 1987; and World Bank 1992). Poor peasants, it is pointed out, often over-cultivate their land in order to survive, and, in their desperation for land, they sometimes are the destroyers of rain forests. More generally, it is alleged that poverty forces people to give high priority to matters of immediate survival and little attention to the longer-term concerns of environmental preservation. There is evidence, however, that it is not low income per se that brings the poor into conflict with the natural environment. In examining the relation of the poor to the environment in the Philippines, Robin Broad (1994) argues that when the rural poor live in stable communities and depend on the local natural environment for their livelihood, then they can become effective, politically active protectors of the environment. When, however, people's sense of 'permanence' is undermined, when, for example, people are forced to migrate, their relation to the environment has no long-term base. Their communities then lack security, and they often do come into conflict with the environment. The cause of the conflict with the environment is not low income, but a lack of community stability, a lack of a sense of 'permanence'.

This argument regarding the potentially mutually supportive relation between community stability and environmental protection is given further support by other experiences. In the Brazilian Amazon, for example, relatively poor independent rubber-tappers organized themselves in the 1970s and 1980s to preserve the rain forests, the basis of their livelihoods, from destruction by cattle ranchers. Although the short-run incomes of the rubber-tappers might have been improved by taking jobs clearing land for the ranches, their long-term and relatively stable relation to and dependence on the natural environment led them to political action as environmentalists (Mendes 1992). Another example of the connection between communities with 'permanence' and environmental protection arises in the case of the much publicized Monarch butterfly preserve in Mexico's state of Michoacan. The establishment of the preserve in 1986 threatened the traditional livelihood of some rural communities by limiting their use of forest resources. Although the reaction was not uniform, many communities responded with efforts to maintain their livelihoods through efforts to protect both the forests and the butterflies. In fact, some rural communities are using the newly appreciated aspect of their environment – the international interest in the Monarch butterfly – as a basis for explicit programmes of sustainable development (Barkin and Chapela y Mendoza 1995; and Barkin 1998). These experiences suggest a strong positive relation between the stability of local communities and political action that would preserve the environment. They provide good examples of the sorts of mutually supportive connections among social programmes, the virtuous circles, on which a democratic development strategy could build.

It is sometimes alleged, however, that, while the expansion of education and perhaps health-care can contribute to economic growth, the expansion of most other social programmes is in conflict with economic growth. For example, much can be made of the statistical analysis by Robert Barro (1991) that finds a negative association between government consumption and economic growth rates in a cross-country analysis (where 'government consumption' includes expenditure on many social programmes, though also expenditures on, for example, government bureaucracies). Barro's findings are consistent with analyses of 'populism' in Latin America that explain the weakness of populism with the argument that strategies focusing on the distribution of wealth – through the expansion of social programmes – undermine the creation of wealth (Dornbush and Edwards 1991). These sorts of analyses provide useful cautionary tales, but they do not rule out a positive connection between social programme expansion and growth any more than the general finding of a positive correlation (discussed in Chapter 3) between income equality and growth assures a positive connection between programmes of income equalization (social programme expansion, for example) and growth.

Experience in India's Kerala, however, presents some special problems for the argument that social programmes can provide a foundation for development in general and economic growth in particular. Kerala's social achievements are undeniable, especially in the realm of education (including general literacy) and health-care, and its various social programmes combined with land reform appear to have given Kerala minimal inequality in the distribution of income. Kerala's success is constrained by the state's low level of income; in 1991/92 Kerala's per capita state domestic product was 17 per cent below that for India as a whole. Most important, however, precisely at the time its social successes had become firmly established (and internationally recognized), its growth rate was very low, lagging far behind that for the rest of the country. In the 1980s, while India as a whole saw per capita domestic product rise at 3.1 per cent per year, Kerala's state per capita product rose at the meagre rate of 0.3 per cent per year (Dreze and Sen 1995: Table A.3).

There is an active debate over the causes of Kerala's poor economic growth performance and the extent to which the social successes themselves account for the low rate of economic growth – or, more precisely, the extent to which the form by which those social successes have been achieved accounts for the low rate of growth (Tharamangalam 1998; and BCAS 1998a and 1998b). Certainly there are other factors that contribute to an explanation of the state's poor growth record, including poor treatment by the central government of India (and the inherent difficulties of implementing social reforms in one state of one country in a global capitalist economy). Yet there are also factors in the Kerala experience that suggest a causal connection between the successes of the social programmes and the virtual failure in terms of economic growth. One of these, for example, is that the strong popular movements that have been the basis for the social successes do not provide the most attractive ambience for business investment; another is that the power of unions may create an inflexibility in state government, making it difficult to reduce bureaucratic ineptitude (to say nothing of corruption); and popular demands and the state's political structure (both bases for the successes of social programmes) have generated an educational system which, however large and successful at the basic levels, may be poorly connected to skill formation at the higher levels. While there is ample room for dispute over the causes of Kerala's slow growth, this experience calls into question the extent to which growth can be built on social programmes and belies any simplistic claim that the success of social programmes automatically generates growth.

Whether or not the general expansion of social programmes enhances economic growth depends, as does the education–growth relationship, on the way social programmes are constructed and on the particular social programmes that are expanded. As I have argued above, for example, it is not enough simply to expand the educational system. It is also important to consider the form that the education should take to make its most effective contribution to economic growth and, also, to give attention to the connection between the form of education and the structure of organization in productive enterprises. In the realm of public health expenditures some programmes (ones that would reduce the incidence of malaria, for example) might have substantial impact on productivity, while others (ones that would reduce the incidence of age-related heart disease, for example) might have little or no positive impact on growth. More broadly, health expenditures that are directed towards curing diseases would likely have lesser impacts – on both immediate social well-being and economic growth – than would equal expenditures on preventative programmes such as inoculation and clean water projects. (I hasten to add that programmes may be of great social value even when they make minimal contribution to economic growth, and there are plenty of non-growth reasons to care for and cure the ill and aged.) Similarly, in most circumstances public housing programmes are likely to have less of a positive impact on growth than would programmes involving equivalent expenditures but directed towards the expansion of the transportation infrastructure (while both programmes might have similar direct employment impacts). Yet in some circumstances – a situation where the lack of adequate housing is a prime factor in generating social instability – public housing expenditures could be an important, if not essential, foundation for economic growth.

All social programmes have a dual and potentially contradictory impact on worker productivity. On the one hand, because they provide security and income (the social wage), an extensive system of social services can undermine workers' efforts in so far as those efforts are based on a coercive incentive system. If work is organized in a hierarchical manner, with tight control over workers by supervisors and rigid discipline, effective social services are likely to undermine productivity by weakening the force of coercive incentives. On the other hand, when social programmes are part of a system where work is organized on the basis of shared decision-making and positive incentives, the security they provide can enhance workers' efforts and raise productivity. In general, the impact of social programmes on productivity, however complex, is tied to the way work is organized. This is an issue that will be developed more fully in Chapter 8, dealing with 'shaping the private sector', when I examine the distinction between the 'high road' and the 'low road' of technological organization.

Social programmes are not something apart from the more general organization of economic activity. A development strategy may be defined by its emphasis on social programmes, but it cannot be defined *solely* by that emphasis. Even the best shaped social programmes (in terms of their impact on productivity) are likely to have limited impact on economic growth unless the strategy also contains explicit consideration of growth-generating policies. The macroeconomic framework discussed in the previous chapter is one set of such policies, and the means to shape the private sector discussed in the next chapter are another.

In any case, it is useful to recognize – and practice would suggest that it is not as obvious as it seems – that the expansion of social programmes does not necessarily lead to economic growth, or, for that matter, to other desirable ends. Seemingly well-motivated economic development programmes in many parts of the world provide examples of roads that are built without allowances for future maintenance or school buildings and medical centres that are constructed only to remain unstaffed and insufficiently supplied. Public officials are often under pressure to 'do something' and the political costs of doing something that has no long-run positive impact on economic growth are minimal. Such experiences are often used as evidence in the argument against a heavy role for government social programmes in a development strategy.

At the same time, the expansion of social programmes is an essential part of a democratic development strategy, and the challenge for such a strategy thus becomes one of finding ways to construct social programmes that avoid the débâcles sometimes associated with government projects. One way to reduce the likelihood that social projects will be economically wasteful, a way especially appropriate within the context of a democratic development strategy, is to implement such projects in a democratic manner. Instead of designing and deciding upon projects through central ministries, the locus of authority could be shifted downwards. Moreover, decision-making processes concerning social projects need not be confined to traditional political processes, but could include extensive opportunities for direct participation by the people who would be affected. Such participation could have multiple benefits, including the assurance that the projects would be serving a perceived need by the beneficiaries and increasing the likelihood that local resources would be provided to complement any central expenditures. Directly participatory democracy is not a panacea, but it can be a strong antidote to bureaucratic processes. It also has value in itself.

There are other ways to reduce, if not avoid, the inefficiency often associated with government 'consumption' expenditures. For example, the extremely rapid expansion of social programmes is likely to be inefficient and thus counter-productive in the long run. The binding constraint on public investment is often one of organizational capacity, and when funds are expended without regard to organizational capacity they have limited positive impact. Also, consistent with the principle of local participation in the planning and implementation of projects, local responsibility can help assure the reduction of waste. When funds for a new school building are provided wholly by the central authorities, there is minimal pressure on local authorities to make sure the building is both necessary and will operate effectively. When, however, the central authority's role, both in planning and financing, is more limited, there is greater pressure on local authorities to ensure efficiency. These sorts of procedures go back to the 'common sense' criterion cited towards the end of Chapter 5. It would seem that there is no way to ensure 'common sense', however, without some mechanism of accountability. Those who oppose a large role for social programmes view the market as the only mechanism by which to ensure this accountability. The suggestion here is that democracy can also be such a mechanism.[5]

Notes

1. In practice, the same workplace can be characterized by a complex of contradictory characteristics, with employers demanding both initiative and conformity from their employees. Consider, for example, the following from a *Business Week* article (28 March 1994) describing a new training initiative and the organization of work at Motorola, a firm that *Business Week* describes as a model of responsiveness, adaptability and creativity: 'The goal [at Motorola] is a workforce that is disciplined yet free-thinking. The initiative will aim to inculcate them with company procedures so they're a well oiled machine but also to develop the knowledge and independent-mindedness that Motorola will need to conquer rapidly changing technologies and markets.'

2. Martin Carnoy and Henry Levin (1985) argue that the schools offer an entry point that can be used to effect democratic change in the entire economy. Their focus is on the United States, where work in the private sector is thoroughly undemocratic but the schools are subject to substantial democratic intervention. They argue that by

changing what goes on in schools in a democratic direction, there are possibilities for influencing change in the organization of work as well. While their explanation of the change does not focus on the relative availability of different kinds of labour (as above), the argument is similar and parallel.

3. In this section, I have not tried to develop links between education (or schools) and the environmental issues that are part of democratic development. I expect there are such links, having to do at least with the importance of equality and stability, which a 'good' educational system helps build, as foundations for environmental preservation.

4. Until fairly recently, there was only weak empirical support for the claim that health-care has a causal role in raising productivity. According to John Strauss and Duncan Thomas (1998), who provide an extensive review of relevant studies, however, this causal role of health-care is now relatively clear, especially in low-income settings.

5. The multiple values of democracy, including its value in promoting a more effective operation of the state, is recognized by James Boyce and his colleagues (1996) in the context of developing economic policy for post-war El Salvador. Also, Dreze and Sen remark: 'The quality of governance ultimately relates, to a considerable extent, to the practice of domestic politics and to "public action" in the broad sense of action *by* the public (rather than just *for* the public, by the government)' (Dreze and Sen 1995: 190).

8

Democratic Development and the Shaping of Private Activity

Simple dichotomies are appealing. Pure 'good' versus pure 'evil' is enshrined in fairy tales, and, perhaps with no more connection to reality, public activity is often counterposed to the private sector as the foundation of social analyses. Social programmes, as I have discussed them in the previous chapter, are the principal initiatives of a democratic economic development strategy, and they are certainly public. Their importance as a foundation for democracy is relatively clear and direct, and the extent of their expansion in a democratic strategy would be considerably greater than that which is envisioned (let alone implemented) in other development strategies. Nevertheless, a strategy based on social programmes should not be counterposed to a strategy involving a substantial role for the private sector. Social programmes alone cannot form an economic development strategy. A democratic strategy also requires a clear set of policies towards the private sector.

All development strategies embody policies that structure and affect the direction of private economic activity. The difference between a democratic strategy and a neo-liberal strategy is not that the former involves the state in managing the economy while the latter 'relies on the market' to manage the economy. Even in a thoroughly market-dominated economy, the state manages private economic activity, both by establishing and enforcing rules that structure markets and by direct interventions – including taxing and spending practices – that favour particular private actors and groups of private actors. (As I argued at length in Chapter 4, markets do not exist outside government policy, and the slogan of 'leaving things to the market' is simply a slogan, not a prescription for policy.) So what distinguishes a democratic strategy is not *that* the state manages the economy, but the *way* that the state manages the economy.

Some Principles for Directing the Private Sector

In a market-dominated economy, society is organized as 'an adjunct to the market', to use Karl Polanyi's formulation. Social goals are then subordinated to the need of private individuals and groups to use the market to make profits, to enrich themselves. In the sort of democratic economic development strategy I am describing here, capitalism still exists, markets operate and the private sector still plays a large role. Policies for directing the private sector, however, are guided by the principle that markets are instruments to pursue social goals, and the object of the policies is to structure markets accordingly. Capitalists will still seek to enrich themselves, and some will succeed, at least in relative terms. Within a democratic strategy, however, their actions would be constrained and guided by policy so as to assure, in so far as possible, that in enriching themselves they would be contributing to larger social goals. (Ever since Adam Smith, advocates of liberal economic policy have maintained that it is precisely by each individual pursuing her or his own well-being through a market system that the well-being of society at large is advanced. The invisible hand is supposed to ensure this fortuitous outcome if capitalists, and everyone else, work to enrich themselves. This argument, however, defines the well-being of society at large simply in terms of maximizing market output. Even then it is a deeply flawed argument – and Adam Smith, unlike his followers, recognized many of the argument's limitations. When social goals are defined more broadly, as they must be in a democratic development strategy, the liberal argument completely falls apart.)

Policies that are designed to constrain and guide capitalists so that their actions will serve social goals are policies that involve considerable tension. Capitalists as capitalists will not embrace policies that subordinate their profit-making to larger social interests, even when as private individuals they believe in those social interests. There will be continual tension (overt and covert political conflicts) between society's efforts to implement state policies that subordinate private profit-making – the operation of the market – to social ends and capitalists' efforts to pursue their profit-making with a set of policies that provide them with maximum support and, willy nilly, subordinate social ends. There is, for all practical purposes, no way to eliminate this tension, and it seems best to recognize it as a first step in the formulation of policy to shape the private sector.

The existence of tensions in the formulation of policy to shape the private sector is most apparent in the creation of incentives designed to encourage certain decisions by business. Such incentives have a long history in capitalist economies in the form, for example, of tax holidays and tax credits designed to encourage certain kinds of investments or simply to increase the overall level of investment. The owners of businesses benefit directly from these incentives, and the rest of society is supposed to benefit from a 'trickle down' effect as more investment generates more economic growth, more jobs and more income. These sorts of incentives often, however, involve considerable pay-offs to business and minimal social benefit. The extreme case occurs when business does what it would have done without the incentive, receives the incentive, and society obtains nothing that it would not otherwise have obtained; the result is no increment to growth and a more unequal distribution of income. Leaving aside the extreme cases, however, the distributional implications of such investment incentives are always problematic. Their direct and immediate impact raises profits, while their impact in terms of incomes for the rest of society (or in terms of other gains for the rest of society) are indirect and long term. Such a sequence of events can result in a more equal distribution of income in the long run, if, for example, the employment-creating effects of the new induced investment increase the bargaining power of workers. The result can also be to exacerbate inequalities, and this is certainly how investment incentives are widely perceived. Perceptions of policies' impacts are themselves important, for perceptions affect the extent to which those policies can gain popular support. Popular support, as I have argued in Chapter 5, is a prerequisite for a democratic development programme because the implementation of a democratic programme must be democratic.

These considerations imply that any incentives offered to business should have clear, identifiable benefits for society at large – clear, identifiable connections to the goals of democratic development. Government authorities should tend to rule out broad, general incentives to business. Tax incentives directed towards, for example, simply raising the level of investment (nationally or in a particular region) might serve long-run social interests, but their positive impacts would tend not to be clear and identifiable. (Also, such incentives often do not serve long-run social interests.) Instead, when government does offer incentives to business, they should be focused in ways that yield clear social gains. This approach will not eliminate the tensions involved in the formulation of policies to direct the private sector, but it may help contain those tensions and help assure the primacy of social goals. I will offer specific examples shortly.

The tensions inherent in using incentives to work through markets to regulate the private sector also arise when the incentives are negative, as with taxes that are imposed to proscribe (or limit) imports of certain products or eliminate (or reduce) environmentally destructive activity. Here the problems appear to be different, since the immediate impact is a cost, not a benefit, to business. Yet the issues are largely the same because a negative incentive on one activity is an implicit, relative positive incentive for substitute activities. In the case of import duties, the benefit to the domestically competing businesses is fairly clear. In other cases – those involving taxes on environmentally destructive activities, for example – the implicit beneficiaries might not be so readily apparent, but they are none the less real. When costs are imposed on one means of meeting consumers' demands, those who would meet the demands in other ways gain. None of this is necessarily a 'bad thing'. Indeed, it is often a good thing, and precisely the object of policy, to promote new, alternative ways to meet consumers' demands. Yet it always needs to be recognized that in a market economy these demands will generally be met by private producers, and this means that certain businesses will reap positive gains (and enrich themselves) from the negative incentives. As with positive incentives, the tension cannot be eliminated, but it is likely to be handled most effectively when the incentives are focused and their relation to social goals is clear.

The indirect impacts of negative incentives are only a special case of a larger problem associated with any effort to regulate a market economy, namely that regulations have numerous indirect and sometimes distant effects that can be of substantial importance. Some of these are relatively obvious, as is the case with the direct negative employment impacts of regulations designed to curtail environmentally destructive activity (the reduction of logging and various kinds of agriculture in rain forests, for example). Others are more subtle, as is the case when tax incentives for export-processing industries shift the demand for labour in ways that upset traditional communities, undermine the production of agricultural staples and alter gender relationships. The point here is not that all of these indirect impacts are 'bad'. Most of us who would advocate a democratic development strategy might, for example, favour the shifts in gender relationships that often come with the promotion of export processing. Nevertheless, complications arising from the indirect impacts of incentive policies and other forms of regulation are one of the general dangers that come from efforts to control private activity.

There is nothing particularly noteworthy in recognizing the sorts of problems that can arise from the indirect impacts of regulatory policies. Economists are fond of pointing out that everything is connected to everything else, and private actors' responses to policy incentives can lead to unintended and sometimes perverse results. It is worth invoking these points and recognizing that policy should proceed from analyses directed towards identification of indirect as well as direct impacts, but this amounts to no more than an injunction that policy should be based on 'common sense'. There are at least two ways, however, that we might move beyond the traditional concept of common sense in these matters:

- *Popular participation* in the formulation of policy, which is important because it promotes democracy (and in this sense is a good thing in itself), can also be useful because it can help identify and force into consideration the complex and indirect impacts of government policies. People know things, and in some realms of policy the knowledge provided by popular participation is especially important. Perhaps the best example is in environmental policy – or, more generally, in assessing the environmental impacts of any policy. Indigenous peoples and farmers often have knowledge about local environments that provides an essential part of any analysis of policy impacts. Also, in understanding the impacts of policies on the structure of communities, the knowledge of people in those communities can be very valuable. The importance of popular participation in policy formulation, however, is not simply a matter of knowledge, but is also a matter of power. Formal mechanisms for popular participation provide a means by which various groups whose interests are affected by a policy can make their voices heard, both positively and negatively: people whose livelihoods would be affected, for example, by the implementation of new foreign trade regulations (or by elimination of existing regulations), those whose employment is affected by environmental policy, communities that feel the impact of new infrastructure investments. The voices expressing the interests of affected groups can be overridden, but, when there are mechanisms for those voices to be heard, it is less likely they will be ignored (Campen 1986).

- *Experimentation*, prior to any general implementation, can serve to reveal the impacts of policy more thoroughly than the most sophisticated formal analyses. When policies generate unforeseen negative consequences, experimentation can dramatically reduce the social cost and may allow the reformulation of policy. With regard to policies that have environmental impacts, literal disasters can be avoided through experimentation and incremental implementation. Even in the mundane realm of policies that create tax incentives for businesses to develop technology (of the type that will be discussed below, for example), experimentation – that is, implementation on a limited scale accompanied by appraisal of the impacts – could be extremely valuable. Likewise, in transforming agricultural production and rural social organization, where a democratic strategy would probably support various forms of cooperative organization, costly errors could be avoided were new programmes confined to small regions. (The same logic that calls for experimentation should make one leery of very large-scale projects, the very nature of which prevents experimentation. Large water control projects are a prime example. They have often been undertaken with promises of huge economic gains, but their most obvious impacts have sometimes been huge social costs. The popular opposition that has emerged to these large-scale water control projects – for example, in India – both illustrates the problem and underscores the importance of formal mechanisms that would assure popular participation.)

Finally, in considering the basis for shaping private sector activity, we should keep in mind that there are limits on the extent to which the private sector can be bent to the dictates of a democratic strategy. Businesses exist to make a profit, and regulations that eliminate that profit, however desirable their ends, will eliminate the businesses. Private business may not be the goose that lays golden eggs for us, as it is portrayed in neo-liberal fairy tales, but it might be likened to the mundane chicken that supplies our real eggs each morning for breakfast. We can do well by controlling our chicken, by regulating its diet and fencing it in. But if we insist that our chicken get its sustenance from the field, saving us money on feed, then we may have to start looking for another source of breakfast food. Excessive regulation can have substantial costs.

Also, even when the private sector continues to exist under heavy regulations, the regulations can pervert its operations to such a degree that they become counter-productive. Regulation will lead private actors to give less effort to production and, instead, to devote their efforts to finding ways to manipulate those regulations to make a profit. This is often called 'rent-seeking behaviour' because profits are obtained by positioning oneself in relation to a law rather than by productive activity, as a landlord's income comes from the position he or she holds rather than from any production. When businesses are regularly adding accountants and lawyers to their payrolls instead of production workers, there is a problem.

Society should attempt to structure and regulate markets so as to control the behaviour of private business because otherwise business will generally fail to provide most effectively for social needs. Nevertheless, there is no assurance that all will be well when society controls private actors through the government. There are 'government failures' as well as 'market failures'. While direct popular participation and strong democratic institutions can be effective devices to limit government failure, our reaction to neo-liberalism and an aversion to market failures should not drive us into a situation where we create a fertile ground for government failures.

Pushing towards a Technological 'High Road'

In Chapter 5, I asserted that economic development involves a change in the way production takes place, a change in technology, that allows greater output per amount of labour time. While this is not a controversial statement, it is incomplete. Technological change is not a straightforward, well-defined process, and there are different ways that progressive changes (changes that raise output per amount of labour time) in the organization of production might be accomplished. To provide a crude but telling example from the realm of industrial activity: progressive technological changes can be accomplished by mass-production assembly-line techniques, with managers exercising tight control of the activities of workers; and progressive technological change can also be accomplished by organizing production in teams, where workers are expected to cooperate, develop their own methods of operation and play a significant role in decision-making. These different modes of technology, which can both bring about expansions of output, have very different implications for wage levels and income distribution. In general, in poorer countries today, assembly-line mass-production techniques are coupled with low wages, as is the case, for example, in the *maquiladoras* along the US–Mexican border or in shoe and garment production in Indonesia, export-oriented manufacturing in which the labour force is largely female. (In the history of the advanced countries mass production sometimes emerged along with high wages in the pattern of classical Fordism, but different labour market conditions and the export-orientation of much manufacturing has undermined the likelihood of this pattern emerging in today's poor countries.) A pattern of team production, which to date has had little application in manufacturing in low-income countries, offers possibilities for higher wages and a more equal distribution of income. Beyond the issue of wages and income distribution, these different methods of work organization have impacts on broader aspects of social relations and political power and, through their different impacts on social relations and political power, different implications for a whole range of other social variables.

These examples of different modes of technological progress are representative of two different routes of economic change that are often referred to as the 'low road' and the 'high road'. David Gordon offers the following defining comment:

> The 'high road' seeks to build economic growth and prosperity through cooperation and strong worker rewards, including relatively rapid real wage growth. The 'low road' relies on conflict and insecurity, control and harsh worker punishments, and often features relatively stagnant or even declining real wage growth. Both are coherent strategies, both can conceivably work. (Gordon 1996: 144)

The high road and low road concepts of technological change and economic development are not so much descriptions of entire economies as they are characterizations of directions of change and, particularly important here, of the tendencies of economic policy. The fact that each can in some sense 'work', at least in the sense of bringing about rising output per unit of labour time and economic growth, makes them useful concepts around which to understand policy alternatives. (Gordon, as is the case with most authors who use the high road, low road distinction, is concerned with economic organization in the advanced countries. The application of this distinction in the analysis of low-income countries is not well developed, as the high road is at most a marginal mode of organization in these regions of the world.)

A high road approach to work organization – that is, a high road approach to technology – can 'conceivably work' because it raises output per unit labour time by providing strong positive incentives to workers in the form of payments and quality of work-life. Also, implicit in the high road is a heavy reliance on the development of workers' skills – not simply in the sense of proficiency at particular technical tasks, but skills in the sense of the ability to make decisions about one's work and the ability to engage in group tasks. Thus the technology of the high road is to a large extent embodied in workers. The formation of the high road skills, the embodiment of technology in workers, is a complex process, involving considerable education and training. There is good reason to believe that considerable education and training can 'conceivably work' as a means to help bring about economic development. In addition, as I have pointed out in Chapter 7, there needs to be a correspondence between the nature of education and the way in which work is organized. So a high road does not just imply the need for extensive education and training, but for education and training of a particular kind.

As Gordon points out, however, a low road approach to technology can also 'conceivably work'. The negative incentives, tight discipline and heavy supervision of the low road can also elicit rising output per unit of labour time and economic growth; and the low road demands the development of workers' skills, both technical and behavioural skills. Yet on the low road, decisions about the work process are thoroughly dominated by management, and regulation of work is top-down and often effected through the use of machinery – the assembly line being the classic example. In this sense, the technology of the low road is largely embodied in capital, both in the sense of owners (and their manager representatives) and in the sense of machinery. Adherence to the demands of this sort of work organization and the development of the technical proficiency involved in mass-production techniques also require that workers undergo education and training. The educational and training demands of low road technology, however, are considerably less than those of the high road. Equally important, the type of education and training that corresponds to the low road is very different from that of the high road.

Whether or not a particular society has its economy organized on a high road towards economic change or a low road depends on a number of historical factors. The characteristics of the labour force, the nature and extent of the schooling system, the patterns of labour–management relations, the extent of the social welfare system, the role of foreign trade, and the types of products that are most important in the society's economy are all factors that play roles in shaping the direction of change and are all factors that have emerged through long processes of historic evolution. Nevertheless, there is a considerable role for policy in affecting each of these factors, and in this sense policy can affect whether or not the direction of a society's economic development is along a high road or low road of technological change.

It is readily apparent that a democratic economic development strategy is necessarily associated with high road technology. Although both the high road and the low road might achieve success with regard to economic growth, only the former is consistent with the broader set of goals that define democratic development. When, for example, technology is embodied in workers and incentives depend on relatively high wage rates, greater income equality is one part of the outcome. When people are involved in decision-making in their work, they are better prepared to participate actively in all spheres of society. Also, a school system that prepares people for a high road mode of technology is likely to be a school system that is more egalitarian and that prepares people for political participation. The implications for policy towards the private sector are relatively clear: policy should be organized so as to push private decision-makers towards technological choices that move towards a high road of development.

Another way of saying the same thing, a way that incorporates the argument of Chapter 4 regarding the social construction of markets, is that policy should be designed to construct markets in ways that move society towards a technological high road. Important parts of this task have been given attention earlier in Chapter 7. The heavy role of social programmes in a democratic development strategy effects changes in the distribution of income and broader aspects of social relations (power relations) in ways that are likely to induce private decision-makers to opt for the sort of work organization that defines the high road. Also, the extensive development of schooling, especially the type of schooling that would be favoured in a democratic strategy, would affect the characteristics of the labour force in ways that would push towards the high road. There are many other ways that markets can be shaped so as to encourage movement in this same direction, and two will be given attention here: focused investment incentives that push private firms towards the high road, and regulation of foreign trade that supports high road technology. (A caveat is necessary: to push private decision-makers along a high road is not at all the same thing as imposing particular technologies – particular modes of work organization – on private enterprises, not at all the same thing as, for example, proscribing assembly-line production in favour of production through teams. By 'pushing' the private sector, I mean using policy to shape markets in ways that will, while maintaining the realm of choice that typically exists for capitalist firms, raise the likelihood that firms will make certain choices. As I have emphasized in defining the sort of strategy I am describing here, we are dealing with a market economy in which capitalists maintain their prerogatives about investment decisions; the problem is one of shaping the context of and thus affecting the direction of those decisions.)

Focused investment incentives As I have suggested in Chapter 7, changes in the labour market, as it is affected by social programmes generally and schools in particular, create powerful incentives for private firms to move towards a high road technology. The connection between labour supply and choice of technology, however, is limited. Labour supply affects employers' choices through its impact on wage rates, but for a number of reasons wage rates do not change very quickly. Wage rates of highly educated workers tend not to fall very quickly as the relative supply of such workers rises, and wage rates of poorly educated workers tend not to rise very quickly as the relative supply of these workers declines. Thus it may take a long time before private employers have sufficient incentive to shift towards technologies that use more highly educated labour even when the relative supply of highly educated labour is rising substantially. In addition, even when relative wage rates do shift, the introduction of more sophisticated technologies (technologies that use more educated labour) does not follow quickly. The introduction of new technologies usually requires new investments in plant and machinery, all of which take time. Therefore, simply to ensure that there are employment opportunities consistent with the abilities of a more highly educated workforce, a democratic strategy needs to complement its initiatives in education and other social programmes with initiatives that would give the private sector a focused push towards more rapid technological change.

One mechanism by which to give the private sector this push would be the introduction by the government of a 'training-for-jobs' programme. In such a programme, the government sponsors training programmes that would give workers the specific skills needed by an investor; in return the investor would agree to provide employment for these newly trained skilled workers. The arrangement would be similar to, but more focused than, other forms of investment incentives, such as tax holidays or tax credits for capital investments. Here the incentive would be the provision of a labour force trained to meet the investor's needs; it would thus lower unit labour costs for the investor without the investor undertaking the costs (and risks) involved in training. In return for this incentive, the investor would be contributing to a structural shift in the technological composition of industry towards a high road.

Training-for-jobs incentive programmes are widely used by state governments in the United States. Many of these state government programmes have played a role in efforts to attract European and Japanese investors in recent decades. However, some programmes emerged well before the influx of foreign investment to the United States, such as the state of Georgia's 'Quick Start' programme that began in 1967. These programmes vary a good deal in the way they operate. Some, such as the Texas 'Smart Jobs Fund Programme', supply training grants to employers who then design and control the training process. Others, such as the Georgia programme and a programme in South Carolina, use networks of technical schools and community colleges to do the training (Sellers 1990; Harrison 1993; and Froiland 1993).

A training-for-technology programme has a special advantage over many other investment incentive schemes: if the investor does not survive, the workers – and through them the society – still have the skills in which they have been trained. In describing the success of South Carolina in attracting new investment, the *Financial Times* notes: 'Training ... is one of the few incentives that has no controversy attached. Generous tax abatements and other such give-aways are sometimes viewed as virtually "buying" a company's investment. But tax dollars spent on training are considered well-spent. The state gains more and better trained workers, who are an asset even if that company moves away' (Harrison 1993). Though some skills are highly industry-specific or even firm-specific, most skills have a large transferable component. Moreover, even if the skill per se is not transferable, the process of learning, regardless of its content, almost necessarily generates an important skill, namely the capacity to develop new behavioural and cognitive traits (that is, the capacity to learn).

A second policy mechanism that could push the private sector towards a technological high road is the levy-grant system that exists in many countries (but is often used ineffectively). A small tax (for example, 1 or 2 per cent of earnings) would be imposed on all firms (the levy), but firms implementing training programmes that would raise the technological level of their operations would receive a rebate (the grant) of the tax. Such a programme is readily justified by the divergence between private and public gains that accrue from firms' training programmes. Its implementation would have the advantages of leaving the operation of training programmes in the hands of the private sector, thereby minimizing the bureaucratic burden on government, and of not involving any new commitment of government funds.

In its 1997 'Green Paper' on 'Skills Development Strategy for Economic and Employment Growth in South Africa', the South African Ministry of Labour proposes the implementation of a levy-grant system that would impose a levy of a 1.5 per cent payroll tax. The Minister of Labour notes that the levy 'spreads the cost of training across all firms. Firms which do not train contribute to the costs of training carried out by others. And this is as it should be because these firms benefit indirectly when they recruit skilled labour from the labour market' (Mboweni 1997). He might also have justified the tax on these non-training firms by pointing out that, by the methods of work organization they choose, they are failing to create positive technological externalities that have long-run social benefits.

The problems with existing levy-grant systems are largely political. Sometimes the programmes exist in name only, and the funds from the tax are 'raided' for various other uses. Also, and of special importance here, representatives of workers' organizations generally and employers often are not involved in the development and operation of the programmes, having no say on such matters as the legitimate training uses for the funds or how training will be organized. Thus, part of what is needed to make levy-grant programmes work is their incorporation within a general democratic strategy – a strategy where those immediately affected by policies have a direct involvement in their development and operation. (See World Bank 1996b; and ILO 1993, for discussion of some of these issues in the specific context of Indonesia.)

Training-for-jobs and levy-grant programmes are two examples of policies that would help shape the activities of the private sector in a way that would support a democratic development strategy. The programmes would build upon the social programmes that are at the base of the strategy, and, by pushing the private sector towards the technological high road, would further the general goals of the strategy. In addition, they offer opportunity for and their effectiveness could be enhanced by extensive participant involvement in their design and operation. While there are surely other programmes that could also accomplish these ends, my purpose here has been only to provide illustrations of specific mechanisms that would shape markets and push the private sector in ways that would advance democratic development.

Controlling foreign trade In Chapter 2, I argued that a country's economic development, whether defined in terms of democratic development or in a more conventional manner, is most effectively achieved by some substantial government regulation of foreign trade. A considerable body of historical experience supports this position, as does an examination of causal links that lie at the base of economic change. Of special importance, protection of domestic industry from foreign competition has often been an essential feature promoting technological progress. Coupled with education and training, other social programmes and focused incentives of the sort discussed above, regulation of foreign trade could be useful in pushing economic activity towards a technological high road. A recognition of the desirability of regulating foreign trade, therefore, is one of the bases for policies towards the private sector in a democratic strategy.

Nevertheless, there are several problems that can and often do arise in efforts to regulate international trade and investment in ways that would promote economic development. Here I will focus my comment on those problems:

To begin with, *regulation of foreign commerce can be costly*. In general, such regulation involves the protection of domestic producers from foreign competition, usually through a tariff or quantitative restriction on an import. This protection allows a relatively high-cost domestic producer to compete with foreign producers, and the high-cost is reflected in the price of the protected good. The protection is justified if the domestic production activity generates sufficient positive social results not captured through the market – for example, the location of specific technological externalities discussed in Chapter 2. The costs involved in protection can thus be viewed as the costs of an investment, an investment in the development of technology (or some other social benefit). As with any other investment, regulation of foreign trade is reasonable only if it is based on a comparison of the benefits and costs and if the former exceeds the latter.

In the same sense that there would be no justification in undertaking a particular investment because 'investment is necessary for economic growth', there would be no justification for a particular tariff or quantitative restriction on imports simply because 'regulation of foreign commerce is necessary for economic growth'. A particular action requires a particular justification. Measuring benefits and costs of foreign commerce regulation is difficult, involving as it does the estimation of the gains from expected technological change, other social benefits and indirect as well as direct costs. The problems are further complicated by the distributional impacts of such regulation, as the benefits and costs are generally borne by different people. Benefit–cost analysis is none the less an essential basis for government actions in any democratic programme, and is especially important when, as is the case with trade regulation, there are substantial opportunities for the narrow interests to affect the decision-making process (about which, more shortly).

One of the benefits of applying benefit–cost analysis to regulatory decisions is to ensure that those decisions are reasonable in the sense that their benefits exceed their costs. In addition, benefit–cost analysis can facilitate democratic oversight because it both requires an explicit statement of the gains and losses associated with the regulations and establishes a formal process by which regulations are enacted (or maintained). The former provides bases on which the public can judge the validity of the regulations and the latter can provide the mechanism by which the public can be heard in the decision-making process. Thus, democratic exposure can become a means by which wasteful – that is, high-cost – regulations of foreign trade might be contained. (Benefit–cost analysis can also be used to remove decisions from democratic oversight by turning the consideration of those into purely analytic exercises to be carried out by experts; on this whole issue, see Campen 1986.)

Aside from the issue of their costs, *protectionist measures do not necessarily yield technological advances.* Often an important part of the justification for a particular foreign trade regulation is the expectation that, in some reasonable period of time, the high-cost domestic producer will become a low-cost producer as it attains economies of scale and reaps the gains of learning-by-doing. (In terms of the benefit–cost analysis, this expectation greatly lowers the costs of the regulation.) Yet, while this justification has been widely used in the form of the 'infant industries argument' to support protectionist measures, it is quite clear that the transition from high-cost to low-cost production does not take place automatically but requires some sort of pressure; also, even when production costs decline, lower costs do not automatically lead to lower prices. Consequently, regardless of the social benefits alleged to justify their creation, protectionist measures often simply support some combination of inefficiency and high profits for the protected firms. (It is conceivable that protection could be justified without any expectation of cost reductions in the protected industry; the benefits in such a case would lie entirely in externalities.)

When the domestic market is sufficiently large so as to support several firms in a protected industry (as was the case, for example, with the nineteenth-century US textile industry), then domestic competition may be sufficient to drive out inefficiency and excess profits. Even when development is based on relative income equality, however, in many countries for many industries the domestic market would not be large enough to support sufficient domestic competition. In general, if protection is to yield cost and price reduction it needs to be accompanied by mechanisms to create pressure for this reduction. One general mechanism exists when protection is established for a clearly limited period of time.

Performance criteria are another sort mechanism that can force protected firms to become efficient. The use of performance criteria requires that protection come in the form of subsidies to individual firms rather than as an import barrier that would protect an entire industry; as subsidies the protection could be maintained or removed subject to a firm's performance. One performance criterion, used effectively in South Korea, can be the ability of the protected firms to penetrate export markets (Amsden 1989). Another set of performance criteria could be directly tied to the progress of the firm towards high road organization of production, where measures of success would be defined, for example, in terms of a firm's expenditures on training or the reduction in the ratio of supervisory employees to production employees. (Gordon [1996] emphasizes this ratio as a quantitative distinction between high road and low road technology.) In general, the existence of performance criteria would mean that protectionist measures would be subject to frequent review and would be maintained only for firms meeting the pre-specified criteria. If frequent review were public review, it would also create the opportunity for democratic procedures to have a role in bringing about efficiency gains in protected firms.

The regulation of foreign trade, even when carried out in ways that generate efficiency and contain costs, appears to involve the state in the chore of 'picking winners'. There are good reasons to be sceptical about the general ability of state functionaries – or, for that matter, the general ability of a group of private individuals – to select which industries or firms will be most successful in contributing to a country's technological transformation and economic development. There are the inherent problems of predicting changing economic circumstances, and history provides a limited guide because those industries that were winners in one era are surely not the winners of the next. When success is achieved in the private sector, it is accompanied by numerous failures – far more of the latter than the former. If the state uses its powers of protection from foreign competition to select winners, it would seem that it would have at least as high a failure-to-success ratio as the private sector.

As a matter of fact, however, in some countries (as I noted in Chapter 2) the state has been very successful at picking winners; experiences in Japan, South Korea and elsewhere in East Asia provide numerous particular instances. Even in countries where neo-liberals have attempted to characterize protectionism as inept and wasteful, states have achieved some notable successes at picking winners. For example, both protection of the national market and requirements that foreign investors develop local sources of supply contributed to the emergence of Mexico's efficient automobile production well before NAFTA. Still, whether the explanation is ineptitude or corruption, there are also many cases where states have used protectionist measures to 'pick' highly inefficient firms or industries. Even when the operations are not particularly inefficient, they may make only minimal contribution to the economic transformation of the domestic economy, and thus fail to be 'winners' in terms of the broader justification of protectionism.

The cases of success and failure do suggest ways that the 'picking winners' problem can be substantially reduced, if not eliminated, and protectionist policies can be used effectively. Although history may not provide a guide as to which industries should be protected, it may provide guides about how protection can work. The central issue is the nature of a firm's or industry's performance, not its product, and in this sense 'picking winners' can be accomplished by the application of the performance criteria already discussed. In order to push a country's technological development along the high road, the issue is not so much *what* is produced but *how* it is produced. For example, an agricultural activity or agricultural processing activity that involves extensive worker training programmes, builds productivity on the basis of worker innovation, and places strong demands on a corresponding expansion of the schooling system is a good candidate for protection. An electronics industry, however, where production is based on assembly lines, using poorly educated and relatively unskilled workers who have little say in and learn less from their work, would make little contribution to technological progress and would be a poor candidate for protection. (There may, however, be reasons other than contribution to high road technological development that would justify protection, and employment could be one of these. This matter will be taken up shortly.)

The basic issue here is performance criteria. With protection organized by performance criteria, the task of the state is not one of picking winners but of allowing firms to gain protection as they show they are winning in terms of longer-run development goals. Protection of this sort cannot be implemented with broad tariffs or other direct import restrictions that would apply to a product, but must be implemented through some sort of subsidy that would apply to the individual firm.

Organizing protection through performance criteria, as with the use of benefit–cost analysis, could create opportunities for democratic exposure and popular participation in the evaluation process. Most important, it thus could set up a means by which the intense pressure of immediately affected groups could be balanced by larger democratic interests. The reason why governments are often bad at picking winners is not that state functionaries are stupid but that they are subject to intense pressure from the owners of firms and workers in those firms who would be the direct winners or losers from any change in trade regulations. Democratic exposure and firmly established performance criteria are protections against the domination of policy by various particular groups. Another way to protect development policy from being subverted by such particular interests is to ensure that people are provided with security and assured that their lives will not be devastated by policy changes, as happens to workers in an industry from which protection is removed – an issue that will be addressed in the following section.

The Value of Local Production

In a sense, the regulation of foreign commerce is no different from any other regulation of private economic activity within the context of a democratic development strategy. It involves structuring markets in ways that will lead most effectively towards society's social goals, while at the same time recognizing that private actors cannot be prevented from making a broad realm of decisions that are a necessary part of making the profit that will keep them in business. As with other efforts to shape the activity of the private sector, regulations affecting foreign commerce need to be focused and have a clear relationship to social goals.

While the regulation of foreign commerce can thus be viewed as a pragmatic issue, as an instrument by which larger strategic goals are pursued, it is not a simple pragmatic issue because the social goals towards which it is directed are multiple and complex. In particular, to treat the issue, as I have above, simply in terms of technological change, would be to confine the discussion largely to the goal of economic growth. I have emphasized that regulation of foreign trade can be an instrument in pursuing a particular kind of technological advance, a high road form of progress, that is justified in terms of its broad social implications as well as its growth implications. Yet international trade has numerous other sorts of impacts on economic and social relations, and decisions about the regulation of trade cannot be reduced to a direct growth or technology accounting.

An example that has broad social implications is the impact of foreign trade and foreign trade regulation on employment. As far as the overall level of employment is concerned, there is unlikely to be a significant distinction between the employment-generating impact and the economic growth impact of foreign trade or foreign trade regulation. If regulation is justified because – through its technological effects, for example – it enhances economic growth, then it is almost surely also justified because it enhances overall employment. Policies that ensure maximum growth and overall employment, however, may be very disruptive to employment in particular sectors of the economy and create substantial employment insecurity; they may also have large impacts on income distribution, the viability of local communities and the natural environment. The interests of a particular group of workers or a local community, for example, versus the larger society's interest in economic growth may appear as a conflict between a special interest and the general interest. Yet society at large has a general interest in the well-being of its constituent parts – that is, particular groups of workers and local communities – as well as a general interest in economic growth. The well-being of the constituent parts has direct value to society at large, and, moreover, instability generated by the displacement of particular groups of workers and destruction of local communities has widespread indirect impacts – often seen in terms of a worsening in the distribution of income.

There is no simple general rule by which these sorts of trade-offs, these apparent conflicts between economic growth and other social goals, can be resolved. One of the essential features of a democratic economic development strategy is that it is defined by multiple goals, and a strategy with multiple goals is a strategy that will involve conflicts among those goals. The conflicts are, furthermore, not simply conflicts among abstract goals but usually take a social form in conflicts among groups of people. This is a necessary part of economic change and development, and it would be folly to pretend that trade-offs among goals and the social conflicts they generate could be eliminated by an appropriate strategy. There may be ways, however, in which a democratic strategy could affect the trade-offs and reduce the frequency and degree of conflict.

In general, the nature of trade-offs among economic goals is a function of the way markets are structured. When, for example, labour markets operate within the framework of a high road technology, including both policy incentives for certain technological choices and the extensive development of schooling, a relatively equal distribution of income and economic growth probably go together. In the framework of markets that are structured by low road technology, however, there is probably a trade-off between equality and growth. The same sorts of issues arise with regard to growth and the environment. For example: when property rights, the labour market and the system of social services provide low-income agriculturalists with a high degree of economic security, they are likely to be effective stewards of the environment; if, however, markets are structured so that low-income agriculturalists have little economic security, they are likely to be poor environmental care-takers (Broad 1994).

These examples suggest the larger observation that issues of economic security have profound impacts on the nature of trade-offs and social conflicts in economic development. A people's economic security is of value in itself, but it is also important in terms of how it affects other aspects of economic life. This is readily apparent in the conflicts over employment in relation to foreign trade regulation. In the context of a labour market and social services that provide them with minimal economic security, working people, in factories and offices and on farms, will tend to oppose change – both in general and in the particular case of change in foreign trade regulations that might eliminate their current employment. With no assurance that other work would be available or that social services would be available to support them in the absence of work, opposition to the change is a rational response.

Recognition of this phenomenon, of the manner in which economic insecurity tends to force people to oppose change, leads to an important part of the solution to the problem posed by conflicts that arise because groups with particular interests appear to be in conflict with the more general social interest on issues of foreign trade regulation. When markets are structured in ways that provide more economic security, the severity of such conflicts is likely to be reduced. This does not mean, however, that by providing economic security, impediments to the deregulation of foreign trade can be eliminated and the vision of free trade advocates can be realized. On the contrary, one of the ways to structure markets so as to ensure greater economic security is to regulate foreign trade.

Neo-liberals and other orthodox economists tend to place a direct value on international trade, and there is no doubt that trade has had a significant value in stimulating economic growth in many circumstances. Nevertheless, as I have already argued, regulation – not autarky, by any means, but regulation – is the most effective way to take advantage of the growth-enhancing role of foreign trade. Local production can have great value, as I have pointed out, in shaping technological change in a way that can both raise the rate of economic growth and shape that growth in the most socially desirable manner. Now I am emphasizing another value of local production. Aside from the way it affects technology and growth, foreign trade is also very disruptive, undermining existing economic activity and creating considerable uncertainty and insecurity in people's lives. There are ways to attenuate this insecurity; through the extensive provision of social services, for example. Yet advocates of a democratic approach to development should recognize that in terms of achieving economic security and a broad array of social goals that are connected to that security, important gains can be attained from recognizing the value of local production.

The value of local production is given poignancy by experience in many countries where peasant food production has been replaced by imports of low-cost grain from the United States, Canada and other, often high-income, grain-producing countries. These changing patterns of trade and production can destroy a way of life for millions of people and generate widespread economic and social instability. An illustration of the process is provided by Mexico, where neo-liberal reforms initiated in the 1980s and furthered by the adoption of the NAFTA in 1994 thoroughly altered the country's food supply system. (The emergence of the change and its background are described in Austin and Esteva 1987; and Barkin 1990.) Similar processes, however, have occurred in many other countries, where production by small-scale agriculturalists has been undermined by a set of factors, including: government promotion of export crops; increasing income inequality, shifting market demand away from the food crops traditionally grown by small-scale producers; price policies designed to assure low-cost food for the urban workforce; protection of industry, which shifts the internal terms of trade against agriculture; failure by the government to provide credit and agricultural extension; lack of rural social services, particularly education; and lack of land reform (often government support for consolidation by large landholders). Then, as neo-liberal policies deregulating foreign trade take hold and low-price imported grain becomes available, small-scale producers cannot survive.

A programme to support the viability of small-scale producers would have to reverse the factors that have weakened their position. In most parts of the world, it would begin with a land reform programme (or at least a programme that would protect the existing landholding rights of small proprietors). It would continue with the extensive provision of both production support in the form of agricultural extension and credit and social support in the form of education and health-care. If the overall development strategy included low-cost food programmes for urban workers, those low costs could not be based on low procurement prices.

In addition, a programme supporting small-scale agricultural producers would eliminate policies of *general* industrial protection and subsidies for export crops that have discriminated against the prices of goods produced by smallholders. According to some estimates by World Bank economists, general policies of industrial protection have often resulted in a 30 per cent to 40 per cent downward bias of agricultural prices (Shiff and Valdes 1995). I have argued above for *focused* regulation of foreign trade, and certainly this would involve protection for some segments of industry. Focused policies are, however, very different from general industrial protection. The South Korean experience demonstrates the feasibility of simultaneously promoting technological advance through protection of segments of industry while maintaining internal terms of trade favourable to agriculture (Shiff and Valdes 1995), though a substantial shift of resources from agriculture to industry does appear to have taken place in South Korea, as I noted in Chapter 4.

Yet all of these actions to reverse the factors that have weakened the position of small-scale farmers would not be sufficient to secure their position. Long before these policies had their full impact, small farmers would face competition from low-cost imported foodstuffs. Their viability would depend on protection from this import competition.

A programme of this sort would be in direct conflict with development strategies that involve deregulation of markets and reduction of the state's economic roles. The advocates of these neo-liberal policies would argue for unrestricted food imports that would provide the rural poor and everyone else with the lowest cost foods. Moreover, they would argue that the programme of support involves subsidies – in the form of agricultural extension, credit, social services – that would strain the fiscal capacity of the state. There are several flaws in the neo-liberal argument. It is based on a set of unreasonable assumptions: for example, that peasants and workers displaced by food imports will find employment elsewhere and that short-run cost considerations are necessarily the best guide to long-run growth. I discussed these issues at length in Chapter 2.

In addition, the advocates of unregulated foreign trade ignore a set of particular issues associated with the value of local production. A programme supporting the viability of small-scale food producers would have a number of interconnected benefits to society beyond those captured in the price of the food itself. These would include:

- A favourable impact on the distribution of income. The most severe poverty in most parts of the world is located in rural areas, and a programme that would support the viability of small-scale producers would directly raise their incomes, overcoming absolute poverty and contributing to equalization in the distribution of income. The poorest of the poor in rural areas, landless labourers, would benefit directly from such a programme in so far as it involved land redistribution, and would also benefit from the increased employment opportunities that the programme would create and the social support it would provide. Were the programme successful, it would not simply raise the amount of food locally produced, but would also provide the poor with the necessary 'entitlements' – that is, the buying power – to have claim to this food. (It is the distribution of such entitlements that holds the key to the elimination of absolute hunger and famine; see Sen 1981; and Dreze and Sen 1989.)
- A positive impact on the stability of rural communities. By raising incomes and providing income security in rural areas, the programme

would reduce out-migration, a process that imposes considerable non-market costs on those who must migrate. The stability of local communities would reduce severe pressures on urban centres, pressures that create substantial costs to government and non-market environmental costs. The savings of public expenditures on urban services and environmental repair would tend to balance the subsidies involved in the programme of support for agricultural production.

- Beneficial impacts on the environment. By raising rural incomes and providing security for the rural poor, the programme could tend to reduce over-cultivation with its attendant consequences of forest destruction and soil erosion and depletion (Broad 1994). Nevertheless, while insecurity and poverty often lead to environmental degradation, their elimination is only a necessary but not sufficient condition for environmental preservation. Programmes aimed at rural development and local production can generate substantial environmental problems (Barbier 1989; and Panayotou 1993), and any development programme designed to support the rural poor would have to deal with environmental issues directly.

- A progressive transformation of agricultural technology. The viability of small-scale agriculture depends on establishing a context in which methods of production could be advanced, raising both output per unit of labour time and output per unit of land. The extension work and the social services, especially the education component, would aim precisely at establishing that context. As Foster and Rosenzweig (1996) have suggested, for example, there is evidence that schooling contributes to peasants' ability to take advantage of new technologies. Technological progress, in agriculture as in industry, can have far-reaching, long-term impacts on economic growth.

A programme that would support the viability of small-scale producers of basic foodstuffs is similar to a food self-sufficiency programme, but it is important to point out that the two are not the same. Food self-sufficiency is a popular goal of development policy, touted at least rhetorically by governments as varied as those in Mexico, China, Indonesia, India and Cuba; the goal has received endorsements from international organizations, including the Food and Agricultural Organization and even the World Bank. Yet food self-sufficiency is a problematic goal, both conceptually and in practice. Conceptually, there is no clear connection between a country's or region's food self-sufficiency and its economic well-being, the former being neither a necessary nor sufficient condition for the latter. Jean Dreze and Amartya Sen (1989) point out what should be obvious: many countries and regions of countries that have no problems with food supply are by no means self-sufficient. When famines develop, the problem is generally not food supply per se, but the capacity of people to purchase the food – that is, they lack the 'entitlement' or purchasing power (Sen 1981).

In practice, the rhetoric of food self-sufficiency has often been empty, and, most important, where programmes have actually been implemented they have at times proved counter-productive. For example, in China, according to Carl Riskin:

> Chief among the negative policies pre-1978 was that of local foodgrain self-sufficiency. Government policy strongly encouraged all regions to be self-sufficient in grains, including those with a long history of specialization in raising economic crops or livestock or in other non-grain activities ... The result was that grain basket areas were deprived of their markets, while non-grain regions produced grain inefficiently. (Riskin 1991)

Another example is described by Patrice Levang (1997) where peasants in an Indonesian transmigration project in South Sumatra, rejecting the advice of 'experts' and the plans of the government authorities, abandoned food self-sufficiency in favour of cash crops. According to Levang, the essential fact explaining the peasants' actions was that the combination of crops and conditions in the self-sufficiency programme involved too high a level of risk. 'In fact, peasants (like non-peasants) do not seek self-sufficiency but security' (Levang 1997: 27).

These sorts of experiences suggest an important lesson: when development projects are conceived, designed and organized from the top they are likely to be ineffective or counter-productive. As I have argued above, one of the principles that needs to guide policy towards the private sector in a democratic development strategy is a reliance on popular participation in the formulation of policy. Popular participation is important as a goal in itself and because the people most directly affected by projects have essential knowledge. Also, people's participation in policy formulation generates a commitment that raises the likelihood of success.

To generate such participation, it would be necessary to develop rural cooperatives or some other form of organization that would strengthen the political as well as the economic position of small-scale farmers. As I noted in Chapter 1, in the general implementation of a democratic development strategy, there is a need for promoting various forms of organization in civil society as counter-weights to both the market and the state. Rural cooperatives are one means to give new voice to small farmers. In the countryside, where political power is often monopolized in the hands of various elite groups, democratic economic policy is particularly dependent on new organization. Without new, democratic organization, efforts to promote progress are likely to founder as they are absorbed in and perverted by the existing political inequalities (Edelman 1980). Also, cooperatives could provide a mechanism for organizing many of the particular programmes that would form the substance of a support programme. Agricultural extension, education and other social services, and credit programmes can be most effective and provided with least cost when their implementation takes place through the organization of the peasants themselves.

The connection between political participation and the development of programmes that recognize the value of and promote local production works in both directions: while political participation is a basis for the success of the programme, a programme that emphasizes local production can promote political participation. One of the great values of local production is that people have knowledge of and understand it. They know ways that it can be improved, and they know the sorts of support services that they need. They are, therefore, more likely to become involved in the political processes surrounding a programme focused on local production. The real value of a programme that focuses on local production and supports the viability of small-scale farmers is that it deals with people where they are, both literally in the physical sense and also in the more abstract sense of their knowledge, understanding and commitment. Instead of demanding that people adjust – by changing where they live and what they do – a democratic programme could, through such programmes, seek to adjust economic life to the people. It could provide people with opportunities to maintain stability in their lives while at the same time becoming increasingly productive.

Part III

Conclusions

9

Power and Politics in the Pursuit of Democratic Development

Sherlock Holmes became the world's most famous detective in large part because he had an uncanny ability to penetrate to the core of a problem, figure out the connections among a series of events, and decipher a mystery. In story after story, Holmes was able to solve the seemingly unsolvable.

The problem of how to achieve democratic economic development is not nearly so simple as the numerous puzzles that Holmes attacked, nor are the problems of development ones that can be settled primarily by the clever reasoning of a sharp intellect. The barriers that block democratic economic development are social and political; they are problems of power. In any effort to solve them, we appear to be caught in a paradox: in order to achieve democratic economic development, we need to have democratic power; it seems that we need to have a large part of what we want in order to get what we want.

So it is easy to look at the proposals I have offered in the previous chapters, either individually or in their entirety, and be very sceptical. In many low-income countries privileged elites are thoroughly entrenched in power, even when formal democracy exists. Often these elites enjoy the support of the US government and the governments of other wealthy countries, the international lending agencies, and large, internationally operating private firms. Efforts to bring about democratic development that would reduce the power and privilege of the ruling groups in the low-income countries can be, and often have been, countered by a broad array of economic, political and military forces. There is no denying that the success of democratic economic development is improbable.

Here there is something to be learned from Sherlock Holmes. In his approach to seemingly unsolvable mysteries, the great detective's most famous maxim was: 'when you have eliminated the impossible, whatever remains, *however improbable*, must be the truth.'[1]

To the extent that we can say anything is impossible in social affairs, it is impossible to achieve the goals of democratic economic development if economic policy in low-income countries continues to be defined as it was in most of the twentieth century. The neo-liberalism that dominated at the end of the century, the liberalism that prevailed in the early years of the century, and the various forms of undemocratic statist policy that held the stage at times during the century – none has worked. It is true that some economic growth, some very significant economic growth, has been attained. As I emphasized at the beginning of this book, there were great changes in the world economy during the twentieth century, and those changes involved tremendous improvements in people's material well-being. Yet, as I also emphasized, the development gap remains essentially as it was in 1900, and the basic needs of hundreds of millions of people remain unmet. Moreover, in spite of the material progress that has been achieved, most people in the world are still thoroughly excluded from any substantial role in shaping the economic contexts of their own lives; environmental destruction continues apace and threatens catastrophe on a global level; and the bonds among people, the social communities that can provide the basis of secure and meaningful lives, are continually weakened if not destroyed. The old approaches to development have not done the job. However improbable it may be to establish new alternatives, some new alternatives for development 'must be the truth'.

Still, the problem remains: how to get there? How can people who want to move towards a democratic economic development strategy overcome the very considerable forces that stand in their way and that protect the status quo of power and privilege? This is not a book about political strategy, and I will make no pretence of offering formulas for political work in low-income countries, or anywhere else for that matter. Economic strategy is enough for one book.

Nevertheless, this is also not a book that simply offers idealistic visions. The proposals I have set out in the previous chapters are, I maintain, practical democratic initiatives. My strategy for democratic economic development is practical, I have argued, both because it could gain wide popular support (since it would meet real, popular needs) and because it would not cripple the operation of a still capitalist economic order – though it could certainly change that order. Yet the strategy would still be impractical if we could not even conceive of a political process by which it could be attained.

My principal purpose in this final chapter is to suggest – but only suggest – some of the basis for the political work that could lead towards democratic economic development. I believe that the key lies in taking advantage of democratic openings, however small, to build popular organizations that increasingly involve people in having a say in the economic and social programmes that affect their lives; these popular organizations and the people in them can become the 'agents' of change. If popular organizations can use their strength to build a democratic economic development strategy, then the economic strategy will enhance their strength. Viewing things this way, we are no longer caught by the paradox that we need democracy in order to attain democracy. Instead, the paradox of democratic development is transformed: *if we have some democratic power, then it can be used to expand democratic power.*

The Agents of Change

In their study of development issues in India, which I have referred to at various points in this book, Jean Dreze and Amartya Sen (1995) offer an analysis of gender inequality that provides insights into the question of power and change. Their analysis starts from the distressing observation that millions of women are 'missing' in India. In the relatively wealthy countries of the world, where men and women have roughly equal access to health-care and nutrition, the ratio of females to males is about 105 to 100. Yet in India the ratio is about 93 to 100, and is similarly low in many other low-income parts of the world: 94 to 100 in China, 96 to 100 in North Africa, and an abysmal 91 to 100 in Pakistan. It seems reasonable to assume that if females in India had the same access to nutrition and health-care as do males, then literally tens of millions more would be alive. Instead, they are 'missing'. (Throughout the world, there are about 95 females born for each 100 males. Under conditions of relatively equal access to nutrition and health-care, however, and excluding the impact of wars, the mortality rate for males is higher, generating the ratios that are typical in high-income countries. Dreze and Sen show that the low ratios in India cannot be explained by infanticide, but result from nutritional and health-care disadvantages of females over time.)

Taking the female–male ratio as an indicator of the general state of gender equality, we could easily conclude from these data that higher income is the decisive factor in bringing about an improvement in the situation of women. Reality, however, is not so simple. By examining the data more thoroughly and, in particular, by looking at the data for the several different states of India, Dreze and Sen establish that there is no automatic relation between higher income in a region and greater gender equality. There is evidence that in some circumstances a region's higher income is associated with a worsening of women's relative position. Most important, when higher income does lead to greater gender equality, it seems to operate through such factors as higher female labour force participation rates and higher female literacy rates. Dreze and Sen argue that these factors are indicative of 'women's agency', that is, of the ability of women to have a role in social, political and economic affairs so as to affect their own conditions. Through gaining some elements of economic power, women in parts of India have been able to expand that power to obtain the most tangible of results, an improvement in their life expectancy.

Dreze and Sen extend their argument by a discussion of conditions in the Indian state of Kerala. Kerala's female–male ratio of 103.6, by far the highest of any state in India, is only the most dramatic indicator of the state's social achievements. As I have suggested in Chapter 7, the expansion of various social programmes in Kerala, particularly education and health-care, appears to have established a virtuous circle whereby improvements in different social arenas are mutually supportive. Furthermore, this virtuous circle has a firm foundation in a history of extensive popular involvement in civic affairs. In part this civic involvement has taken the form of traditional electoral politics, and parties of the left have played a major role in advancing social reform in Kerala. But in addition, Kerala has well-established trade unions, peasant organizations and social action organizations, including organizations of women, involved in advocating and overseeing the state's social reforms.

The story of social progress in Kerala is one in which people have gained some measure of democratic power, used that power to build social change, and that social change has in turn become a basis for the further expansion of democratic power. The situation in Kerala is not without problems (as discussed in Chapter 7), but it does provide an important illustration of the connections between democratic power and socio-economic progress.

Experiences with environmental struggles in many different countries also provide illustrations of the way small opportunities for democratic action can be built upon to advance the agenda of democratic development and thus widen the opportunities for the emergence of democratic power. One especially interesting set of cases has been analysed by Robin Broad (1994; also see, Broad and Cavanagh 1993). Examining experience in the Philippines, Broad calls into question the traditional argument that the poor are principal agents in the destruction of the natural environment. As I pointed out in the previous chapter, she argues that when the rural poor live in stable communities and depend on the local natural environment for their livelihood, then they can become effective, politically active protectors of the environment. Beyond their sense of permanence, however, there is an additional crucial variable affecting the response of the poor when environmental degradation is threatening the resource base on which they live. This additional variable, Broad argues, is the extent to which civil society is politicized and organized. In the Philippines:

the richness of ... environmental activism is directly related to the historical vibrancy of [Philippine social movements, the organized part of civil society], creating what could be called a culture of empowerment (even during periods of authoritarian rule). For activity related to the environment, Philippine civil society has become a web of pressure groups – a mixture of new and old social movements, groups that see themselves as environmental and others that see themselves as struggling for land rights, fishing rights, and a wide array of development issues. (Broad 1994: 816)

If a foundation for democratic action is provided by the extent to which, historically, civil society has been politicized and organized, it is also true that democratic action deepens that politicization and organization. Broad is, in effect, describing a virtuous circle of activism and change. She points out that 'environmental activism involves people becoming agents of social change'. That involvement in environmental struggles has been facilitated by a history of various forms of social activism encompassing a wide range of issues. In turn, people's engagement in environmental struggles furthers the foundation for democratic action on that wider set of issues, the elements of a democratic economic development strategy.

Broad's story of the Philippines finds a parallel in the experience of Brazilian rubber-tappers in the Amazon rain forest (Mendes 1992). Building on the narrow political space that existed for labour union activity under the country's dictatorship in the 1970s, rubber-tappers saw their own economic well-being tied to the preservation of the rain forest and advanced a programme of sustainable development. Their actions both contributed directly to the broad efforts to preserve the Amazon rain forest and served to expand the movement for democracy in Brazil. They were able to build on the history of activism in Brazil and amplify a small political space to have substantial impact.

The Brazilian rubber-tappers' story also provides a sobering reminder of the obstacles to social change and economic progress. Their efforts have come up against powerful interests, principally the cattle ranchers and large firms that would prosper from unregulated expansion into the rain forests. The rubber-tappers have seen their leaders murdered as a consequence of their struggles, and the destruction of the Brazilian rain forest has hardly been halted by their efforts. (In fact, at the beginning of 1999, under pressure from the IMF to reduce its spending, the Brazilian government slashed funding to the central project in its programme for protecting the natural environment of the Amazon.) Yet the success of the Brazilian rubber-workers, as is the case with any democratic activism, cannot be measured simply in terms of tangible and direct results; their contributions lie also in the foundation they help establish for democratic change.

The civic struggles in South African townships were an element in establishing the foundation of one of the most important democratic changes of the late twentieth century (Mayekiso 1996). Also, the civic organizations (the 'civics') of South Africa provide another useful example of the way a small, very small, democratic space can be enlarged through local actions, and the organizational experience gained in that action can become a basis for implementing the programmes of a democratic development strategy.

Civic organizations, community-based and independent local organizations in South Africa's black townships, became an important part of the struggle against apartheid in the 1980s. They were outside and independent of the national political resistance and labour organizations such as the African National Congress (ANC) and the Congress of South African Trade Unions, but they worked in connection and in alliance with these larger groupings. The civics organized boycotts and community defence, demanded local services and provided political education to the people in the townships. As part of the broad struggle for change, they also created a wealth of organizational experience at the grass-roots level that could be called upon in the economic reconstruction programmes of a new, post-apartheid South Africa.

How the civic organizations will function in the new South Africa – whether they will be coopted, shunted aside, or able to maintain an independent existence – is an issue of continuing struggle. Their programmes for reconstruction and development at the local level could play an important role in complementing national economic programmes, provide a basis for popular participation in those national programmes, and give them a more thoroughly democratic content. For example, the civic organizations can maintain pressure on the government to meet strongly felt community needs, such as more housing and more extensive social services for women. Without local pressure and input, national programmes are likely to meet community needs less effectively, if at all (even with the most well-intentioned of government planners). While the role of civic organizations in post-apartheid South Africa remains in flux, by establishing grass-roots organizational experience they have helped create the possibility of a democratic foundation for development.

Experiences in many other countries provide additional examples of this basic process by which the organizations of civil society can provide small wedges that can enlarge political space and provide the political experience that may form a foundation for a democratic economic development strategy. These organizations range from the long-standing labour unions to the newly burgeoning environmental protection organizations, from neighbourhood self-help groups forced into existence by the ravages of neo-liberal structural adjustment programmes to women's organizations struggling for both immediate welfare and a larger feminist agenda, from peasant cooperatives attempting to protect their livelihoods to student or parent associations dealing with the quality of the schools. Such groupings can be successful when, beyond the immediate gains on which they are focused, they move people towards being agents in changing their own lives; they then become the instruments of creating 'popular agency' or 'democratic agency'.

Even the broadest and strongest network of such organizations, however, does not automatically translate into a society-wide programme of change or the implementation of a democratic development strategy. The creation of democratic agency can establish a political environment that pushes towards larger programmes of change, but the traditional mechanisms of political authority must be set in motion for that change to become reality. Strong and extensive organizations of civil society are not a substitute for formations, such as political parties, that focus directly on the state. However, the reverse is also true: in any effort to achieve democratic development, political parties that focus directly on the state are not a substitute for organizations of civil society.

These two approaches to politics – building the organizations of civil society and working to affect state action – are complementary components of a democratic strategy. There is no necessary competition between local and wider struggles; their imports can be cumulative and mutually supportive.[2] As I pointed out above in describing South African civic organizations, while they are independent local groupings, they worked with the ANC to liberate the country from apartheid. If the civics are successful in affecting the course of development in the new South Africa, it will be because they are able to influence – either directly or through political parties, trade unions or other national associations – the actions of the state. Likewise, in Brazil the work of the rubber-tappers which I have noted above has been connected to the development of the country's Workers' Party (PT). The PT, while failing to win elections at the national level, has won several municipal elections where its success in implementing democratic programmes has relied heavily on the role of independent social movements. Describing the PT's work in Porto Alegre, for example, Ricardo Tavares notes: 'Porto Alegre [during the PT's administration] has been a successful example of both efficiency and popular participation. A tradition of strong urban social movements that pressured the city to democratize its public life – even during the military dictatorship (1964–1985) – is an important factor behind this success' (Tavares 1995).[3]

There is no great originality in my emphasis on the organizations of civil society as a political foundation for democratic economic development.

In recent years, many people have given attention to the concept of civil society and the growth of new social movements. I emphasize this form of politics in the context of this book in order to suggest three points:

1. *Independent social movements, the organizations of civil society, are an essential foundation of democracy generally and of a democratic economic development strategy in particular.* While, as I have noted, this form of politics is complementary to traditional, state-focused political work, the latter can exist without the former. Yet when traditional politics operates without a foundation in social movements, then, regardless of the substance of the programmes that are initiated by the state authorities, those programmes will be lacking a crucial dimension of democracy and, sooner or later, are likely to lose much of their democratic substance. As I said in the first chapter: democratic initiatives, non-reformist reforms, cannot simply be for the people; they need to be of the people and by the people as well.

2. *The extensive organization of civil society is probably the best safeguard, perhaps the only ultimate safeguard, against state domination – bureaucratic or tyrannical – of economic and social life.* The formal aspects of democracy – open elections, civil liberties, the rights of opposition – are also important, but they are made most effective when they exist within a well-organized civil society. My focus on this aspect of politics should help define the anti-statist character of the strategy I have proposed, even while that strategy depends heavily on state action.

3. *In many low-income countries there is a rich history of social movements and civic organizations; they are a reality, not an idealistic notion.* When formal democracy has existed, they have often flourished. Even under dictatorial situations, they have sometimes been able to push the limits of the small political space that has existed for independent activity. Thus, in suggesting that this form of politics can bring into existence the sort of democratic economic development strategy that I have set out in this book, I am proposing to build on foundations that already exist.

There are problems, of course. Certainly not all organizations of civil society further democracy, even when their existence is an element of democracy. Vigilante groups, for example, can serve as instruments of repression and conformity. At times, organizations defined by a religious commitment have been thoroughly undemocratic – though at other times religious identity has also served democratic goals. Also, because the strength of civil society is a counter-balance to the power of the state, it can become a means to weaken the democratic programmes that require state action. In fact, the slogan of 'local empowerment' has at times been used by neo-liberals who seek a decentralization or devolution of political authority as a means to block state regulation of the market and limit the extent to which the state can mobilize resources for democratic reform. If the organizations of civil society are to serve as a basis for the sort of economic strategy that I have proposed here, they must find ways to deal with the continuing tension between limiting the state's domination over democratic initiatives and using the state both to support those initiatives and to control powerful private actors.

The Globalization of Politics

There is an additional problem. By emphasizing civil society and the development of popular organizations as the means by which to establish a foundation for a democratic economic development strategy, I might imply that the national arena is a sufficient locus for political organization. That would be a mistake. As I have noted both at the beginning of this book and at the beginning of this final chapter, it is not only the local elites that block democratic initiatives in low-income countries. The US government, the international lending agencies dominated by the US government and its allies, and the world's largest private firms all work to subvert efforts at democratic change. Imperialism is a powerful force; any political programme that does not recognize this reality is unlikely to have much success.

In low-income countries, an increasingly organized civil society and growing social movements are a good foundation for limiting the negative impact of imperialism. Furthermore, as I have argued in Chapter 2 and Part II, the economics of globalization does not eliminate the possibilities for national policy in low-income countries. Governments still have options in selecting strategies for the control of their countries' foreign commerce and fiscal policies; and in the ability to exercise control over fiscal policies lies the power to implement more extensive social reforms. In economic terms, globalization does not close the door on efforts to find alternative, democratic economic strategies in low-income countries. Furthermore, to the extent that this economic reality is recognized, the political situation is affected: people are not paralysed by a belief that they must submit to the inexorable forces of globalization.

Yet, not only does economic life operate on a global level, but it is also buttressed by imperial power that operates globally. Political efforts to change the way the economy operates also need a global dimension. This is exactly what is happening, as during the final decades of the twentieth century elements of global democratic activity have actually begun to expand. The current era of globalization has generated many reactions, and some of these are distinctly positive (MacEwan and Tabb 1989b).

Perhaps the most widely recognized democratic reaction to globalization has been the move of some labour unions towards international alliances and international organizing. With workers in all parts of the world producing the same sorts of products in the same ways and often working for the same companies, many unions are forced to move away from a traditional, national focus. In the United States, for example, textile and garment workers' unions have recognized that the only way they can protect the position of their members is to campaign against the poor working conditions and low wages of textile and garment workers in low-income countries. Also, the advent of the North American Free Trade Agreement (NAFTA) brought with it an initiation of cross-border organizing; as their protection through import limitations declined, US workers had little choice but to seek common cause with their Mexican counterparts. Beyond the impetus that NAFTA gave to cross-border labour organizing, the struggle in the early 1990s over the ratification of the NAFTA treaty led to some embryonic formations of cross-border ties and a broader realization of the importance of international alliances among democratic, oppositional groups in Canada, Mexico and the United States (Hunter 1995).

As with the labour movement, the current era of globalization has led to growing international activity among environmental organizations. Although problems of environmental destruction far pre-date the modern era, the modern spread of capitalism has generated problems that are truly global in nature: including, for example, global warming, the depletion of the ozone layer, the pollution of the oceans, the international shipping and dumping of waste materials (Foster 1994). Even when problems appear to be local, as with the pollution exuded by a particular factory, they often have important international dimensions: the factory is, for example, the subsidiary of a large internationally operating firm or it will move internationally if required to limit its pollution (or both). Because solutions can only be found on an international level, environmental organizations increasingly seek international ties.

Women's organizations, too, have moved towards the development of an international dimension in their activities. Links among women's organizations in different parts of the world, sometimes facilitated by the work of the United Nations and the World Conferences on Women that it has sponsored, have served as catalysts in many low-income countries for the growth of women's organizations dealing with issues such as health, education, physical abuse and child-care. One aspect of the international linking of women's organizations has been directly associated with the increased participation of women in the paid labour force, as women workers have faced special difficulties. Discussing experience in the global textile and garment industry, for example, Diane Elson (1989) cites the way women workers in the Sri Lankan Free Trade Zone have been aided by their international links in fighting the repression of trade unions by government and the multinationals. Elson points out that struggles against the employment practices of multinational firms are limited when they are defined simply as workers' struggles, but she suggests that the role of women workers creates new opportunities for the development of worker–community links that may raise the likelihood of democratic change.

Globalization is not some monolithic force that pushes in one direction, limiting the possibilities for democratic economic and political change. Like all powerful social forces, it has many facets and generates its own counter-forces. The developments I have noted with regard to the labour unions, environmental organizations and the women's movement are all examples of the way globalization creates opportunities for progress. Even the development of the technology of communications and transportation that has been so important in the current wave of globalization has facilitated the international connections among democratic organizations. As rapidly as globalization throws up barriers to democratic change, it creates both the demands and the possibilities for the globalization of politics that might advance that democratic change.

A reasonable person might be sceptical of the optimism implicit in these observations. I began this book by noting that in spite of the remarkable economic expansion that took place in the twentieth century, there was also a remarkable lack of change in the dramatic inequalities that exist in our world. It appears, moreover, that as the twentieth century came to an end, these inequalities – the development gap – were getting even worse. In this context, one might find it difficult to accept my optimism. Yet I believe it is an optimism that does follow from the analysis I have offered throughout this book. That analysis shows that there are possibilities for doing things differently, more democratically and with better results for economic development. Democratic economic development will certainly be difficult. Yet, *however improbable*, it is certainly possible. It is worth a try.

Notes

1. Holmes fans will, most likely, need no guide but, for others, I believe the statement of this maxim first appears in *The Sign of Four* and then, in slightly varying form, in 'The Adventure of the Beryl Coronet', 'The Adventure of the Bruce-Partington Plans' and 'The Adventure of the Blanched Soldier'.

2. This perspective differs from that of analysts who see social movements as distinct from and as an alternative to traditional state-focused political parties. See, for example, Frank and Fuentes (1990) and Castells (1983).

3. The success of the PT in several municipalities is part of a general pattern that emerged in Latin America during the early 1990s, whereby local electoral gains had been made possible by the opening of some democratic 'space' in Latin America in recent years. Jonathan Fox notes: 'state power is not limited to the "commanding heights" alone. If one looks at electoral contests for local and state offices in the 1990s, alternative parties – including those that are unconventional but not strictly speaking of the left – have done quite well ... local and state politics have turned out to be the most viable arenas in which the left can compete for power, experiment with progressive reforms, and learn how to govern' (Fox 1995: 15). Also see Winn (1995) and Nylen (1995).

References

Adelman, Irma, and Cynthia Taft Morris. 1973. *Economic Growth and Social Equity in Developing Countries*, Stanford, CA: Stanford University Press.

Agarwal, Bina. 1991. 'Under the Cooking Pot: The Political Economy of the Domestic Fuel Crisis in Rural South Asia', in Sontheimer (ed.), 1991.

Ahluwalia, Montek. S. 1976. 'Inequality, Poverty and Development', *Journal of Development Economics*, Vol. 3.

Akerlof, George, William Dickens and George Perry. 1996. 'The Macroeconomics of Low Inflation', *Brookings Papers on Economic Activity*, No. 1.

Albert, Michael, and Robin Hahnel. 1991. *Looking Forward: Participatory Economics for the Twenty-first Century*. Boston: South End Press.

Alesina, Alberto, and Dani Rodrik. 1994. 'Distributive Politics and Economic Growth', *Quarterly Journal of Economics*, May.

Althusser, Louis. 1970. 'Contradiction and Overdetermination', in *For Marx*. New York: Vintage Books, Random House.

Amsden, Alice. 1989. *Asia's Next Giant: South Korea and Late Industrialization*. Oxford: Oxford University Press.

Armstrong, P., A. Glyn and J. Harrison. 1984. *Capitalism Since World War II: The Making and the Breakup of the Great Boom*. London: Fontana.

Arrighi, Giovanni. 1991. 'World Income Inequalities and the Future of Socialism', *New Left Review*, No. 189, September–October.

— 1994. *The Long Twentieth Century: Money, Power, and the Origins of Our Times*, London and New York: Verso.

Arrow, Kenneth, et al. 1995. 'Economic Growth, Carrying Capacity, and the Environment', *Science*, Vol. 268, April.

Ascher, Carol, Norm Fruchter and Robert Berne. 1996. *Hard Lessons: Public Schools and Privatization*. New York: Twentieth Century Fund Press.

Ashton, David, and Francis Green. 1996. *Education, Training and the Global Economy*. Cheltenham: Edward Elgar Publishing.

Auerbach, Paul. 1994. 'Markets', in Philip Arestis and Malcolm Sawyer (eds), *The Elgar Companion to Radical Political Economy*. Cheltenham: Edward Elgar Publishing.

Austin, James, E. and Gustavo Esteva (eds). 1987. *Food Policy in Mexico: The Search for Self-Sufficiency*. Ithaca, NY and London: Cornell University Press.

Baran, Paul. 1956. *The Political Economy of Growth*. New York: Monthly Review Press.

Barbier, Edward B. 1989. 'Cash Crops, Food Crops, and Sustainability: The Case of Indonesia', *World Development*, Vol. 17, No. 6, June.

Barkin, David. 1990. *Distorted Development: Mexico in the World Economy*. Boulder, CO: Westview Press.

— 1998. *Wealth, Poverty and Sustainable Development*, Centro de Ecologia y Desorrollo. Mexico City: Editorial Jus.

Barkin, David, and Gonzalo Chapela y Mendoza. 1995. *Monarcas y Campesinos: Strategia de desarrollo Sustentable en el oriente de Michoacan*. Mexico City: Centro de Ecologia y Desarrollo.

Barro, Robert. 1991. 'Economic Growth in a Cross Section of Countries', *Quarterly Journal of Economics*, May.

Barry, Tom. 1995. *Zapata's Revenge: Free Trade and the Farm Crisis in Mexico*. Boston: South End Press.

BCAS (Bulletin of Concerned Asian Scholars). 1998a. 'The Kerala Model of Development: A Debate (Part I)', *Bulletin of Concerned Asian Scholars*, Vol. 30, No. 3, July–September.

— 1998b. 'The Kerala Model of Development: A Debate (Part II)', *Bulletin of Concerned Asian Scholars*, Vol. 30, No. 4, October–December.

Bello, Walden, and Stephanie Rosenfeld. 1990. *Dragons in Distress: Asian Miracle Economies in Crisis*. San Francisco: Institute for Food and Development Policy.

Berlan, Jean-Pierre, and Richard Lewontin. 1986. 'The Political Economy of Hybrid Corn', *Monthly Review*, Vol. 38, No. 3, July–August.

— 1995. 'Inside the Black Box: Hybrid Corn Revisited', paper presented to the Eleventh World Congress of the International Economics Association, Tunis, December.

Birdsall, Nancy, David Ross and Richard Sabot. 1995. 'Inequality and Growth Reconsidered: Lessons from East Asia', *World Bank Economic Review*, Vol. 9, No. 3, September.

Bowles, Samuel. 1972. 'Unequal Education and the Reproduction of the Social Division of Labor', in Martin Carnoy (ed.), *Schooling in a Corporate Society: The Political Economy of Education in America and the Alternatives Before Us*. New York: David McKay.

— 1978. 'Capitalist Development and Educational Structure', *World Development*, Vol. 6, No. 6, June.

Bowles, Samuel, and Herbert Gintis. 1976. *Schooling in Capitalist America: Educational Reform and the Contradictions of Economic Life*. New York: Basic Books.

— 1982. 'The Crisis of Liberal Democratic Capitalism: The Case of the United States', *Politics & Society*, Vol. 11, No. 1.

— 1993. 'Agency, Incentives, and Democratic Accountability', in Samuel Bowles, Herbert Gintis and Bo Gustafsson (eds), *Markets and Democracy: Participation, Accountability and Efficiency*. Cambridge: Cambridge University Press.

— 1995. 'Escaping the Efficiency–Equity Trade-off: Productivity-Enhancing Asset Redistribution', in Gerald Epstein and Herbert Gintis (eds), *Macroeconomic Policy After the Conservative Era*. Cambridge: Cambridge University Press.

Bowles, Samuel, Herbert Gintis and Peter Meyer. 1975. 'The Long Shadow of Work: Education, the Family, and the Reproduction of the Social Division of Labor', *The Insurgent Sociologist*, Summer.

Boyce, James K. (ed.) 1996. *Economic Policy for Building Peace: The Lessons of El Salvador*. Boulder, CO: Lynne Rienner.

Braverman, Harry. 1974. *Labor and Monopoly Capital: The Degradation of Work in the Twentieth Century*. New York: Monthly Review Press.

Broad, Robin. 1994. 'The Poor and the Environment: Friends or Foes?', *World Development*, Vol. 22, No. 6, June.

Broad, Robin, with John Cavanagh. 1993. *Plundering Paradise: The Struggle for the Environment in the Philippines*. Berkeley, CA: University of California Press.

Bruno, Michael, and William Easterly. 1996. 'Inflation and Growth: In Search of a Stable Relationship', *Federal Reserve Bank of St. Louis Review*, Vol. 78, No. 3.

Bryant, Ralph C. 1987. *International Financial Intermediation*, Washington, DC: Brookings Institution.

Buchele, Robert, and Jens Christiansen. 1992. 'Industrial Relations and Productivity Growth: A Comparative Perspective', *International Contributions to Labor Studies*, Fall.

Cable, Vincent. 1995. 'The Diminished Nation-State: A Study in the Loss of Economic Power', *Daedalus*, Vol. 124, No. 2, Spring.

Campen, James T. 1986. *Benefit, Cost and Beyond: The Political Economy of Benefit–Cost Analysis*, Cambridge: Ballinger.

Carnoy, Martin, and Henry M. Levin. 1985. *Schooling and Work in the Democratic State*. Palo Alto: Stanford University Press.

Castells, Manuel. 1983. *The City and the Grassroots: A Cross-Cultural Theory of Urban Social Movements*. Berkeley and Los Angeles: University of California Press.

Cecelski, David S. 1994. *Along Freedom Road: Hyde County, North Carolina, and the Fate of Black Schools in the South*. Chapel Hill: University of North Carolina Press.

Clapham, J. H. 1961. *The Economic Development of France and Germany, 1815–1914*. Cambridge: Cambridge University Press.

Cohen, Morris R. 1982 [1927]. 'Property and Sovereignty', reprinted in *Law and the Social Order: Essays in Legal Philosophy*. New Brunswick: Transaction Books.

Cohen, Stephen S., and John Zysman. 1987. *Manufacturing Matters: The Myth of the Post-Industrial Economy*. New York: Basic Books.

Collins, Joseph, and John Lear. 1994. *Chile's Free-Market Miracle: A Second Look*. San Francisco: Institute of Food and Development Policy.

Commons, John R. 1974 [1924]. *Legal Foundations of Capitalism*. Clifton, NJ, Augustus M. Kelly Publishers.

Crotty, James. 1983. 'Keynes and Capital Flight', *Journal of Economic Literature*, March.

— 1989. 'The Limits of Keynesian Macroeconomic Policy in the Age of the Global Market Place', in MacEwan and Tabb (eds), 1989a.

Crotty, James, and Gerald Epstein. 1996. 'In Defense of Capital Controls', in Leo Panitch (ed.), *Are There Alternatives? Socialist Register 1996*. London: Merlin Press.

Cumings, Bruce. 1989. 'The Abortive Abertura: South Korea in the Light of the Latin American Experience', *New Left Review*, No. 173, January–February.

Daly, Herman E., and John B. Cobb, Jr. 1989. *For the Common Good: Redirecting the Economy Toward Community, the Environment, and a Sustainable Future*. Boston: Beacon Press.

de Janvry, Alain. 1981. *The Agrarian Question and Reformism in Latin America*. Baltimore: Johns Hopkins University Press.

Dicken, Peter. 1992. *Global Shift: The Internationalization of Economic Activity*. 2nd edn. New York: Guilford Press.

Dornbush, Rudiger. 1992. 'The Case for Trade Liberalization in Developing Countries', *Journal of Economic Perspectives*, Vol. 6, No. 1, Winter.

Dornbush, Rudiger, and Sebastian Edwards (eds). 1991. *The Macroeconomics of Populism in Latin America*. Chicago: University of Chicago Press.

Dreze, Jean, and Amartya Sen. 1989. *Hunger and Public Action*. Oxford: Clarendon Press.

— 1995. *India: Economic Development and Social Opportunity*. Delhi: Oxford University Press.

Dutt, A. K. 1984. 'Stagnation, Income Distribution and Monopoly Power', *Cambridge Journal of Economics*, Vol. 8.

Dutt, Romesh. 1963 [1884]. *The Economic History of India, Volume One, Under Early British Rule, 1757–1837*. 2nd impression. Delhi: Publications Division, Ministry of Information and Broadcasting, Government of India.

Easterly, William, and Sergio Rebelo. 1993. 'Fiscal Policy and Economic Growth: An Empirical Investigation', *Journal of Monetary Economics*, Vol. 32, No. 3, December.

Edelman, M. 1980. 'Agricultural Modernization in Smallholding Areas of Mexico', *Latin American Perspectives*, No. 27, Fall.

Edwards, Richard C. 1976. 'Individual Traits and Organizational Incentives: What Makes a "Good Worker"?' *Journal of Human Resources*, Spring.

— 1977. 'Personal Traits and "Success" in Schooling and Work', *Educational and Psychological Measurement*, Vol. 37, No. 1, Spring.

Elson, Diane. 1989. 'Bound by One Thread: The Restructuring of UK Clothing and Textile Multinationals', in MacEwan and Tabb (eds), 1989a.

— 1995. 'Gender Awareness in Modeling Structural Adjustment', *World Development*, Vol. 23, No. 11.

Evans, Peter. 1979. *Dependent Development: The Alliance of Multinational, State, and Local Capital in Brazil*. Princeton NJ: Princeton University Press.

— 1987. 'Class, State and Dependence in East Asia: Lessons for Latin America', in Frederic Deyo (ed.), *The Political Economy of the New Asian Industrialism*. Ithaca, NY: Cornell University Press.

Fagen, Richard R. 1969. *The Transformation of Political Culture in Cuba*. Stanford, CA: Stanford University Press.

Fainaru, Steve. 1995. 'From Miracle to Mess in Latin America', *The Boston Sunday Globe*, 27 August 1995.

Fischer, Stanley. 1993. 'The Role of Macroeconomic Factors in Growth', *Journal of Monetary Economics*, Vol. 32, No. 3, December.

— 1995. 'Reform Can Reduce Poverty and Boost Growth in India', *IMF Survey*, 22 May.

Foster, Andrew D., and Mark R. Rosenzweig. 1996. 'Technical Change and Human-Capital Returns and Investments: Evidence from the Green Revolution', *American Economic Review*, Vol. 86, No. 4, September.

Foster, John Bellamy. 1994. *The Vulnerable Planet*. New York: Monthly Review Press.

Fox, Jonathan. 1995. 'The Crucible of Local Politics', *NACLA Report on the Americas*, Vol. XXIX, No. 1, July–August.

Frank, André Gunder. 1972. *Lumpenbourgeoisie, Lumpendevelopment: Dependence, Class, and Politics in Latin America*. New York: Monthly Review Press.

Frank, André Gunder, and Marta Fuentes. 1990. 'Civil Democracy: Social Movements and Recent World History', in Samir Amin et al., *Transforming the Revolution: Social Movements and the World System*. New York: Monthly Review Press.

Franke, Richard W., and Barbara H. Chasin. 1994. *Kerala: Radical Reform as Development in an Indian State*, A Food First Book. Oakland, CA: Institute of Food and Development Policy.

Friedman, Milton. 1962. *Capitalism and Freedom*. Chicago: University of Chicago Press.

Froiland, Paul. 1993. 'Training as Bait', *Training*, June.

Furtado, Celso. 1976. *Economic Development of Latin America*. 2nd edn. Cambridge: Cambridge University Press.

Gerschenkron, Alexander. 1962. *Economic Backwardness in Historical Perspective*. Cambridge, MA: Harvard University Press.

Gillis, Malcolm. 1989. 'Tax Reform: Lessons from Postwar Experience in Developing Nations', in Malcolm Gillis (ed.), *Tax Reform in Developing Countries*. Durham, NC, and London: Duke University Press.

Glyn, Andrew, and David Miliband (eds). 1994. *Paying for Inequality: The Economic Costs of Social Injustice*. London: IPPR–Rivers Oram Press.

Glyn, Andrew, and Bob Sutcliffe. 1992. 'Global but Leaderless? The New Capitalist Order', in Ralph Miliband and Leo Panitch (eds), *New World Order? The Socialist Register 1992*. London: Merlin Press.

Gomes, Ciro, and Roberto Mangabeira Unger. 1996. *O Próximo Passo: Uma alternativa práctica ao noliberalismo*. Rio de Janeiro: Topbooks. (An English version of the book appeared as *The Next Step: A Practical Alternative to Neoliberalism*, translated by Alfred P. Montero, prepared for the roundtable on 'An Alternative to the Neo-Liberal Model of Development', 22 March 1996, Global Studies Research Program, University of Wisconsin, Madison.)

Gordon, David M. 1994. '"Twixt the Cup and the Lip": Mainstream Economics and the Formation of Economic Policy', *Social Research*, Vol. 61, No. 1, Spring.

— 1996. *Fat and Mean: The Corporate Squeeze of Working Americans and the Myth of Managerial 'Downsizing'*. New York: Free Press.

Gorz, André. 1964. *Strategy for Labor: A Radical Proposal*. Boston: Beacon Press.

Green, Francis. 1988. 'Neoclassical and Marxian Conceptions of Production', *Cambridge Journal of Economics*, Vol. 12.

Habakkuk, H. J. 1962. *American and British Technology in the Nineteenth Century: The Search for Labour-Saving Inventions*. Cambridge: Cambridge University Press.

Hamilton, Alexander. 1966 [1791]. *Report on the Subject of Manufactures*, in Harold C. Syrett (ed.), *The Papers of Alexander Hamilton, Volume X*. New York: Columbia University Press.

Harbison, Ralph W. 1970. 'Colombia', in W. A. Lewis (ed.), *Tropical Development, 1880–1913*. Evanston: Northwestern University Press.

Harrison, Barbara. 1993. 'The Incentive that Passes the Test', *Financial Times*, 28 October.

Hart-Landsberg, Martin. 1993. *The Rush to Development: Economic Change and Political Struggle in South Korea*. New York: Monthly Review Press.

Helpman, Elhanen, and Paul Krugman. 1985. *Market Structure and Foreign Trade*. Cambridge, MA: MIT Press.

Hicks, Norman L., and Paul Streeten. 1979. 'Indicators of Development: The Search for a Basic Needs Yardstick', *World Development*, Vol. 7, No. 6, June.

Hill, Richard C. 1989. 'Divisions of Labor in Global Manufacturing: The Case of the Automobile Industry', in MacEwan and Tabb (eds), 1989a.

Hirschman, Albert O. 1958. *The Strategy of Economic Development*. New Haven: Yale University Press.

Hobsbawm, E. J. 1968. *Industry and Empire*. Harmondsworth: Penguin Books.

Horwitz, Morton J. 1977. *The Transformation of American Law, 1780–1860*. Cambridge, MA: Harvard University Press.

— 1992. *The Transformation of American Law, 1870–1960*. New York: Oxford University Press.

Hunter, Allen. 1995. 'Globalization from Below? Promises and Perils of the New Internationalism', *Social Policy*, Summer.

ILO (International Labour Organization). 1993. *A Comprehensive Women's Employment Strategy for Indonesia*, Final Report of an ILO-UNDP TSSI Mission, ILO, Regional Office for Asia and the Pacific, Bangkok, June.

Jaynes, Gerald David. 1986. *Branches without Roots: Genesis of the Black Working Class in the American South, 1862–1882*. New York: Oxford University Press.

Jenkins, Glenn P. 1991. 'Tax Reform: Lessons Learned', in Dwight H. Perkins and Michael Roemer (eds), *Reforming Economic Systems in Developing Countries*, Harvard Institute for International Development. Cambridge, MA: Harvard University Press.

Jenkins, Rhys. 1991. 'Learning from the Gang: Are there Lessons for Latin America from East Asia?', *Bulletin of Latin American Research*, Vol. 10, No. 1.

Kenyon, Daphne A., and John Kincaid (eds), 1991. *Competition Among State and Local Governments: Efficiency and Equity in American Federalism*. Washington, DC: Urban Institute Press.

Kolko, Gabriel. 1962. *Wealth and Power in America: An Analysis of Social Class and Income Distribution*. New York: Praeger.

Kozol, Jonathan. 1991. *Savage Inequalities: Children in America's Schools*. New York: Crown Publishers.

Krugman, Paul (ed.). 1986. *Strategic Trade Policy and the New International Economics*, Cambridge, MA: MIT Press.

— 1992. *The Age of Diminished Expectations: U.S. Economic Policy in the 1990s*. Cambridge, MA: MIT Press.

Kuznets, Simon. 1955. 'Economic Growth and Income Inequality', *American Economic Review*, Vol. 45, No. 1, March.

— 1966. *Modern Economic Growth*. New Haven: Yale University Press.

Lahera, Eugenio, Ernesto Ottone and Osvaldo Rosales. 1995. 'A Summary of the ECLAC Proposal', *Cepal Review*, No. 55, April.

Lee, Dwight R., and Richard B. McKenzie. 1989. 'The International Political Economy of Declining Tax Rates', *National Tax Journal*, Vol. 42, No. 1, March.

Leibenstein, Harvey. 1966. 'Allocative Efficiency vs. X-Efficiency', *American Economic Review*, Vol. 56, No. 3, June.

Levang, Patrice. 1997. 'From Rags to Riches in Sumatra: How Peasants Shifted from

Food Self-Sufficiency to Market-Oriented Tree Crops in Six Years', *Bulletin of Concerned Asian Scholars*, Vol. 29, No. 2, April–June.

Levin, Henry. 1987. 'Education as a Public and Private Good', *Journal of Policy Analysis and Management*, Vol. 6, No. 4.

Lewis, Cleona. 1938. *America's Stake in International Investments*, Washington, DC: Brookings Institution.

Lewontin, Richard, 1998. 'The Maturing of Capitalist Agriculture: Farmer as Proletarian', *Monthly Review*, Vol. 50, No. 3, July–August.

Lewontin, Richard, and Jean-Pierre Berlan. 1986. 'Technology, Research, and the Penetration of Capital: The Case of U.S. Agriculture', *Monthly Review*, Vol. 38, No. 3, July–August.

— 1990. 'The Political Economy of Agricultural Research: The Case of Hybrid Corn', in C. Ronald Caroll, John V. Vandermeer and Peter Rosset (eds), *Agroecology*. New York: McGraw Hill.

List, Frederich. 1928 [1841]. *The National System of Political Economy*. London: Longmans, Green and Co.

MacEwan, Arthur. 1990. *Debt and Disorder: International Economic Instability and U.S. Imperial Decline*. New York: Monthly Review Press.

— 1991. 'What's "New" about the "New International Economy"?', *Socialist Review*, Vol. 21, Nos 3 & 4, July–December.

— 1992. 'Alternatives to Free Trade: A Critique of the New Orthodoxy', *Monthly Review*, Vol. 44, No. 6, November.

— 1994. 'Globalization and Stagnation', in Ralph Miliband and Leo Panitch (eds), *Socialist Register 1994: Between Globalism and Nationalism*. New York: Monthly Review Press.

— 1995. 'Technological Options and Free Trade Agreements', *Science and Society*, Vol. 59, No. 1, Spring.

MacEwan, Arthur, and William K. Tabb (eds). 1989a. *Instability and Change in the World Economy*, New York: Monthly Review Press.

— 1989b. 'Instability and Change in the World Economy', in MacEwan and Tabb (eds), 1989a.

Maddison, Angus. 1989. *Dynamic Forces in Capitalist Development*. New York: Oxford University Press.

Magdoff, Harry. 1992. 'Globalization – To What End?', in Ralph Miliband and Leo Panitch (eds), *The Socialist Register 1992: New World Order?* London: Merlin Press.

Mamdani, Mahmood. 1976. *Politics and Class Formation in Uganda*. New York: Monthly Review Press.

Marglin, Stephen. 1974. 'What Do Bosses Do? The Origins and Functions of Hierarchy in Capitalist Production', *Review of Radical Political Economics*, Summer.

Marx, Karl. 1961 [1867]. *Capital: A Critical Analysis of Capitalist Production*, Vol. I. Moscow: Foreign Languages Publishing House.

Mayekiso, Mzwanele. 1996. *Township Politics: Civic Struggles for a New South Africa*. New York: Monthly Review Press.

Mboweni, Tito. 1997. 'Keynote Address by the Minister of Labour Tito Mboweni at the Launch of the Green Paper on a Skills Development Strategy for Employment and Growth in South Africa,' 24 March.

Mendes, Chico. 1992. *Fight for the Forest: Chico Mendes in his Own Words.* 2nd edn. Latin America Bureau. New York: Monthly Review Press.

Mill, John Stuart. 1976 [1848]. *Principles of Political Economy.* Fairfield, NJ: Augustus M. Kelly Publishers.

Moock, P. 1976. 'The Efficiency of Women as Farm Managers', *American Journal of Farm Economics*, Vol. 58.

Muller, Ronald. 1979. 'The Multinational Corporation and the Underdevelopment of the Third World', in Charles Wilbur (ed.), *The Political Economy of Development.* 2nd edn. New York: Random House.

Murnane, Richard J., and Frank Levy. 1996. *Teaching the New Basic Skills: Principles for Educating Children to Thrive in a Changing Economy.* New York: Free Press.

Murphy, Kevin M., Andrei Shleifer and Robert Vishny. 1989. 'Income Distribution, Market Size, and Industrialization', *Quarterly Journal of Economics*, Vol. CIV, No. 3, August.

Myrdal, Gunnar. 1957. *Rich Lands and Poor: The Road to World Prosperity.* New York: Harper and Row. (Published in the UK as *Economic Theory and Underdevelopment.* London: Duckworth.)

NEER (New England Economic Review). 1997. *The Effects of State and Local Public Policies on Economic Development*, Proceedings of a Symposium, *New England Economic Review*, March–April.

North, Douglas C. 1990. *Institutions, Institutional Change and Economic Performance.* Cambridge: Cambridge University Press.

— 1991. 'Institutions', *Journal of Economic Perspectives*, Vol. 5, No. 1, Winter.

Nurkse, Ragnar. 1953. *Problems of Capital Formation in Underdeveloped Countries.* New York: Oxford University Press.

Nylen, William R. 1995. 'The Workers Party in Rural Brazil', *NACLA Report on the Americas*, Vol. XXIX, No. 1, July–August.

OECD (Organization for Economic Cooperation and Development). 1998. OECD Economic Outlook, No. 63, June.

Ongaro, W. A. 1988. *Adoption of New Farming Technology: A Case Study of Maize Production in Western Kenya*, PhD Thesis, University of Gothenberg.

Osmani, Siddiqur Rahman. 1996. 'Is Income Equality Good for Growth?', in Abu Abdullah and Azizur Rahman Khan (eds), *State, Market and Development: Essays in Honor of Rehman Sobhan.* Dhaka: University Press.

Panayotou, Theodore. 1993. *Green Markets: The Economics of Sustainable Development.* San Francisco: Institute for Contemporary Studies Press.

Papanek, G. 1978. 'Economic Growth, Income Distribution and the Political Process in Less Developed Countries', in Z. Griliches et al., *Income Distribution and Economic Inequality.* New York: John Wiley.

Pastor, Manuel, Jr, and Jae Ho Sung. 1995. 'Private Investment and Democracy in the Developing World', *Journal of Economic Issues*, Vol. 29, No. 1, March.

Persson, Torsten, and Guido Tabellini. 1994. 'Is Inequality Harmful for Growth?', *American Economic Review*, Vol. 84, No. 3, June.

Pieper, Ute, and Lance Taylor. 1998. 'The Revival of the Liberal Creed: The IMF, the World Bank, and Inequality in a Globalized Economy', in D. Baker, G. Epstein and R. Pollin (eds), *Globalization and Progressive Economic Policy: What are the Real Constraints and Options?* New York: Cambridge University Press.

Polanyi, Karl. 1944. *The Great Transformation: The Political and Economic Origins of Our Time*. Boston: Beacon Press.

Prebisch, Raul. 1950. *The Economic Development of Latin America and Its Principal Problems*. Lake Success, NY: United Nations Department of Social Affairs.

Psacharopoulos, George, et al. 1993. *Poverty and Income Distribution in Latin America: The Story of the 1980s*. World Bank, Human Resource Division, Latin America and the Caribbean Technical Department, Regional Studies Program, Report No. 27, revised April.

Putterman, Louis, John E. Roemer and Joaquim Silvestre. 1998. 'Does Egalitarianism Have a Future?', *Journal of Economic Literature*, Vol. XXXVI, No. 2, June.

Quisumbing, A. 1993. 'Women in Agriculture', World Bank Education and Social Policy Department, Washington.

Republic of China. 1989. *Statistical Yearbook of the Republic of China 1989*. Directorate-General of Budget, Accounting and Statistics, Executive Yuan.

Reynolds, Morgan, and Eugene Smolensky. 1977. *Public Expenditure, Taxes, and the Distribution of Income, 1950, 1961, 1970*. New York: Academic Press.

Ricardo, David. 1966 [1817]. *The Works and Correspondence of David Ricardo, Vol. 1, On the Principles of Political Economy and Taxation*. Cambridge: Cambridge University Press.

Riskin, Carl. 1991. 'Feeding China: The Experience since 1949', in Jean Dreze and Amartya Sen (eds), *The Political Economy of Hunger, Vol. 3, Endemic Hunger*. Oxford: Clarendon Press.

Rosenberg, Nathan. 1972. *Technology and American Economic Growth*. Armonk, NY: M. E. Sharpe.

Rosenstein-Rodan, Paul N. 1943. 'Problems of Industrialization of Eastern and Southern Europe', *Economic Journal*, June–September.

Rosovsky, Henry. 1961. *Capital Formation in Japan, 1868–1940*. Glencoe, IL: Free Press.

Russell, James. 1992. 'Free Trade and the Concentration of Capital in Mexico', *Monthly Review*, Vol. 44, No. 2, June.

Rutter, John. 1993. 'Recent Trends in International Direct Investment: The Boom Years Fade', US Department of Commerce, International Trade Administration, Trade Development, August.

Schiavo-Campo, Salvatore. 1978. *International Economics*. Cambridge: Winthrop.

Schultz, Theodore. 1961. 'Investment in Human Capital', *American Economic Review*, Vol. 51, No. 1, March.

Schumpeter, Joseph A. 1954. *History of Economic Analysis*. New York: Oxford University Press.

Seers, Dudley. 1972. 'The Meaning of Economic Development', in Nancy Bastor (ed.), *Measuring Development: The Role and Adequacy of Development Indicators*. London: Frank Cass.

Sellers, Patricia. 1990. 'The Best Cities for Business', *Fortune*, 22 October.

Sen, Amartya. 1981. *Poverty and Famines: An Essay on Entitlement and Deprivation*. Oxford: Clarendon Press.

— 1992. *Inequality Reexamined*. Oxford: Clarendon Press.

Shiff, Maurice, and Alberto Valdes. 1995. 'The Plundering of Agriculture in Developing Countries', *Finance & Development*, Vol. 32, No. 1, March.

Singer, Hans. 1950. 'The Distribution of Gains between Investing and Borrowing Countries', *American Economic Reveiw*, Vol. 40, No. 2, May.

Smith, Adam. 1937 [1776]. *The Wealth of Nations*. New York: Random House.

Solow, Barbara L., and Stanley L. Engerman (eds). 1987. *British Capitalism and Caribbean Slavery: The Legacy of Eric Williams*. New York: Cambridge University Press.

Sontheimer, Sally (ed.) 1991. *Women and the Environment: A Reader – Crisis and Development in the Third World*. New York: Monthly Review Press.

Stern, David I., and Michael S. Common. 1996. 'Economic Growth and Environmental Degradation', *World Development*, Vol. 24, No. 7.

Stiglitz, Joseph. 1998a. 'More Instruments and Broader Goals: Moving Toward the Post-Washington Consensus', WIDER Annual Lecture, Helsinki, Finland, 7 January.

— 1998b. 'Redefining the Role of the State: What Should It Do? How Should It Do It? And How Should These Decisions be Made?', presented on the tenth anniversary of the MITI Research Institute, Tokyo, Japan, 17 March.

Strauss, John, and Duncan Thomas. 1998. 'Health, Nutrition, Economic Development', *Journal of Economic Literature*, Vol. XXXVI, No. 2, June.

Sundrum, R. M. 1990. *Income Distribution in Less Developed Countries*. London and New York: Routledge.

Sutcliffe, Bob. 1995. 'Development after Ecology', in V. Bhaskar and Andrew Glyn (eds), *The North, the South and the Environment: Ecological Constraints and the Global Economy*. London: Earthscan.

Sutcliffe, Bob, and Andrew Glyn. 1999. 'Still Underwhelmed – Indicators of Globalization and their Misinterpretation', *Review of Radical Political Economy*, Vol. 31, No. 1, March.

Taussig, F. W. 1931. *The Tariff History of the United States*. New York: Putnam Sons.

Tavares, Ricardo. 1995. 'The PT Experience in Porto Alegre', *NACLA Report on the Americas*, Vol. XXIX, No. 1, July–August.

Taylor, Lance. 1988. *Varieties of Stabilization Experience*. Oxford: Clarendon Press.

Taylor, Lance, and Ute Pieper. 1996. *Reconciling Economic Reform and Sustainable Development: Social Consequences of Neo-Liberalism*. New York: Office of Development Studies, United Nations Development Programme.

Tharamangalam, Joseph. 1998. 'The Perils of Social Development without Growth: The Development Debacle of Kerala, India', *Bulletin of Concerned Asian Scholars*, Vol. 30, No. 1, January–March.

Todaro, Michael. 1997. *Economic Development*. 6th edn. Reading, MA: Addison Wesley.

Tzannatos, Zafiris. 1992. 'Potential Gains from the Elimination of Labor Market Differentials', in *Women's Employment and Pay in Latin America, Part I, Overview and Methodology*, Regional Studies Report No. 10, World Bank, Washington.

UNCTAD (United Nations Commission on Trade and Development), Division on Transnational Corporations and Development. 1994. *World Investment Report 1994: Transnational Corporations, Employment and the Workplace*. Geneva.

UNCTC (United Nations Centre on Transnational Corporations). 1988. *Transnational Corporations in World Development: Trends and Prospects*. New York.

UNDP (United Nations Development Programme). 1992. *Human Development Report 1992*. New York and Oxford: Oxford University Press.

— 1995. *Human Development Report 1995*. New York: Oxford University Press.

— 1998. *Human Development Report 1998*. New York: Oxford University Press.

USBC (United States Bureau of the Census). 1998. *Current Population Survey*. www.census.gov/hhes/www/income.html

USDC (United States Department of Commerce). 1975. *Historical Statistics of the United States: Colonial Times to 1970*. Washington, DC: US Government Printing Office.

Vilas, Carlos. 1989. 'International Constraints on Progressive Change in Peripheral Societies', in MacEwan and Tabb (eds), 1989a.

— 1997. 'Inequality and the Dismantling of Citizenship in Latin America', *NACLA Report on the Americas*, Vol. XXXI, No. 1, July–August.

Wade, Robert. 1990. *Governing the Market: Economic Theory and the Role of Government in East Asian Industrialization*, Princeton, Princeton University Press.

WCED (World Commission on Environment and Development). 1987. *Our Common Future* (The Brundtland Report). New York: Oxford University Press.

Wilford, John Noble. 1993. 'New Finds Suggest Even Earlier Trade on Fabled Silk Road', *New York Times*, 16 March.

Williams, Eric. 1966 [1944]. *Capitalism and Slavery*. New York: Capricorn Books. (First published: University of North Carolina Press.)

Williamson, John. 1990. 'What Washington Means by Policy Reform', in John Williamson (ed.), *Latin American Adjustment: How Much Has Happened?* Washington DC: Institute for International Development.

Winn, Peter. 1995. 'The Frente Amplio in Montevideo', *NACLA Report on the Americas*, Vol. XXIX, No. 1, July–August.

World Bank. 1982. *World Development Report 1982*. New York: Oxford University Press.

— 1987. *World Development Report 1987*. New York: Oxford University Press.

— 1991a. *World Development Report 1991*. New York: Oxford University Press.

— 1991b. *Global Economic Prospects and Developing Countries*. Washington, DC: World Bank.

— 1992. *World Development Report 1992*. New York: Oxford University Press.

— 1993. *The East Asian Miracle*. New York: Oxford University Press.

— 1995. *World Development Report 1995*. New York: Oxford University Press.

— 1996a. *World Development Report 1996*. New York: Oxford University Press.

— 1996b. *Training and the Labor Market in Indonesia: Productivity Gains and Employment Growth*, Population and Human Resources Division, Country Department III, East Asia and the Pacific Region, 7 June.

— 1997. *World Development Report 1997: The State in a Changing World*. Washington, DC: Oxford University Press for the World Bank.

Zevin, Robert B. 1992. 'Are World Financial Markets More Open? If So, Why and With What Effects?', in Tariq Banuri and Juliet B. Schor (eds), *Financial Openness and National Autonomy: Opportunities and Constraints*. Oxford: Clarendon Press.

Index

Zed Titles on the Political Economy of Capitalism

Intellectual fashion continues to prompt changes in vocabulary. Today, 'globalization', and the 'market', have become the dominant buzzwords. In reality, however, what is happening is an ongoing, perhaps accelerating, spread (as well as transformation) of the market nexus between members of society on the one hand and relations of exploitation of labour on the other. Whatever the terms different writers may use, the world's economic systems are, with the collapse of the socialist project, almost exclusively capitalist and the political economy of capitalism remains a centrally important focus of social understanding. Zed Books has a strong list of titles in this area.

Samir Amin, *Capitalism in the Age of Globalization: The Management of Contemporary Society*

Asoka Bandarage, *Women, Population and Global Crisis: A Political-Economic Analysis*

Robert Biel, *Beyond the New World Order: Global Capitalism: Current Dynamics and Future Trajectory*

Michel Chossudovsky, *The Globalisation of Poverty: Impacts of IMF and World Bank Reforms*

Peter Custers, *Capital Accumulation and Women's Labour in Asian Economies*

Diplab Dasgupta, *Structural Adjustment, Global Trade and the New Political Economy of Development*

Graham Dunkley, *The Free Trade Adventure: The WTO, GATT and Globalism: A Critique*

Terence Hopkins and Immanuel Wallerstein et al., *The Age of Transition: Trajectory of the World-System, 1945–2025*

Saral Sarkar, *Eco-Socialism or Eco-Capitalism? A Critical Analysi of Humanity's Fundamental Choices*

Hans-Peter Martin and Harald Schumann, *The Global Trap: Globalization and the Assault on Prosperity and Democracy*

Harry Shutt, *The Trouble with Capitalism: An Enquiry into the Causes of Global Economic Failure*

Kavaljit Singh, *The Globalisation of Finance: A Citizen's Guide*

David Woodward, *Foreign Direct and Equity Investment in Developing Countries: The Next Crisis?*

For full details of this list and Zed's other subject and general catalogues, please write to: The Marketing Department, Zed Books, 7 Cynthia Street, London N1 9JF, UK or e-mail: sales@zedbooks.demon.co.uk

Visit our website at: http://www.zedbooks.demon.co.uk

Zed Titles on Globalization

Globalization has become the new buzzword of the late 1990s. Despite the very different meanings attached to the term and even more divergent evaluations of its likely impacts, it is clear nevertheless that we are in an accelerated process of transition to a new period in world history. Zed Books' titles on globalization pay special attention to what it means for the South, for women, for workers and for other vulnerable groups.

Nassau Adams, *Worlds Apart: The North–South Divide and the International System*

Samir Amin, *Capitalism in the Age of Globalization: The Management of Contemporary Society*

Asoka Bandarage, *Women, Population and Global Crisis: A Political-Economic Analysis*

Michel Chossudovsky, *The Globalisation of Poverty: Impacts of IMF and World Bank Reforms*

Peter Custers, *Capital Accumulation and Women's Labour in Asian Economies*

Bhagirath Lal Das, *An Introduction to the WTO Agreements*

Bhagirath Lal Das, *The WTO Agreements: Deficiencies, Imbalances and Required Changes*

Bhagirath Lal Das, *The World Trade Organization: A Guide to the New Framework for International Trade*

Diplab Dasgupta, *Structural Adjustment, Global Trade and the New Political Economy of Development*

Graham Dunkley, *The Free Trade Adventure: The WTO, GATT and Globalism: A Critique*

Bjorn Hettne et al., *International Political Economy: Understanding Global Disorder*

Terence Hopkins and Immanuel Wallerstein et al., *The Age of Transition: Trajectory of the World-System, 1945–2025*

K. S. Jomo (ed.), *Tigers in Trouble: Financial Governance, Liberalisation and the Economic Crises in East Asia*

Hans-Peter Martin and Harald Schumann, *The Global Trap: Globalization and the Assault on Prosperity and Democracy*

Harry Shutt, *The Trouble With Capitalism: An Enquiry into the Causes of Global Economic Failure*

Kavaljit Singh, *The Globalisation of Finance: A Citizen's Guide*

Henk Thomas (ed.), *Globalization and Third World Trade Unions*

David Woodward, *Foreign Direct and Equity Investment in Developing Countries: The Next Crisis?*